PREPARING FOR THE FOODSERVICE INDUSTRY

An Introductory Approach

PREPARING FOR THE FOODSERVICE INDUSTRY

An Introductory Approach

Earl R. Palan

Department of Institution Administration
University of Southern Mississippi
Hattiesburg, Mississippi

Judith A. Stadler

Food and Nutrition Consultant
Appleton, Wisconsin

AVI Publishing Co., Inc
Westport, CT

© Copyright 1986 by
THE AVI PUBLISHING COMPANY, INC.
250 Post Road East
P.O. Box 831
Westport, Connecticut 06881

Library of Congress Cataloging-in-Publication Data

Palan, Earl R.
    Preparing for the foodservice industry.

    Bibliography: p.
    Includes index.
    1. Food service.   I. Stadler, Judith A.
II. Title.
TX911.P354   1986   647'.95023   86-3634
ISBN 0-87055-521-9

Printed in the United States of America

A B C D E 5 4 3 2 1 0 9 8 7 6

Contents

Contents

13   Sandwiches

14   Stocks, Soups, Sauces

15   Seasonings: Herbs, Spices, Flavorings, Condiments

x   **Contents**

Preface

Preparing for the Foodservice Industry is designed to meet the needs of the student in the secondary or postsecondary foodservice curriculum. The focus of the book is on the practical. It presents the student with firsthand knowledge he or she will need when entering that first job. It is not a text for a cook, manager, or chef; rather it is a "how to do it" guide for the beginning student. It is not a theoretical book that has no application in the workplace nor is it a recipe book; instead it presents all of the basic concepts underlying the development of skills for the foodservice industry. Students will find the text usable in the classroom, in the laboratory, or in the institutional or commercial operation. The instructor will find the text relevant and helpful, whether his or her background is predominantly in teaching or in foodservice industry work.

The text is competency based, with clear objectives laid out in each chapter.

The first seven chapters discuss the entry-level skills needed to become familiar with the foodservice industry, to learn about job possibilities in the industry, and to get the first job. These chapters explore communications, human relations, sanitation, safety, and nutrition. Together, skills in these areas will help prepare the entry-level worker to be an effective member of the foodservice team, perhaps beginning as a cook's helper.

Chapters 8 and 9 acquaint the student with the language and equipment of the foodservice operation.

Chapters 10 through 24 help provide the student with a working knowledge of basic food preparation principles and methods, and quality standards for preparing various food products. These sections give insight into real-life applications in the industry.

The chapters are all structured similarly: Following an introduction, appear the objectives of the unit, the terms to be discussed, and basic information appropriate to the chapter topic. In food production chapters, this includes information about selecting, purchasing, storing, and preparing foods that are important in every foodservice operation. Most chapters include a final section on merchandising food produced in various units of the foodservice operation.

The organization of material is easily adaptable to the typical two-semester year. The first six chapters might be covered during the first quarter, with the remaining eighteen chapters covered in the next three quarters. The course could also be adapted to the three-quarter system, or to a single semester, if necessary.

The accompanying laboratory manual and instructor's guide will help make the student's beginning foodservice coursework even more concrete and practical.

Acknowledgments

The authors are indebted to the people at the Mid-America Vocational Curriculum Consortium for their help; to their colleagues and friends at Oklahoma State University; to Kathy Grossarth Palan for her creative assistance; to the many food and equipment manufacturers and trade organizations that provided photos, tables, and background information; and to their families for their support and encouragement.

1
Introduction to the Foodservice Industry

If you asked all the foodservice operators you know what qualifications they want in an employee, what would they say? Most would say that they want their workers to understand communications. They want them to deal with people well. They want them to follow principles of safety and sanitation. And they want their workers to know something about nutrition. An operator can train a worker with those basic qualifications or competencies to fit into the foodservice or hospitality team. A study of these skills, along with an orientation to the foodservice industry, make up the basic lessons of the first seven chapters.

After finishing these chapters, the student is ready to enter the foodservice industry as a worker at the lowest level—an unskilled worker. He or she would have to spend a long time working in the business to learn all the practical skills of food production.

The next 17 chapters are designed to make that process go more quickly by examining food production in depth. After completing all 24 chapters, a student could go into a foodservice operation and understand what is expected. He or she could work as a semiskilled worker, and with some extra training, become a baker, a service supervisor, a fast-food supervisor, or a management trainee.

Our main purpose in writing this text is to give you the basic concepts and skills you will need to enter the foodservice industry. We hope that this book will help you become a successful member of an exciting, satisfying, and expanding industry.

Objectives. This section should help you:

- Describe the growth of the foodservice industry since its beginnings.
- Discuss reasons for the continued future growth of the food-service industry.
- List types of foodservice operations.
- List the four types of foodservice jobs and an example of each.
- Describe two advantages and two disadvantages of employment in the foodservice industry.
- Discuss the characteristics of a good worker.

Terms to Know

Foodservice Industry. The business of preparing food for people to eat away from their homes.

Hospitality Industry. Foodservice, hotel and motel, and entertainment businesses.

Institutional Foodservice. Operations that prepare food more as a service than for profit.

Commercial Foodservice. Operations in business to make a profit from food service.

Career Ladder. Steps in moving from one job to another, from unskilled worker to professional, in the foodservice business.

History of the Foodservice Industry

Modern-day restaurants and fast-food places developed from European roadside inns. Those inns served travelers on horseback or in carriages long before people had ever dreamed of automobiles. The early inns offered simple food and drink and a bed.

As European society progressed, more roads were built and travel became easier, so that there were many more travelers. In large cities, hotels developed, and some of them set up dining rooms that in many cases became quite famous. Even small boarding houses began to include food as part and parcel of their service.

At the end of the 1800s, when the young railroad industry had grown quickly, the number of travelers increased dramatically. As people moved from rural towns to industrial cities, small inns and taverns made way for big hotels, which often became the centers of social life in the cities. Restaurants became well known for their food specialities. By 1938 the United States Department of Labor reported that over one million people were working in the restaurant business in the United States. Another 300,000 were employed in hotels and hotel dining rooms.

As these hotels and restaurants changed, so did their menus. The food served in the early European inn was simple—fresh fish, wild game, seasonal vegetables and fruits, and some preserved foods. Menus in the United States changed as the population changed. As waves of immigrants arrived between 1860 and 1920, they brought their food choices with them. Neighborhood restaurants sprang up. They served foods that were favorites of the people who lived in the neighborhoods.

This growth and change continued until the Great Depression of the early 1930s. The economy got so bad that the foodservice industry suffered along with other industries. It did not fully recover until the end of World War II in 1945. World War II was also responsible for one of the major changes in the industry. Women went to work outside of their homes in large numbers, and for the first time families began eating away from home on a regular basis. As a result, the postwar foodservice industry soon became one of the fastest growing sectors in the U.S. economy.

Employment in the industry rose from 1.5 million in 1958 to 2.3 million in 1968. By 1980 it had grown to 8 million. Sales grew from 10 billion dollars in 1958 to 130 billion dollars in 1980.

What are some reasons for this increasing demand for prepared food?

1. Good economic conditions
2. An increase in population.
3. An increase in the number of working women.

Today the foodservice industry is changing rapidly. What shall we see in the future? No doubt the industry will continue to grow at a rapid pace. There will probably be an increase in both volume of food served and in the variety of food served.

We can predict that this increasing variety in foodservice operations will reach out even more to these markets:

1. Women who work.
2. Families with higher incomes and more leisure time.
3. People who eat out frequently, not just once or twice a week.
4. People who are increasingly accustomed to the fast-food operation.

Table 1.1 lists some facts about today's foodservice industry.

Needs of the Future.   The foodservice industry of today is creating a very definite set of needs for the future.

New Equipment.   The microwave oven will be an essential tool. Because the operator can use it to cook frozen foods, it is a time saver and helps the operator run the business with fewer employees. It also makes it possible to stock a great variety of frozen convenience foods, which will decrease the need for some conventional tools and equipment. At the same time, they mean the operation will need more of certain types of specialty equipment.

New Packaging.   Foods with a longer shelf life will be coming into the foodservice storeroom. There will be a move away from frozen or refrigerated foods to foods that can be stored safely at room temperature. We shall also see packages that do more than just hold food—it is already possible to store, heat and serve foods in the same package.

New Foods.   While the public is not likely to forget its favorite foods soon, there may be more new foods entering the marketplace. Soybeans are already being used as a protein source. We may see greater use of cotton seed, whey, nuts, and other foods. Consumer demand for fresh vegetables may turn the restauranteur into a part-time gardener.

Table 1.1: Facts about Today's Foodservice Industry

Sales Projections 1983 (billion $)

1. Commercial feeding	
Eating places	87.8
Drinking places	9.2
Foodservice contractors	8.3
Hotel/motel restaurants	8.1
Other: retail, vending, recreation	9.1
	122.5
2. Institutional feeding: business, schools, hospitals, nursing homes, others that operate their own foodservice	20.7
3. Military feeding: base exchange, officers and NCO club foodservice	0.8
TOTAL	144.0

Food Service—The Number One Retail Employer

- Employment in the foodservice industry is 8 million persons
- 66% are women
- 24% are teenagers
- Household income of foodservice employees compares favorably with average for all workers
- Total annual foodservice wages and benefits is $48 billion.

Food Service—First in Daily Customer Contact

- The average person eats out 3.5 times a week
- Over 77 million customer transactions occur each day in commercial foodservice
- 78% of all families report eating at commercial foodservice establishments regularly
- The average per-person check size is $2.79
- Men eat away from home more frequently than women
- Singles eat out more frequently than families
- As income increases consumers eat away from home more frequently

Eating and Drinking Places Are Mostly Small Businesses

- 94% have sales under $500,000
- 85% are single units
- 61% are sole proprietorships or partnerships

Food Service Is a Ladder to Management Opportunity

- 31% of industry employees are managerial or administrative personnel
- Foodservice employs more minority managers than any other industry
- Half of all foodservice managerial and administrative personnel are women

Courtesy: National Restaurant Association, Foodservice Industry Pocket Factbook, 1983.

Types of Foodservice Operations

We speak of foodservice operations as either institutional or commercial.

Institutional Foodservice Operations. Institutional operations prepare food more for service than for profit. They include the following:

Schools. School feeding programs, subsidized by the U.S. Department of Agriculture (USDA) are the largest school operations. They provide meals (lunch or breakfast) according to a food group plan. In addition, school feeding programs serve as a learning environment where children can learn about balanced meals and good nutrition.

Colleges and Universities. These institutions provide three meals a day, seven days a week. Operators follow the NRC's recommended dietary allowances (RDA) in planning balanced meals. Variety is also an important consideration for the college age patron.

Military Bases. Military installations prepare food in very large quantities. The cooks are military personnel who are specially trained, and food production is well standardized.

Hospitals. Hospital foodservice operations serve many needs, and so there are usually several feeding units. In addition to feeding patients, the hospital dietary department operates a cafeteria for employees, snack bars, or visitor restaurants. Because of the many different needs of patients, a great variety of food is prepared. Some patients need special diets that are part of their total care plan.

Nursing Homes. The volume of food prepared is naturally smaller than in hospitals. Operators must consider the age of residents, who are mostly elderly. Since people usually stay in nursing homes for a long time, it is important to include as much variety as possible. Some residents will also require special diets.

Correctional Institutions. Inmates of prisons are usually healthy adults or juveniles. Again, there is a great volume of food produced. Because of the long-term stays, variety in foodservice is important.

Child Care Facilities. Since small children eat small quantities, the volume of food produced is relatively small. Menus should be well planned to provide one-third of the child's nutrient needs for the day. There should also be snacks. Eating should provide learning experiences for children.

Commercial Foodservice. Commercial operators are in business to make a profit. Types of operations include the following:

Hotel. Hotels often offer quality foodservice that is expensive. Catering meetings is a big profit gainer for hotels. Most of the hotel's income comes from the rental of rooms, but a good hotel operation will use food sales as a moneymaker, too.

Motel. Since motels are not usually centers for gatherings but rather just places to stop before moving on, their foodservice operations are usually small. Foodservice is not fancy and is often contracted out to a franchise operator.

Restaurant. Restaurants vary from the plain fried chicken place to the fancy, sit-down restaurant. Meals are usually produced on the premises. There are three types of restaurants:

Full-service. The guest selects from the menu, which features quality foods. The server is a trained waiter or waitress who takes the order and brings the food. The decor is usually an important part of the guest's dining experience.

Self-service. Guests help themselves by going through a cafeteria or buffet line. Employees provide little service but the quality of food and service can still be high.

Specialty restaurant. Specialty restaurants can be full-service, self-service, or a combination. These family-type restaurants offer sit-down meals with menus and some table service. The menu is usually limited to steaks, pizza, pancakes, or fried seafood. The price is in the medium range. They are popular for families with children.

Fast-Food Operations.   Fast-food operations are not restaurants because they offer the least amount of service to the public—even less than the self-service operation. The well-known hamburger place is a typical fast-food operation. Operators produce a large volume of food. Prices are low and quick turnover is a feature. The customer orders and picks up food at the counter. The meal may be eaten on the premises or carried out. Popular fast-food specialities are hamburgers, fried chicken or seafood, and Mexican food.

Clubs.   A select group of customers visits a club for meals or snacks. It may be a country club with a variety of social purposes, including regular food service as a major part of the operation, or it may be a tennis or golf club with snacks offered as a sideline.

Retail Operations.   Some department stores or large variety stores offer foodservice as a convenience to customers. The menu

Fast-food operations are among the most common foodservice institutions.

usually features convenience foods or quick foods that are not prepared on the premises.

Recreation or Amusement Centers.   Foodservice is like that in retail stores. Quick convenience foods are usually offered.

Foodservice Jobs

Foodservice jobs fall into four groups: semiskilled, skilled, technical, and professional workers.

Semiskilled Workers.   Semiskilled workers usually have a high school degree. They complete a foodservice training program and advance through on-the-job training. Workers who are considered semiskilled are:

Cook's Helper.   The helper helps the cook in general food preparation. He or she is training to be a cook.

Many unskilled and skilled jobs are available in the foodservice industry.

Fast-Food Worker.   This worker serves the customer by taking orders and preparing beverages. The worker can assemble or cook simple food items to order.

Waiter/Waitress.   The waiter or waitress serves food and beverages to the customer.

Pantry Worker.   The pantry worker usually works in the cold-food preparation area. He or she prepares sandwiches, salads, and dressings.

Fountain Worker.   This worker prepares desserts, soft drinks, and ice cream to order.

Counter Worker.   The counter person prepares and serves simple food in fast-food operations.

Tray Line Worker.   The line worker dishes up food in cafeterias or health care facility kitchens.

Baker's Assistant.   This helper works closely with the baker and may prepare simple baked items.

Dietary Aide.   The dietary aide helps with simple preparation and service tasks in the dietary department of a health care facility.

Skilled Workers.   Skilled workers have a high school diploma and have completed a foodservice program. They have an intermediate level of working skills, knowledge, and experience. They can advance upward through on-the-job training. Included among skilled workers are:

Cook.   The cook is responsible for preparing entrees and their accompanying dishes listed on the menu. The cook also supervises helpers and other cooks.

Baker.   The person who prepares baked goods—breads, rolls, muffins, pies, cakes, and pastries—is the baker. Some operations have a pastry chef to prepare the pies, cakes, and pastries.

Host/Hostess.   The host or hostess greets guests, checks reservations, seats guests, and has charge of the dining room.

Cashier.   The cashier receives payment for meals, makes change, keeps records, and may handle complaints.

Butcher.   The butcher prepares meat, poultry, and fish for cooking.

Dietary Assistant.   The dietary assistant is a skilled worker in the foodservice area of the dietary department of a health care facility.

Technical Foodservice Workers.   The technical worker usually has an associate (two-year) degree in Food Service or Institutional Administration. This worker has a high level of working skill, knowledge, and experience. He or she advances both through on-the-job training or continuing education. Some technical foodservice workers are:

Chef.   In a large-volume business the chef supervises and coordinates the food preparation area. He or she may direct many cooks. The quality of food in these operations in usually high.

Dining Room Manager.   The dining room manager supervises, coordinates, and trains dining room workers.

Catering Manager.   The catering manager arranges details and supervises the catered meal. (Banquets are examples of catered events.)

Storeroom Manager.   The storeroom manager supervises the receiving, inspection, storing, and issuing of food.

Foodservice/Kitchen Supervisor.   This worker supervises food production for a kitchen or section of a large kitchen.

Dietary Technician.   This skilled worker assists the dietitian in a health care facility food preparation area.

Professional Foodservice Workers.   Professional workers have college degrees in foodservice management, restaurant management, or dietetics. They have management level skills, knowledge, and experience and usually advance by completing a man-

agement training program. The most familiar professional workers are:

Dietitian.   The administrative dietitian is the administrator in
charge of a large foodservice operation. The dietitian is responsible for the nutritional planning and management needed to produce and control meals. A clinical dietitian plans and supervises
the production of special diets in a health care facility. This dietitian also has responsibility for patient education.

**Foodservice or Food Production Manager, or Executive
Chef.**   This manager has responsibility for general supervision
of all production in all kitchens of a large institution.

Table 1.2: Occupational Employment 1982–1995

Occupation	1982	1995 (projected)	Change (%)
Bakers (bread, pastry)	36,000	46,000	28
Bartenders	384,000	505,000	32
Butchers, meatcutters	191,000	179,000	−6
Cooks			
institutional	423,000	536,000	27
restaurant	351,000	500,000	42
short order	437,000	578,000	32
Food preparation, service workers, fast-food restaurant	809,000	1,106,000	37
Host/hostess—restaurant lounge, coffee shop	113,000	154,000	36
Kitchen helpers	850,000	1,155,000	36
Pantry—sandwich and coffee makers	84,000	112,000	34
Waiter/waitress	1,665,000	2,227,000	34
assistant	302,000	388,000	29
Restaurant, cafeteria, and bar managers	574,000	711,000	24
Other	559,000	734,000	31
Total	6,778,000	8,931,000	32

All figures have been compiled from Bureau of Labor Statistics data.

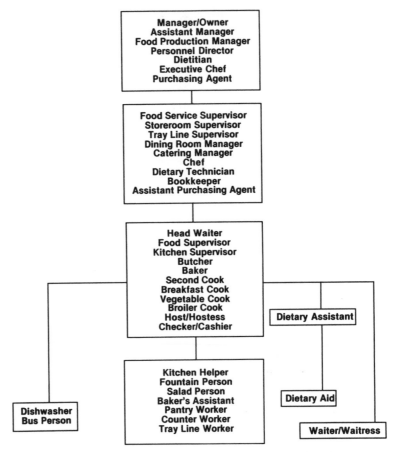

Unskilled, beginning positions can lead up the career ladder.
Courtesy: Mid America Vocational Curriculum Consortium.

Restaurant Manager/Owner. The restaurant manager or owner is responsible for the entire operation, from production to service.

Purchasing Agent. Some large operations have a purchasing agent who buys all food, supplies, and equipment.

Table 1.2 lists projections for employment in the hospitality industry from 1982 to 1995. According to the U.S. Bureau of Labor Statistics (BLS) food service workers rank sixth on the list of most rapid employment growth in the 1980s.

Advantages of Employment in the Foodservice Industry

Among the benefits of foodservice industry work are working conditions, availability of jobs in all locations, excellent training, and promotion opportunities.

Steady Work.   The foodservice industry has been growing consistently for a number of years. Predictions are that this trend will continue for a long time.

Constant Demand.   As Table 1.2 shows, there is a constant demand for employees.

Working Conditions Good.   Foodservice is gratifying to those who enjoy working with the public. It offers an opportunity to work with talented and interesting people.

Availability.   Foodservice jobs are available anywhere in the country.

Promotion.   The industry offers excellent opportunities for training and promotion. There is also the opportunity to become an owner/operator.

Table 1.3: Wages and Salaries in the Foodservice Industry, 1983

Position	Average	
	Commercial	Noncommercial
Chef (annual)	$20,634	$18,217
Manager (annual)	21,003	16,424
Assistant Manager (annual)	15,183	17,481
Management Trainee (annual)	14,958	15,409
Cook (weekly)	207	232
Dishwasher (weekly)	152	180
Server (weekly)	138	181

Compiled from Labor Cost Index, Restaurants and Institutions Magazine, Dec. 28, 1983.

Fits Schedules.   Part-time jobs in the foodservice industry are there for those who need them.

Fringe Benefits.   Benefits often include one or more meals a day, uniforms, paid vacations, and health insurance.

Wages Are Good.   Table 1.3 lists some average wages for positions in the foodservice industry.

Disadvantages of Employment in the Foodservice Industry

Not everyone is cut out for the foodservice business. It is important for you to recognize that there are some disadvantages to this kind of work.

Hours.   Working hours can be inconvenient. Employees may have to work evenings, weekends, and holidays.

Seasonal Nature.   In some areas foodservice industry jobs are very seasonal and short term.

Work Pressure.   The food business is a fast-paced business. Food will spoil quickly. That is why it is essential that operators serve food correctly and at the right time. Customers can become critical for many reasons.

Physical Labor.   A worker must be physically fit enough to handle some heavy equipment and demanding work.

Working Conditions.   A food preparation area can be warm, cramped, and uncomfortable for some people.

Characteristics of a Good Foodservice Worker

A good foodservice worker needs several important assets:

Good Work Habits.   A worker should be punctual, proud of himself or herself (dress and job), willing to work, eager to learn, able to get along with others, and able to accept and learn from criticism.

Good Physical and Mental Health. A worker needs stamina, positive attitude, good posture, self-confidence, and the ability to give and follow directions.

Math Skills. A good worker should be able to understand basic math, fractions, percentages, and units of measure.

Human Relations Skills. Because the foodservice worker deals with the public every day, he or she should be able to work with customers, other workers, supervisors, employers, and suppliers.

Communication Skills. The worker should be able to send and receive written and verbal communications. It is important to use correct grammar, to have a clear voice, and to express ideas clearly.

Ways to Achieve Job Advancement

Job advancement depends on length of service, policy of promoting from within, on-the-job training, recommendations, and additional education.

Sources of Career Information

Get in touch with any of the following organizations for more information on careers:

- National Institute for the Food Service Industry (NIFI)
- National Restaurant Association (NRA)
- American Culinary Federation (ACF)
- American Dietetic Association (ADA)
- American Home Economics Association (AHEA)
- American School Food Service Association (ASFSA)
- Club Manager's Association of America (CMA)
- American Hotel and Motel Association (AHMA)
- Local restaurant association
- State restaurant association
- Local foodservice operation

2
Getting a Job

When you finish this course, you will be ready to get a job in the foodservice industry. You may even have a part-time or full-time job already. To get the job you really want, you will need the skills you are learning in school. However, it is even more important to know how to find the right job, how to be considered for the job, and how to sell yourself to the person doing the hiring.

Objectives and Terms

Objectives. This section should help you:

- Do a self-inventory.
- Look for a job.
- Write an appropriate resume.
- Have a satisfactory job interview.
- Describe how laws affect the employee and employer.

Terms to Know

Interview. A face-to-face meeting and conversation with a possible employer.

Letter of Application. A letter written to a potential employer in which you express interest in a job and reasons for feeling qualified.

Application Form. A form developed by an employer, to be completed by you when you are asking to be considered for a job.

Qualifications.   Those characteristics that may help you get a particular job.

Resume.   A document that tells an employer about your schooling, training, and experience.

References.   People who know something about your abilities to do a job.

Self-Inventory.   An evaluation of your own personality, experience, interests, wants, and desired working conditions.

Follow-Up Letter.   A letter written to a potential employer after an interview to say thank you and express interest in the job again.

Self-Inventory

The first step in getting a job is to do a self-inventory—this will help you decide which type of job suits you best. Consider your experience, personality, ability, wants, and desired working conditions. Think about all these points and you will have a clearer idea of what you want in a job.

Experience.   Think about jobs you have already held. What did you think of them? What interests, hobbies, and activities do you have outside school? What kind of vocational preparation have you had?

Personality.   What are your likes and dislikes? Do you work well with others or do you perform better on your own? How do you feel about authority? And how do you work under pressure?

Ability.   What are your special talents, strengths, and weaknesses? Have you shown the ability to improve yourself when you set your mind to it? How are your grades?

Wants.   What are your goals in the near future and in the long run? Do you want to help other people? Do you want or need money, personal satisfaction, and personal recognition?

Working Conditions.　Do you want to work in a small or large operation? Do you like working with the public or would you prefer to be in the kitchen? Do you like indoor or outdoor work? How do you feel about the possibility of moving?

Going After a Job

In order to get a job, you first need to find out what is available. Tne next step is to apply for the job. Finally, you interview with the person who does the hiring.

Looking for a Job.　Many jobs will be listed in local newspaper want ads. State and private employment agencies also have listings of available jobs. The services of the state employment agency are taxpayer supported and free to you. Most private agencies charge a fee.

Besides checking those formal job listings, check with local businesses that interest you. It is possible that you will show up just as an employer is getting ready to advertise. Labor unions also keep listings of job possibilities.

The counselor at your school may keep track of job possibilities for students. Perhaps the principal or a teacher also does this. Some large schools even have a placement officer, who has the responsibility to help graduates find a job.

Check with people who are already working in the foodservice industry—they may know of openings. Friends and neighbors can also give your suggestions. The yellow pages of the phone book will give you a list of the foodservice establishments you may want to survey. You will find that want ads and employment services list jobs under standard titles. Be sure you know what they are talking about before you apply for a job. Check the Dictionary of Occupational Titles (DOT) prepared by the BLS or

Newspaper want ads often list many jobs in the foodservice industry.
Courtesy: Stillwater News Press.

PART TIME food/cocktail waiters, waitresses and buspersons. Must be 21 and willing to work weekends. Apply in person, Bobo's Cantina. No phone calls.

Department of Labor. It is available at your local library. The Occupational Outlook Handbook prepared by the BLS gives information on training needed, educational requirements, advancement possibilities, and earnings possibilities. Guidance counselors usually have copies of this document.

Once you have decided on the job area that interests you, you'll need the right tools for getting a job. These are the resume, application, and interview (including tests in some cases.)

The Resume.   The resume is a document that makes clear to the employer what you have to offer. It is a summary of information about you. A good resume should be neat, logical, honest, and descriptive. It should emphasize your strengths and be not more than two pages long. Follow outline form and organize the resume into the following categories:

Heading.   At the top of the resume, list your name, address, phone number, and social security number.

Job Preference.   Describe the job you want. If you are qualified for several jobs offered, list them in order of your preference.

Education.   List the schools you have attended and when, even if you are still in school, starting with the most recent. Describe major areas of study or courses that are related to the job. List any awards you have received, extracurricular activities, or offices that may have given you experience for the job.

Work Experience.   List your most recent employer first. Give the name and address of the employer and the period of time you worked there. Describe your duties and job title. Be sure to include any special training you received on the job.

Military Experience.   Describe your rank, where stationed, and type of duties you performed.

References.   List people who can give the employer information about you as a worker or as a person. Never use the names of relatives. Good references might be teachers, clergy, doctors, neighbors, former employers or supervisors, or even co-workers.

```
RESUME
TERRY McKRACKEN


ADDRESS:

Present:  774 E. Adams Street        Permanent:  Route #3
          YourTown, YourState 77704              AnyTown, YourState 77702
          (405) 555-7779                         (405) 555-4433

JOB OBJECTIVE:

Cook

ULTIMATE GOAL:

Food Service Manager

EDUCATION:

AnyTown High School, AnyTown, YourState 1976-79

Progress Vo-Tech, Progressville, YourState 1980-81
Certificate:  Food Service, Four Semesters
Grade Average:  3.5 on a 4.0 scale

RELATED SUBJECTS STUDIED:

High School                          Vo-Tech School

Bookkeeping - 2 semesters            Quantity Food - 540 hours
Communications - 1 semester          Baking - 270 hours
Jr. Cooking - 1 semester             Service - 135 hours
Senior Cooking - 1 semester          Nutrition - 30 hours
                                     Management - 60 hours
                                     Safety/Sanitation - 30 hours

STUDENT ACTIVITIES:

President, Senior Class
President, VICA
Treasurer, Baptist Youth Fellowship Organization
Culinary Arts Contest, Second Place State, Fifth Place National
```

The resume describes your background, including education, experience, and references.

Courtesy: Mid America Vocational Curriculum Consortium.

Send the resume to any companies that have jobs that interest you. Give one to your vocational teacher and guidance counselor so that they will have it on hand if a job opening comes to their attention. Carry a resume along if and when you go for an interview.

Letter of Application.   When you send a resume to a possible employer, include a letter of application. Your letter should be informative, clear, attractive, logical, and free from errors.

Give the name of the position that interests you. Summarize your qualifications for the job and mention that there is more detail in the resume, which is enclosed. Tell why you are in-

```
                              Route #3
                              AnyTown, YourState 77702
                              April 15, 1982

Mr. John Jones
Personnel Director
E & P Cafeteria, Box 19
YourTown, YourState 77704

Dear Mr. Jones:

Please consider me for the position of cook which you advertised in the
Daily Chronicle.

The skills I have learned in my food service courses should qualify me for
this job.  A more complete description of my qualifications is given in the
enclosed resume.

I would appreciate the opportunity to come and talk over this job opportunity
at your convenience and can be reached by telephone at 405-555-4433 after
3:30 or at the above address.

Sincerely,

Terry McKracken

Terry McKracken
Encl.
```

The letter of application tells the prospective employer that you are interested in a specific job and why you think you are qualified.

Courtesy: Mid America Vocational Curriculum Consortium.

terested in the job and what experience you have. Ask for an interview. Remember, your letter is your first contact with the person you want to be your boss. Be sure you make a good impression. Type the letter on standard business size (8½ × 11) paper and use a business envelope. Make sure you sign your name.

Application Form.   Most employers require an application form in addition to a resume and letter of application. Common information on the form is very much like your resume information. Make sure that you are completely honest when you fill out the form and that the information is as accurate as what you say in person. Be sure to type the application form or print in dark ink.

The Interview.   If you have sent in a good resume and application, you may get an invitation for an interview. That will be your opportunity to showcase your talents. The employer will be looking for certain characteristics during the interview—keep them in mind. The employer will be looking for a person who is enthusi-

Application for Employment

Name _____ Date_____
                    (Last)   (First)   (Middle)

Present Address _____ Tel. #_____
                         (Street)   (City)   (Zip Code)

Position applying for _____ Social Security # _____

Date available for work _____ Full time_____Part time_____Temporary_____

Do you have any physical defects?_____If yes, describe _____

Are you taking daily medication?_____If so, what? _____

Were you previously employed here?_____If so, when? _____

Who referred you to us? _____Do you have friends or relatives working here?_____

Have you ever been convicted of a crime?_____If so, please explain _____

Has a surety company ever refused to issue, or continue any bond on your behalf? _____

Will you take a verification test?_____Years completed in school _____

Have you had other training?_____If so, what other training? _____

Do you plan to take further training?_____What kind? _____

Are you in the military reserves?_____Can you work any day of the week? _____

Can you work any hours scheduled? _____

Please explain if there are days or hours that you can not work in the next six months _____

If employed will you be able to dress according to the Company's dress code? _____

WORK EXPERIENCE

Start with your present job, or your last, and list each job you have held. Include any military assignments.

Name of Employer _____

Address of Employer _____

Work Performed _____ From _____ To _____ Salary _____

Reason For Leaving _____

Name of Employer _____

Address of Employer _____

Work Performed _____ From _____ To _____ Salary _____

Reason For Leaving _____

The application form must be filled out with correct information about you, the job applicant.

Courtesy: Mid America Vocational Curriculum Consortium.

astic, dependable, honest, cooperative, and willing to work and learn. To help the employer see that you have these characteristics, get ready for the interview.

Appearance.   Look neat and be well groomed. Be sure your hair is neat and trimmed. Do not wear casual clothes such as sandals, t-shirt, or cap. Take along a copy of your resume and carry a pen to fill out forms. Be on time and go for the interview alone. Get information about the business beforehand. It will help you know what to expect in the interview.

Meeting the Interviewer.   You will probably meet a receptionist before going in to be interviewed by the person who does the hiring. Introduce yourself to the receptionist and explain why you are there. The receptionist will tell you where to wait.

Greet the interviewer with a smile and shake hands firmly. Tell the interviewer your name and the reason you are there. Do not sit down until the interviewer invites you to sit. Do not place your belongings on the interviewer's desk. Never smoke or chew gum during the interview.

Answering Questions.   The interviewer will no doubt ask you a number of questions—he or she is simply trying to find out if you are right for the job offered. Think carefully before answering questions. Be truthful and speak clearly, without nervousness. Do not discuss personal problems and do not speak badly of former employers. Try to speak positively. Even if you were fired, point out that you learned from the past. Do not get into discussions of politics and religion if possible. Personal questions are out of order but some interviewers may ask them anyway. Try to respond tactfully and look the interviewer in the eye and speak clearly.

Clarify Your Questions.   If the interviewer does not give all the information you wanted about the job, ask questions. Be sure to ask about schedules, rotations, and fringe benefits. Write your questions so that you do not forget to ask them.

Ending the Interview.   The interviewer will probably let you know when he or she has enough information from the interview.

```
                                        Route #3
                                        AnyTown, YourState 77702
                                        May 1, 1982

    Mr. John Jones
    Personnel Director
    E & P Cafeteria
    Box 19
    YourTown, YourState 77704

    Dear Mr. Jones:

    Thank you for interviewing me for the job of cook with your establish-
    ment.  I feel that working for the E & P Cafeteria would be enjoyable
    and that I could do the general cooking work that the job requires.
    Hopefully you will give me the opportunity to prove my worth.

    The application form you gave me is enclosed.

    I will be available for work May 15.  You may call me at my home after
    3:30 p.m.  The number is 405-555-4433.

    Sincerely,

    Terry McKracken

    Terry McKracken

    Encl.
```

After you have had a job interview, send the interviewer a follow-up letter to let him or her know that you are still interested in the job.
Courtesy: Mid America Vocational Curriculum Consortium.

Be sure you have made the points you want to before the interviewer gets up. Thank the interviewer for his or her time.

Interview Follow-Up.   After your interview, you may not have any definite information about the job for a while. Write a short thank you letter or call to show the employer you are still interested in the job. If you are not selected, do not feel defeated. Analyze the reasons as best you can and learn from them.

The Law and Employment.   You should know what the law requires of employers and employees in your state. All employers must follow the Fair Labor Standards Act, Wage and Hour Laws, and laws regarding unemployment insurance, workman's compensation, taxation, and social security.

Fair Labor Standards Act.   The Fair Labor Standards Act includes a group of laws that control how employment practices are carried out. They include the Federal Child Labor Law, which says that minors under the age of 18 can be employed only under certain conditions.

Children under 16 years of age can work only 3 hours on school days and only 18 hours a week except on weekends, national holidays, and summers. During the summer, a child can work no more than an 8-hour day or 40-hour week. Minimum wage laws say that employees must earn at least $3.35 an hour. They can get tip credits for $2.01 per hour.

Unemployment and Other Insurance. Every employer with a large business must register for state unemployment insurance and worker's compensation programs. This means that employers can deduct a certain portion from your paycheck to pay for that insurance. If you should become unemployed or disabled, you will be able to draw on those funds. Employers also withhold money for your federal and state taxes and for social security (FICA) taxes.

3
Human Relations

Do you get along with your classmates? Your boss? Your teachers? Good relationships with those people and others mean good human relations. It is important to get along with others on the job. It makes satisfied employees, pleased customers, and happy employers. All of this usually results in a better product. The customer who is happy will come back again. And the business makes higher profits. Greater profits for the employer keeps the business open and makes it possible for your employer to give you a raise. In other words, good human relations is good for everyone.

What makes for good human relations? That is not an easy question to answer—every person is different and his or her way of interacting with others is different. Still, the basis for good relations is each person's self-image. If you feel good about yourself, you will do your part to build a good relationship with others. However, like most people, you do not start with a self-image that is 100% positive all the time. That means you have to work on self-development—which means that you must develop a good work attitude and favorable personality traits.

Objectives and Terms

Objectives. This section should help you:

- Describe how personality affects human relations on the job.
- Describe some positive and negative job attitudes.

- Make a list of your own values and goals.
- Make a plan for personal development.
- List some of the reasons why people work.
- Get along on the job.
- List characteristics of a good team worker.
- Get along with the public.

Terms to Know

Personality Traits.   All of your typical characteristics and behaviors.

Assertiveness.   The ability to stand up for your rights.

Attitude.   The manner in which you approach everything in life.

Values.   Those things in life that are important to you.

Goal.   A target or something to shoot for in life.

Teamwork.   A system in which everyone works together to reach a goal.

Personality—You, the Person

All of your characteristics and behaviors make up your personality. Some of those traits are important to the kind of job you will do as a worker. By taking a close look at them, you will be better able to understand yourself and others. You will also get along better in society.

Desirable Personality Traits.   Those characteristics most important to the foodservice worker are friendliness, self-confidence, and humor or cheerfulness. It is also important to be tolerant of others and tactful in dealing with others. Suppose someone carries a pan or tray the wrong way: it would be tactless to say, "You dope, carry it with the potholders." Instead, you should suggest a better, safer way to do the task. Assertiveness is also an important trait—it is hard to get along on an even basis with people if they think of you as a doormat.

Undesirable Personality Traits.   Some characteristics can make it difficult for you to get along well in a work situation. The first is gossiping—a person who repeats rumors is usually not trusted by co-workers. Forming cliques on the job also gets in the way of success. A third undesirable characteristic is blaming problems on others—the person who cannot accept responsibility when something goes wrong usually has trouble getting along. Almost as bad is the trait known as apple-polishing: This is paying extra attention to a superior so that he or she might give special favors.

If you recognize any of these undesirable characteristics, decide now to work toward changing them. Decide that you can eliminate some of those not-so-great traits. Tell yourself which traits you will work on. Then make a plan and stick with it until you have reshaped those characteristics into some listed as "desirable."

Your Attitude

The way you approach everything in life is your attitude. It affects the way you talk, think, and work. Table 3.1 lists some positive and negative attitudes that might show up on the job.

It is important to work at changing attitudes if they are less than the best—it can be and should be done. Good work attitudes can help you get a job, keep a job, and advance in a job. They also help you take pride in your work. All of those benefits add up to job success.

Table 3.1: Positive and Negative Attitudes

Positive	Negative
Shows interest	Seems uninterested
Respects authority	Shows disrespect
Is willing to do more	Does the minimum
Carries out tasks	Does not follow through
Shows appreciation of others' help	Ignores others' help
Listens to criticism	Is unwilling to change or learn from others
Gives ideas	Does not contribute ideas
Deals honestly with others	Makes up excuses
Is even tempered	Complains, is grumpy
Accepts responsibility	Passes the buck

Steps to Improving Attitude. As in anything else, it helps to have a plan for improving attitudes. Start by looking at yourself carefully. Decide which of your attitudes need work. Then set up a schedule of goals. What will you work on first, second, and third? Finally, carry out your plan on a daily basis until you have achieved your attitude improvement goals. Work at it as hard as you can. Stick with it and stay in charge of your behavior. If you backslide, do not give up—keep working at it. Pay attention to the little things, too. Watch your appearance and speech. If you look and speak as though you have a good attitude, you may have one soon.

Here is a summary of steps to improving attitude:

1. Evaluate yourself
2. Decide on attitudes to improve.
3. Schedule your attitude improvement plan.
4. Work at attitude improvement every day.

Your Values and Goals

Values. Your values are important in human relations on the job. Values are those things in life that are important to you. They are based on your experiences with others and are usually first developed in the family. In most cases you take on the same values of those with whom you live. Your friends and co-workers also have some influence on your values. Even the type of television shows you watch can influence your values.

If you have clear values, you are on the way to a life with purpose and meaning. You know who you are and what you want out of life. On the other hand, unclear values make for an unsure path in life. If you do not know what is important to you, you may be confused about where you are going in life.

As you go about developing both as a person and as a worker, you will need to keep your values in mind. They should be the foundation for the goals you set.

Goals for Successful Development. A goal is like a target— something to shoot for. Your personal goals can be a roadmap for your future. There are short-term and long-term goals—both require careful consideration and planning. You will need to concentrate on short-term goals first, but remember that short-term goals lead to lifelong dreams. To obtain your goals:

1. Identify what's important to you—your values.
2. Choose your goal.
3. Think about your personal resources. These are your strengths, attitudes, environment, and values.
4. Develop a plan of action.
5. Carry out your plan to the finish.
6. Review what you did after you have finished. Did you get the results you hoped for? If not, why not? Think about it and start again, perhaps with a revised goal.

The Job—Why People Work

We almost never ask someone why he or she is working. It seems obvious that we all need to work to pay the bills, but there is more to working than that. People work for many reasons other than to bring home a paycheck: They need acceptance from their friends. They like the company of the workplace. They take pride in being able to support themselves and a family. They like the power that comes with some work. They have long-term goals that require working at a particular job today. They may want to be wealthy someday.

Different people have different reasons for choosing a job. Motivating factors depend on your background, abilities, and attitudes. If you grew up in a family that ran a restaurant, you probably value foodservice work. You may even have as a goal buying your own restaurant some day.

Whatever your reasons for working in a particular job, you need some important human relations skills to be successful: You need to learn to get along with people. You need to know what is expected of employees and employers. You need to learn teamwork.

Getting Along.   Try to understand other people. That may not always be possible, but, if you try, you may have better results than if you ignored others. Be cheerful and interested in others. Give pats on the back when they are due. Consider everyone an important person. Be honest and keep your promises. If you must criticize someone's work, help the person to learn from what you say. Keep an open mind in a two-sided argument. Ignore unfriendly comments about yourself. Do not try to get people to praise you—if you do a good job, praise will come soon enough.

What to Expect from the Boss. You as an employee should expect certain things from your employer: The first is that you expect to receive a just wage for the work you do. It should be the same wage as that received by others who do the same kind of work.

You also should expect some chance to grow on the job and perhaps get a promotion. That means job security.

Employers should provide a safe and pleasant workplace. It gives the employee a sense of security and belonging.

Employers should clearly explain duties, responsibilities, and rules and regulations.

What the Boss Expects from You. A boss expects a good worker to do the job, to follow instructions, and always to give his or her best.

Employees should cooperate with other members of the team and be loyal to the job. If necessary, an employee should give a little extra.

Workers should have good daily work habits. They should get to work on time, stay until the workday is over, and follow procedures.

The boss also has a right to expect the employee to be honest and decent.

How to Be a Member of the Team. In most foodservice operations, it takes more than one person to get the job done. The chef cannot prepare food without foodservice workers. And they cannot prepare food without dishroom workers. And they cannot clean dishes without the bus person. And so on. No one person can be more important than another. All members of the team need to know each other and know what they are expected to accomplish. Then they must cooperate to do the job.

Because it takes all members of the team to get the job done, it is important to be a team worker.

To get the job done, team members need to communicate with one another. That will help them know what is expected of each member of the team. They should work together to make decisions and be enthusiastic about working on the team.

It is not easy to make true team decisions. Often one person likes to make the decisions for others. That, of course, is not teamwork. Communication is an important skill in making team decisions. Each team member should consider whether everyone is having his or her say. Is everyone allowed to make suggestions without being shot down? Would you like to be treated as you treat others on the team? Are you trying to control the decision? Will everyone be satisfied with the result? If not, you can be sure that ultimately no one will.

The truly successful team worker does not stop with his or her job either. The team worker helps out in other areas if needed. He or she does not make excuses or say, "That's not my job." He or she works until the job is completely done.

If something changes, let everybody know. It may affect their work, too. Suppose you work in the salad section and a shipment of lettuce did not arrive on time. The salad supervisor decides to substitute spinach in the day's salad. As a responsible team member, make sure the other salad people are aware of the change. It will make the job easier for everyone and the customer will benefit from your extra care.

How to Get Along with the Public.

Use your best human relations skills with the public. Remember, they keep you in business. Always be courteous and helpful. If you are the waiter or waitress, be patient and tolerant. Be especially considerate of children and the elderly. Be cheerful. It will make the customer want to come back. Try your best to get the order right. Be sincere and tactful. If the fish is not the best that day, do not say, "The fish stinks." Say that it is not up to par. Then suggest an alternative. Be sure your appearance is pleasing. Wear a clean, neat uniform and be sure your hair is in place. Have a positive attitude and a cheery voice.

4
Communications

When you ask a friend for a ride to school, you may or may not have communicated with your friend. If your friend answers, "Yes, I'll give you a ride," there has been communication. If you think he will give you a ride, but he does not stop for you, communication has failed.

Objectives and Terms

Objectives.   This section should help you:

- Define communications.
- List the three parts of communication.
- Describe how to be an effective communicator.
- List the communication steps for the sender and receiver.
- List the four types of communication.
- Describe the two elements of verbal communication.
- Name common listening traps.
- Describe some positive and negative characteristics of body language.

Terms to Know

Communications.   The transmission of information, with understanding, from one person to another.

Sender.   The person who sends information to another.

Receiver. The person who receives information from another.

Medium. The means through which a message is sent from one person to another.

Feedback. Questions or comments from the receiver that tell the sender a message is coming through.

Verbal Communication. Transmission of information from one person to another by speaking.

Written Communication. Transmission of information from one person to another by writing.

Body Language. Communication of ideas by the position or expression of the body.

Visual Communication. The use of posters, displays, or other means to communicate ideas.

What Is Communication?

Communication is the transmission of information, with understanding, from one person to another. It does not have to be written. It does not have to be spoken. The key to communication is understanding. Without it, there is no communication.

There are three parts to communication: a sender, a receiver, and a medium or means of transmitting the message.

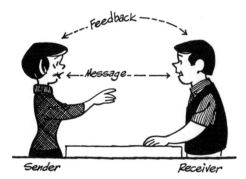

Sender   *Receiver*

For communication to take place there must be a sender, a receiver, and a means of transmitting the message (speech in this case.)

Why Communication Is Important

Communication plays a big role in foodservice operations. It is the key to working with other people. In the foodservice business, we communicate with three different groups: customers, other workers, and supervisors. We may do this by writing, by speaking face to face, by talking on the phone, or by electronic means. No matter how we do it, communication still depends on the message being understood by the receiver as it was intended by the sender.

How to Be an Effective Communicator

In order to get a message across, consider these important elements of good communication. Believability is important: If the receiver does not have basic trust in the sender, there will be no communication. Be sure the receiver has his or her mind on what you, the sender, are communicating. Avoid communicating at times when interruptions or lots of background noise get in the way.

The receiver should work at listening to the sender's message. The receiver should give the sender feedback so the sender knows whether or not the message is coming through as intended. Feedback includes such questions as, "Would you explain what you mean by that?" or "Do I turn the hand guard to the left or right?" A simple nod of the head can be feedback, too.

Communications Steps for the Sender. No matter what type of communication you use, if you are the sender, follow these steps to get your message across:

Be Clear. Tell exactly what you want to happen or the results you expect.

Examples. Make your main points with examples.

Simple Language. Do not use fancy words or beat around the bush. It will complicate your message. On the other hand, do not talk to people as if they are stupid.

Respect.   The listener is an important person. Treat him or her with respect when you communicate.

Communications Steps for the Receiver.   If you are the receiver of the message, follow these steps:

Listen.   Pay attention. Do not let your thoughts wander. Make a point of getting all the information before thinking about your reply.

Questions.   Ask questions to be sure you understand the sender's message.

Be Considerate.   Some people who send messages to you may not be experienced communicators. Be patient and respectful.

Types of Communication

There are four basic types of communication. They all have the same three elements. Let us look at each type more closely.

Verbal Communication.   We use verbal communication, or speech, all day long. It is the most common form for most of us. If we work in the service part of the operation, verbal communication influences sales. If we use incorrect English, slang, vulgarity, or jargon, we can turn off the customer. Verbal communication

Speech is the most common communication form for most of us.

between workers helps the operation run smoothly. It leads to good human relations among workers and also helps create a pleasant environment in which to work.

Communication between workers and supervisors is a key factor in a good or poor work environment. Communications that are below par can lead to low morale, poor production, and small profits.

Verbal communication depends on two processes, speaking and listening:

Speaking.   Speaking is the sending of a verbal message. To make the message clear, speak slowly and carefully. Use a pleasant tone of voice. Always speak in complete sentences—it helps the listener know what you mean. Use correct grammar and acceptable speech. Avoid slang. Do not say "Ah" or "Umm" before every sentence.

Listening.   Listening is the key to receiving the message. Learning to listen can help you improve your work performance. It can help you get along better with fellow workers. And, if you listen well, you will understand what a customer is trying to communicate. Therefore, you can help the customer get what he or she wants. Good listening also makes it possible to follow directions. That results in doing the job better. Watch out for common listening traps:

Try not to fall into listening traps. They can keep you from understanding the message.

Interruptions.   If you interrupt the speaker, you will not be able to understand his or her message.

Pretending Attention.   If you are not interested in what the sender is saying, you will not get the point. Pretending to pay attention does not help clarify the message. It just makes the sender think you have heard the message.

Quick Conclusions.   If your mind rushes ahead, you may decide that the speaker is saying something other than what he or she intends.

Concentrating on Something Else.   Focus your attention on the message rather than the speaker. He or she may be wearing an interesting shirt but do not let it distract you. Try to maintain eye contact.

One special situation that requires good listening skills is taking a message. If you are asked to give a phone or verbal message to another person, listen especially well. Be sure to write down who gave the message, when you got it, what it was about, and where the person can be reached. Spell the name correctly when you write it down. Be sure you have written down all the important points.

If you take business phone calls, answer the phone quickly. Use a pleasant voice and identify yourself. Speak into the receiver and do not be shy about using the phone. Follow the policy of the company. Some businesses want employees to get the name of the caller. Others do not. Avoid putting the caller on "hold"—it may be better to ask if you can call the person back when you have the information he or she needs. If you do put the caller on hold, check back from time to time so that he or she does not think you have hung up. When you return to the phone, thank the person for waiting. If your phone has no hold button, place the receiver on the desk while you get information or call another person to the phone.

A common setting for verbal communication is a first meeting. If you are meeting people for the first time, get off to a good start with good communications. Introduce yourself with your first and last names. Give some details about yourself. Say, for example, "I'm Jane Smith and I'll be your assistant."

Keep written communications simple.

Sometimes casual conversation is important to setting the tone for a good work environment. Learn the art of conversation. Ask the other person about his or her family and other interests. Let him or her do some of the talking. Use good manners if you are talking with a person older than yourself. It is courteous to call a person who is older than you are by Mr., Mrs., or Ms., unless you are asked to use the person's first name. Get into the habit of using friendly phrases such as "good morning," "hello," or "good-bye."

Written Communication.   To make your written communications effective, keep them simple, clear, and neat. Follow those suggestions in anything you write. It may be a letter of application, a telephone message, a standard record, or a report form. Remember, you are still trying to send a message. In the case of written communications, the means of transmitting your message is paper instead of spoken words.

Body Language.   Another type of communication that is sometimes the most expressive of all is the language of the body itself. Have you ever seen someone slouch in a chair? What does that tell

Your body language tells a lot about your attitude.

you about what the person thinks? It may mean that he or she is not interested. That is an example of how your posture "speaks." Other features of our body language include dress, gestures, tone of voice, eye contact, facial expressions, and space.

Posture.   To communicate positively, stand or sit straight. Slouching tells people you are depressed or uninterested.

Dress.   If you wear neat, clean clothing, you tell the world you have confidence and pride in yourself. On the other hand, slovenly or dirty clothes say you do not care.

Gestures.   In our culture, we have some very common gestures. Shaking hands is a routine greeting and a way of saying "welcome," "nice to have you here," or "good-bye." A pat on the back is a common way of telling people, "that was a job well done." Negative gestures include squirming, finger drumming, or shuffling of feet. These gestures tell people you are nervous or bored.

Tone of Voice.   The way you accent words can say a lot about what you mean.

Eye Contact.   If you look a person in the eye as you speak or listen, you show interest. If you turn your eyes away, you have created a barrier to communication.

Sometimes it is helpful to use posters or other visuals to make a point.

Facial Expressions. Everyone knows the difference between a smile and a frown. Other clues to how you feel are the position of the eyebrows, the tilt of the chin, and the tilt of the head.

Space. Most people are comfortable speaking to others if they have a little distance between them. We are not accustomed to standing nose to nose. If you give a message to another, keep in mind that need for distance.

Visual Communication. In some cases, we go beyond plain verbal and written communication and body language. To make a point, we use visuals of some kind—a demonstration, poster, menu, or display. Whatever is used to illustrate the point, the visual should be colorful, neat, and well designed.

5
Sanitation

Sanitation is the process of promoting cleanliness. It involves all of the practices that help to provide the customer with food that is safe to eat. Sanitation includes both personal habits and work procedures. Many government agencies are concerned about cleanliness—those that play some part in sanitation in the food-service area include the following

- Food and Drug Administration (FDA).
- U.S. Department of Agriculture (USDA).
- U.S. Center for Disease Control (CDC).
- Environmental Protection Agency (EPA).
- Federal, state, and local health departments.

These agencies have different responsibilities. Some conduct regular inspections of facilities, where they inspect such things as:

- Food handling.
- Personnel.
- Cleaning and sanitizing procedures for equipment.
- Sanitary services such as toilets, sinks, sewers, drains.
- Construction and maintenance of sanitary facilities.

If inspectors find a problem, they have standard procedures for the foodservice operator to follow to comply with health regulations.

Objectives.   This section should help you:

- Define sanitation.
- List important practices in personal cleanliness.
- List common microorganisms that can cause foodborne illness.
- Describe conditions important for the growth of most bacteria.
- List common pests in foodservice areas and methods of control.
- Describe standards for sanitary food production.
- Describe general steps in cleaning and sanitizing foodservice areas.

Terms

Sanitation.   All practices that help keep personnel, food, and the foodservice area clean.

Hygiene.   Practices that help maintain good health.

Grooming.   Personal and clothing care habits.

Microorganisms.   Very small plants or animals that we can see only with a microscope. They include bacteria, molds, viruses, and yeasts.

Bacteria.   Types of microorganisms. Some can multiply rapidly and cause spoilage and foodborne illnesses.

Foodborne Illness.   Disease or injury that occurs from ingestion of contaminated food.

Food Poisoning.   A traditional term for food infection or food intoxication caused by eating food contaminated by microorganisms.

Contamination.   The presence of harmful substances, especially organisms, in food.

Pasteurization.   A heat process that destroys some microorganisms in milk and some other food products.

Cleaning.   Practices that help remove soil and dirt.

Sanitizing.   Practices that help destroy microorganisms.

Detergents.   Cleaning agents that are used with water to loosen soil.

Germicides.   Strong chemicals that are used to kill germs or bacteria on work surfaces.

Wares.   All tools, utensils, and equipment used in food preparation.

Sanitation and the Foodservice Worker

Each foodservice worker represents the establishment. That is why personal cleanliness is very important. Customers judge the operation by the workers. Employees should do their best to be neat and clean and to maintain a neat clean operation.

Personal cleanliness (or hygiene) is important because it makes a worker more attractive to a customer. Cleanliness also helps prevent disease and the spread of germs or microorganisms that can cause disease.

Personal Habits.   A foodservice worker who does not have good personal habits can make people sick. He or she can contaminate food when handling it. Cleanliness helps to assure that the food that comes out of the worker's area is as sanitary as it can be.

Body Cleanliness.   Foodservice workers should bathe every day. They should put on clean underwear and use a deodorant every day.

Hand Cleanliness.   Germs responsible for foodborne illness usually come from the hands of a foodservice worker. It is therefore extremely important to keep hands clean. Wash thoroughly with a germ-killing soap that comes from a dispenser. Use plenty of very warm water. Wash hands after using the restroom, after eating, and when moving from one kind of food handling to another. Be sure to clean under fingernails. Use a brush if necessary.

Hair Cleanliness.   Wash hair frequently. Wear a simple hair style that is easy to control. Hair should not hang below the collar.

Wash hands with soap and plenty of warm water.

Wear hair back away from the face. Always wear a hair net or hat when working. Loose hair has a habit of ending up in the customer's food.

Mouth Hygiene. Floss and brush teeth every day. This helps control diseases and bad breath.

Feet Care. Keep your feet in good condition. Wash them daily to minimize odor. Use a foot powder in warm weather. Ask a foot specialist to care for calluses or corns. Improper care can lead to infections that could cause you to miss work. Wear comfortable, loose-fitting shoes with a good arch support. Be sure they have rubber, nonslip soles. They will help prevent foot fatigue. Wear good, medium-weight, clean hosiery.

Wearing Apparel and Uniform Care. Each foodservice operation has its own uniform policy. Some workers wear a simple white uniform, others use a vivid trademark uniform that is well remembered by customers. Wear no jewelry except watches, rings, or simple post earrings on the job.

Uniform Policy or Dress Code. The operation may have rules about uniforms. They may include requirements like these:

1.   Uniforms should be neat, clean, and well pressed.
2.   Uniforms should be not too short or too long.

A. Soiled uniforms and poor grooming can cause sanitation problems. B. Good grooming and a neat appearance are important to sanitation in the foodservice business.

3. There should be no ripped seams.
4. Aprons and caps should be kept neat and clean.
5. Uniforms should not be so loose that they create a safety problem.
6. Uniforms should not be so tight that they are uncomfortable.

Grooming for Women Workers.   Use light makeup, if any. Heavy makeup can run or look bad in a hot, steamy kitchen area. If you wear foundation garments, be sure they fit correctly.

Grooming for Men Workers.   Shave or trim beard every day. It will help with personal cleanliness.

Overall Good Health.   As you will read in the unit on nutrition, what you eat affects how you feel and how you do the job. A well-balanced diet will also help you resist colds and other body infections. Remember that a balanced diet means eating foods from the basic food groups in the right amounts.

Preventing Foodborne Illness

Sources of Foodborne Illness.   The goal in preparing food for service is to keep it wholesome and to prevent foodborne illness, that is, any illness caused by food. It can be caused by bacteria or other infectious agents, by toxins produced by bacteria, or by chemical contaminants.

Bacteria-Caused Illnesses.   Bacteria are tiny organisms or microorganisms. Some people call them germs. They grow and multiply if conditions are right. There are many kinds of bacteria. Some are harmless but others can cause serious illness if enough of them are growing in food.

Some bacteria float in the air. Others occur in the mouth and intestines of every person. They also grow on skin and hair. Since body temperature is 98.6°F, you can see that the human body is an ideal environment for bacteria.

Some bacteria that grow in food are "good" bacteria: A few types cause fermentation, which is a changing process that results in foods such as buttermilk, cheese, sauerkraut, pickles, vinegar, alcohol, beer, and wine. Other "good" bacteria help decompose organic waste. If they did not, we would never be able to get rid of our garbage.

Most foodborne illnesses are food infections or food intoxications.

Table 5.1: Common Foodborne Illnesses

Microorganism	Disease: how carried
Salmonella group	Intestinal infection: food contaminated by dirty hands, undercooked or dirty eggs, poultry, meat
Staphylococcus aureus	Intestinal infection: food contaminated by coughing, sneezing, sores, boils on a worker's body
Clostridium botulinum	Botulism (deadly): toxin from bacteria in improperly canned food
Perfringens	Intestinal infection: food contaminated with intestinal wastes from food handlers

Food infection. *Salmonella* and *perfringens* bacteria are examples of food infection. Food infection is caused when a person eats contaminated food. The bacteria in the food causes an infection in the gastrointestinal tract, which may lead to vomiting, diarrhea, nausea, weakness, or abdominal cramps.

Food intoxication. *Staphylococcus aureus* and *clostridium botulinum* are the most common causes of food intoxication. In both cases, the bacteria produce toxins in the food. *Staphylococcus* is transmitted by coughing or sneezing directly onto food. When the food is kept warm for several hours, the toxin develops.

In the case of *Clostridium botulinum,* the conditions for growth are different. It usually comes from a low-acid food that is canned. The toxin develops in the absence of air, and the resulting food poisoning can be fatal! Danger signs are bulging cans, leaks, broken seals, rusty cans, or off-colored or off-flavored products. A common source of botulism is home canning. Table 5.1 lists common foodborne illnesses.

Conditions for growth. Conditions that help most problem bacteria grow rapidly are warmth, moisture, and food. Some bacteria require oxygen, while others (such as *Clostridium botulinum*) do not. Sunlight is the enemy of most bacteria.

Consider one ideal environment for a colony of *Salmonella* bacteria. A few bacteria are floating in the air near an egg, freshly cracked out of its shell. The air temperature is warm—about 85°F. When the bacteria settle on the surface of the egg, they

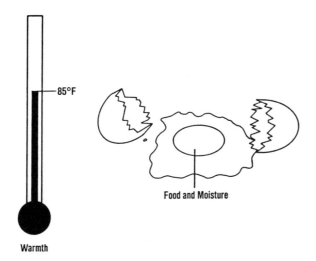

Bacteria need moisture, food, and warmth to grow.

begin to multiply rapidly. There is moisture and food in the egg and the warm air helps bacteria to grow.

By knowing about those three necessary conditions, we can control bacteria growth. Food is always a growth medium for bacteria, but we can control temperature and moisture.

Controlling temperature. Most troublesome bacteria grow best between 45 and 140°F. This is the danger zone. By controlling the temperature of food or its environment, we can slow the growth of bacteria on food. It should be below 45°F or above 140°F. That is why we refrigerate, freeze, or cook food. Above 170°F most bacteria die.

Controlling moisture. Drying has been used to control moisture in food for centuries. When moisture is low, bacteria do not grow well.

Other controls. Over time, people have also learned to control bacteria in food by adding acid, salt, or sugar. Three common food preservation techniques make use of these principles—pickling (acid), curing (salt), and candying (sugar.)

Kitchen Cleanliness. In the kitchen area, the goal of sanitation is to control the growth of microoganisms and pests that carry

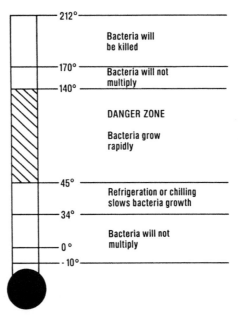

To keep bacteria from multiplying rapidly, be sure food is not in the temperature danger zone—between 45 and 140°F.

them. The best way to do that is to be sure the area is absolutely clean. Why? So that pests do not have food on which to feed.

Pests in the Kitchen.   The most common kitchen pests are flies, roaches, ants, mice, and rats. They feed on waste food and carry germs and viruses from garbage to other food. That is what spreads foodborne diseases. It can also spread the pests themselves (by reproduction). When insects and rodents get into food, it can result in expensive food spoilage, too. This is called food contamination.

To keep pests under control, report signs of bugs and rodents at once. Learn about their favorite hiding places and behaviors. You will be better able to control them if you do. Table 5.2 lists common pests, their habits, and controls.

Kitchen Procedures to Control Pests.   Let us summarize the steps that will help control all kinds of kitchen pests:

To keep pests from coming in.   Remove all spoiled food from the kitchen and throw it out. Do not leave water standing on the

Table 5.2: Pests, Habits, and Controls

Pest	Habits	Controls
Rodents	Build nests in holes, rubbish piles; can jump and swim; eat anything; reproduce quickly; carry fleas with bacteria; urine and feces contaminate food	Seal holes and cracks; deprive of food; cover food, cover garbage; get help from exterminator
Ants	Live in colonies where they store food for young; carry disease germs on feet and bodies	Get rid of waste; clean garbage cans; find colony and use chemicals
Roaches	Feed at night; live in cracks, crevices for 5 years, eat anything, are thirsty, carry disease	Cover food; keep work areas clean; get rid of damp areas; use chemical controls
Flies	Lay 100–200 eggs in any waste; eggs hatch in few days to maggots, which grow to adults in 4 to 5 days; carry filth and germs on bodies	Keep area clean, cover garbage; use screen doors and windows; protect food
Mosquitoes	Breed in water; multiply rapidly	Use screens; eliminate breeding places
Lice	Eggs hatch in 2–3 days; cling to hair; carry typhus	Use chemical controls, special shampoo

Control rodents and insects in the food preparation and service area.

floor, counters, tables, or in drains. Clean all work surfaces thoroughly and regularly. Clean drains with a good cleaner every day. Keep covers on all garbage containers. Be sure doors and windows are closed or screened. If there are any loose tiles, boards, or other problems, report them right away. They could become homes for rodents, roaches, or other pests.

To eliminate pests if they do get in.　Sometimes it is impossible to keep pests from coming into a food production area. After all, there is food around all the time to tempt them. If they do get in, use a regular control program. Some foodservice operators contract with an exterminator. Others do the job themselves. Whatever the choice, use the right control for the pest. Use repellents to keep pests away. Use poison, dust, or powder to kill them. For some pests, bait and traps work best. Whatever the case, be sure the product or procedure is safe to use around food. Follow the policy for your operation.

Standards for Sanitary Food Production.
Foodborne illness almost always comes from mishandling food. It may be due to one or more of the following factors:

- Incorrect food preparation.
- Improper holding of food.
- Improper storage of food.
- Incorrect serving techniques.

There are hazards in preparing any food, but foods most likely to become contaminated by bacteria, viruses, or other microorganisms are

- Milk products.
- Meat.
- Poultry.
- Fish and shellfish.
- Eggs.

These foods are favorite targets for microorganisms because they are protein foods. To protect those and other foods, follow correct sanitation steps for each food. Use only wholesome food that is not spoiled. Refrigerate protein foods. Use clean utensils and equipment and wash food before using it. Here are special instructions for individual foods.

Milk products.   Start with milk that is pasteurized. Pasteurization is a heat process that destroys some bad microorganisms. Pasteurized milk will have a much lower bacteria count than unpasteurized (raw) milk. Store milk and milk products in the refrigerator at 45°F or lower. It keeps well for three to five days if held at 33–37°F. Milk products must be cooked thoroughly.

Meat.   Be sure the meat you buy is USDA inspected. Watch for slimy meat or meat that has a bad odor—both are signs of bacterial spoilage. Pork spoils first where the bone meets the flesh. Beef spoils from the outside in. To prevent spoilage, store meat at 35°F for a short time or freeze it. To assure the safety of cooked meat, be sure it is cooked to the right internal temperature. Pork is cooked to an internal temperature of 165–170°F and other meats to an internal temperature of 140°F.

Poultry.   Be sure birds are not sticky under the wings or above the tail. Dark wing tips are another sign of a bird that has been around too long. To prepare poultry, be sure to wash equipment and hands carefully. If the cutting board has cracks, they can be a hiding place for bacteria and other microbes. Use a clean cutting board (preferably not wooden) with no cracks. Cook poultry to an internal temperature of 180°F.

Fish.   The odor is the best clue for fish—if it smells bad, it is bad. Sunken eyes and grey gills are other bad signs. If fish or shellfish is good, handle it the right way to keep it fresh. Refrigerate until preparation time, but do not wait too long. Use a clean cutting board and equipment. Cook soon after cutting.

Eggs. *Salmonella* bacteria can come from the chicken and infect eggs. If the egg has even the slightest crack, organisms can multiply rapidly. Be sure that any eggs used for cooking are clean and fresh, with no cracks. Hard cooking will stop bacteria from multiplying, but they can begin growing on the surface of the shelled egg once it is cooked. To control microorganisms, plunge hard-cooked eggs in boiling water for 60 seconds. Then drain in a

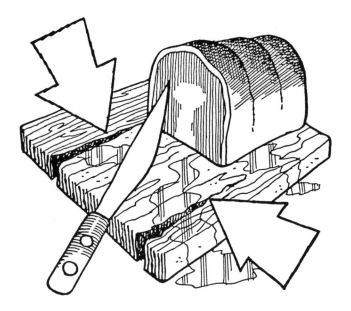

Cracks in a cutting board can be a hiding place for microorganisms.

colander and put in the refrigerator until it is time to cut the eggs or use them whole.

Dried foods.   Keep cereals, sugar, flour, and pasta in covered ratproof containers. Store on shelves that are at least 6 inches above the floor and 2 inches away from the wall. Watch temperature and humidity carefully. Insects grow rapidly in storage areas that are too warm or unventilated. Moisture will help mold grow on these foods. If there is insect or mold damage, throw out the dried food. Be sure to label all containers.

Frozen foods.   Frozen meat usually needs to be defrosted before cooking. Be sure to defrost in the refrigerator, not on a shelf at room temperature. This can cause bacteria to multiply quickly. Keep vegetables and other foods frozen until it is time to cook them. If they stand out for a long time, bacteria growth can lead to spoilage. Heat all frozen meat, vegetables, and prepared dishes to 170°F to destroy any bacteria that have started multiplying.

Leftovers.   Store leftovers in the freezer or in the refrigerator at 42°F or lower. Cover them and use within one day. If there is any sign of spoilage, do not use leftovers.

Fruits and vegetables.   Wash produce well and store in clean containers. Watch out for mold on fruit—it looks like cotton fibers. To prevent mold growth, keep fruit cold and dry.

Canned food.   Canned food is the least likely to spoil from bacterial contamination. Store cans for the right length of time in a cool, dry storage area. Never use food from a can that is bulging, leaking, or dented at the seam. If the contents look or smell unusual, do not use the food.

Rules for Preparing Sanitary Food.   Food poisoning can result from carelessness in the food preparation area. To avoid being responsible for mild or serious illness, or even death from food contamination, follow these rules:

Use chilled ingredients.   Be sure that all ingredients for any food mixture are thoroughly chilled before you start. Do not make potato salad with warm potatoes, for example. Warm potatoes will cause the mixture to become a great incubator for bacteria.

Prepare food quickly.   Try to keep food at room temperature for only a short time. Work quickly, and then heat or refrigerate the prepared food.

Cool at 45°F.   If prepared food goes to the refrigerator, be sure the temperature is 45°F or lower. Store food in shallow pans so that it cools quickly. If containers are too big or deep, the food in the center will stay warm, which will help bacteria to grow. If food has been standing out for several hours, it is probably not safe to store in the refrigerator.

Caution: Refrigeration does *not* kill bacteria—it just keeps them from growing or slows their growth.

Heat food to 140°F.   Heat hot food to at least 140°F. Do not hold foods on serving lines or steam tables at a temperature lower than that. Remember that temperatures between 45 and 140°F are ideal for bacteria growth.

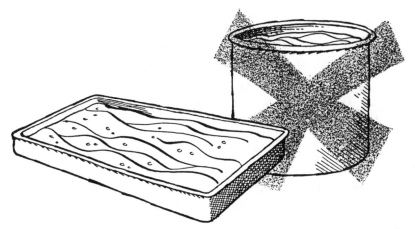

Refrigerate food in shallow pans to cool quickly. If containers are too deep, food at the center will stay warm for a long time.

Follow recipe for meat preparation. Use only meat that comes from inspected packing plants or other approved sources. Let frozen meat thaw in the refrigerator for the correct amount of time. Cook meat to the right internal temperature according to a standardized recipe for that meat cut.

Cook milk and eggs. Milk and eggs are especially good media for bacteria growth. Cook any products that contain milk and eggs thoroughly, but be careful not to overcook. Milk will curdle and eggs will become tough. (See Chapters 21 and 22.)

Taste and stir correctly. Use a separate small spoon to taste food. Never use the stirring spoon. You will introduce bacteria from your mouth into the mixture. Do not taste with the fingers either. They can carry bacteria that will contaminate food.

Standards for Sanitary Storage. Correct storage procedures are the first step toward sanitation in food handling. Keep storage areas clean through a regular cleaning program. Follow these storage procedures:

Separate food. Separate food into cold and dry foods.

Cold storage. Put food for the freezer into a freezer kept at 0°F or lower. Refrigerators should be kept at 40°F.

Dry storage. Place dry food away from heat on shelves that are off the floor and away from the walls. Control moisture and pests.

Cover food. Cover food tightly to prevent contamination.

Store sensibly. Keep like foods together. Do not store foods with an odor next to foods that absorb odors (onions and dairy products.) Be careful not to store raw meat over other food. (Blood or drippings could contaminate food on lower rack.)

Standards for Sanitation in Serving Food. If you have handled food correctly all the way from the loading dock to the steam table, it is foolish to spoil it by serving incorrectly. Follow these guidelines for serving food.

Clean hands. Wash hands thoroughly before serving food. Never lick fingers when serving, and avoid touching hair with hands during serving.

Hair and uniform. Always wear some kind of hair covering— a hairnet, cap, or hat. Be sure your uniform is clean. Do not chew gum while serving.

Handling the place setting. Do not hold forks, knives, and spoons by the eating ends. Handle glassware, dinnerware, and

Do not touch the rims of glasses when serving.

cups correctly. Never touch the rims of cups or the eating surfaces of plates. Use tongs to portion out ice, butter, and pastries.

The right temperature.　Always serve hot food *hot* and cold food *cold*.

Cleaning and Sanitizing.　Everything we do in cleaning is designed to keep food from spoiling, to control odors, and to reduce health hazards. In general we use the term *cleaning* to mean removing soil. *Sanitizing* means removing microorganisms that the eye can not see.

Cleaning.　Clean with water and detergent. Water is the basic cleaning agent and detergent loosens soil. There are four types of detergents, each with a different purpose:

1.　Alkaline detergent is the most common. It removes food, grease, and general soil. Use this type in dishwashing machines.
2.　Acid detergent removes lime buildup and discoloration from equipment such as the dishwashing machine itself. Lime is a calcium compound that comes from water and makes a crust on machine parts over time.
3.　Neutral detergent is especially designed for cleaning floors.
4.　Combination detergents are mixtures of one of these detergents with a sanitizer.

Sanitizing.　As we said earlier, the purpose of sanitizing is to prevent microorganisms from contaminating food. There are several ways to do this.

Heating at a temperature of 170°F or more for 30–45 seconds will destroy most food microorganisms.

Special chemicals destroy microorganisms on dishes and equipment. In selecting these chemicals, a foodservice operator should consider hardness of the water, alkaline content of water, the type of metal used in the equipment, and the amount of contact there will be with employees' hands and with food. The most common chemicals are

1.　Iodine: It is good for hard water but not for alkaline water. It does not harm skin.

2. Chlorine: Chlorine works well in hard water, but not in alkaline water. It is harmful to skin and eyes.

3. Quats Compound: This compound is good in acid or alkaline water, but not in very hard water. It does not control bacteria as well as iodine or chlorine.

4. Germicides (sanitizers): Use these very strong chemicals on tables and counters but avoid contact with food.

Ware Washing. Washing steps are different for hand tools, utensils, small equipment, or pots and pans. In general, soak, wash, rinse, sanitize, and air or heat dry wares. Then store in a clean place. It is important to wash wares correctly. Follow the directions on cleaning supplies. Always store cleaners covered in the correct place, with the correct label.

Washing Dinnerware and Glassware. Wash glasses and dinnerware correctly. Do not put glasses and dishes in the same racks. Check glasses for breaks and chips. Throw out any cracked or broken pieces at once. Do not pretend they are not broken. A customer could be injured if a broken glass stays in circulation.

Floor Care. Clean floors in the foodservice area every day. Never use brooms. They cause dust to rise and spread germs in the air. Instead, dust mop, damp mop, and wet mop foodservice area floors.

Dust mopping picks up dust. Damp mopping takes off surface dirt but not the floor finish. In wet mopping, the worker pushes the mop back and forth on the floor. Cleaning solution helps loosen and lift dirt. Follow the correct procedure for wet mopping floors.

Wall Cleaning. Clean walls regularly with neutral cleaning solution.

6
Safety

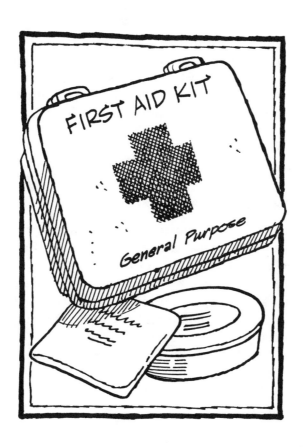

Each year about 100,000 people in the United States die because of accidents. Of those, 17,000 are on-the-job accidents. A far larger number are injured in workplace accidents.

You may say it is too bad that so many people have to die or become disabled, but accidents do happen. In fact, most accidents can be prevented. We need to pay attention, take our time, and be sure we understand how to do a task before trying to do it.

Objectives and Terms

Objectives. This section should help you:

- List the major causes of workplace accidents.
- List three or more causes of fires in the workplace.
- Describe the classes of fires.
- List types of fire extinguishers and types of fires they control.
- List steps in preventing and controlling fires.
- Demonstrate correct lifting and carrying techniques.
- Describe kitchen safety techniques.
- Describe general first aid procedures for simple kitchen accidents.

Terms to Know

Accident. An unintentional event that causes damage.

Safety. Procedures that get rid of unsafe conditions or behaviors that cause accidents.

Hazard. A source of danger.

Obstructed Vision.   Inability to see clearly where you are going or what you are doing.

Combustible.   Material that can start a fire.

Fire Extinguisher.   A container filled with a substance used to put out fires.

Flammable.   Material that burns easily.

Spontaneous Combustion.   The starting of a fire due to the flash burning of materials, apparently without cause.

Burn.   Injury caused by fire, steam, hot liquids, or chemicals.

Electrical Shock.   Dramatic jolt caused by an electrical charge delivered to the body.

Wound.   A break in the skin caused by a strong force.

First Aid.   The first steps taken to help an accident victim until medical help arrives.

CPR.   Cardiopulmonary resuscitation: emergency procedure performed by trained individuals to help a heart stoppage victim.

OSHA.   Occupational Safety and Health Act: federal legislation whose purpose is to ensure safe working conditions.

Major Causes of Accidents and Prevention

Let us take a close look at how accidents happen. They may be due to unsafe conditions or unsafe behavior. Unsafe conditions can be controlled or removed, but unsafe behavior is harder to eliminate. It involves people who have habits that may lead to accidents.

To keep behavior-caused accidents to a minimum, train yourself to be careful. In general, keep your mind on what you are doing. Pick up anything you drop. Wipe up anything you spill.

The major cause of accidents are falls and fires. Accidents can also result from obstructed vision, improper lifting, and unsafe equipment.

Falls.   Try to avoid falls in corridors, in doorways, or on wet or soiled floors by following these precautions:

Walk.   Do not run in halls or kitchen areas. Be very careful on newly washed or waxed floors. Wet floors are a common safety hazard.

Don't wait for someone to trip
over something. Pick up what you drop immediately.

Use Ladders for Climbing.   Do not climb on stacked boxes,
chairs, rickety ladders, or anything not intended for climbing. Be
sure your ladder is tall enough that you do not have to climb all
the way to the top to reach what you want.

Keep Passageways Clear.   Do not store equipment, supplies, or trash in corridors and traffic areas. Report broken tiles,
turned-up carpet, or other problems to a supervisor.

Stay to the Right.   Slow down and stay to the right as you
enter hallways.

Wear Suitable Shoes.   Wear rubber-soled closed shoes, not
open-toe sandals or other unsafe shoes.

Do not climb on boxes, chairs, or other unstable objects. Use a step stool or ladder.

Spills can cause serious falls and injuries. Wipe up anything you spill.

Wipe Spills at Once.   Do not wait for someone to trip. And, if a wet spot comes from a leak, report the cause to a supervisor.

Be Careful on Stairs.   Take one step at a time and keep your eyes on where you are going. Do not run or take two stairs at a time. Keep to the right and walk single file both up and down stairs. Report any missing or damaged safety strips. These are rough, sandpaperlike strips that help keep feet from slipping on stairs.

Obstructed Vision.   Do what it takes to see where you are going.

Do Not Carry Boxes.   Instead of carrying bulky boxes in front of you, push them on a cart or pull them on a dolly. That way they will not interfere with your vision.

Be Careful in Doorways.   Since you may not be able to see what is on the other side of a door, take special precautions.

Approach with Caution.   Go slowly as you come to a door. Assume that someone on the other side is about to open the door.

Be Careful with Swinging Doors.   Walk slowly through swinging or revolving doors. Report sticking doors or doors that are too springy.

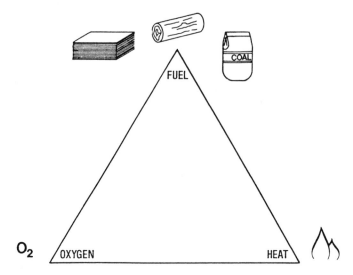

A fire can start whenever these three things are present: a heat source, oxygen, and fuel. This is called the fire triangle.

Open Glass Doors Correctly.   Push on the handle or push plate. Do not open a door by pushing on the glass.

Fires.   The entire foodservice team must respect the danger of fire. If just one worker is careless, a fire can cause serious damage to life, health, or property. Everyone must understand the building's fire safety plan. People must also know what fire fighting equipment is available and how to use it. Most important, they should know where the nearest fire alarm is. Before we get into prevention, let us look at major causes of fires. Remember that three conditions are necessary for a fire to start: heat, oxygen, and a substance that will burn.

Causes of Fires.   Smoking or matches, electrical problems, heating-system defects, spontaneous combustion, and poor rubbish disposal are the major causes of fire. All of them can be controlled.

Smoking or Matches.   About 20% of all kitchen fires are caused by careless habits with smoking materials. Obey the "no smoking" rule. Be sure others obey it, too.

Electricity Misuse.   Misuse of electricity is responsible for 16% of kitchen accidents. Be sure you have heavy-duty outlets for large equipment. Do not use defective outlets. Never use small extension cords or frayed cords. Report any loose connections or equipment that looks defective.

Heating-system problems.   Fires in the heating system are difficult for the average worker to control. Still, it is important to know that they cause about 15% of kitchen fires. Report any problems you notice.

Spontaneous combustion.   Nine percent of all kitchen fires start from spontaneous combustion. The most common source of an unexplained fire is a pile of oily rags tossed into a corner somewhere. Be sure to dispose of oily rags the correct way. Wash them if possible. Do not leave covers off trash cans—that, too, can result in spontaneous flare-ups.

Poor rubbish disposal.   Disposal problems cause 7% of kitchen fires. Remove pressurized cans from trash to be burned. Aerosol cans can explode in the incinerator and may cause a fire.

Classes of Fires.   Three classes of fires, identified by letter, occur in foodservice areas. A companion symbol identifies the correct type of fire extinguisher for each class of fire.

Class A fires.   Class A fires start in ordinary combustible materials such as wood, paper, and rags. The symbol for the correct fire extinguisher is a green triangle with the letter A enclosed.

Class B fires.   Class B fires involve flammable liquids such as gasoline, grease, oil, and paint. The symbol for the correct fire extinguisher is a red square with the letter B enclosed.

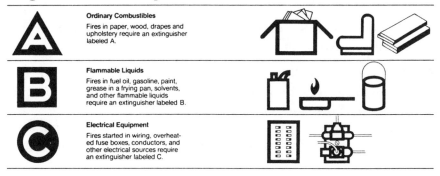

Ordinary Combustibles
Fires in paper, wood, drapes and upholstery require an extinguisher labeled A.

Flammable Liquids
Fires in fuel oil, gasoline, paint, grease in a frying pan, solvents, and other flammable liquids require an extinguisher labeled B.

Electrical Equipment
Fires started in wiring, overheated fuse boxes, conductors, and other electrical sources require an extinguisher labeled C.

Class C fires.   Fires that break out in or near electrical equipment are class C fires. The symbol for the correct extinguisher is a blue circle with a C enclosed.

Note: Class D fires involve combustible metals. They are not commonly found in foodservice areas. However, the extinguisher symbol is a five-pointed green star.

Types of Fire Extinguishers.   Most foodservice areas have fire extinguishers nearby for all workers. State laws require inspectors to check extinguishers regularly. This is to find out if they are working correctly. Inspectors also check to be sure the right type of extinguisher (A, B, or C) is placed near the right fire hazard area. Before starting a job, it is important to know how to operate the fire extinguisher near your area. It is also important to know what kinds of fires it extinguishes.

Pressurized water.   In a pressurized-water extinguisher, water is put under pressure so that it sprays when the extinguisher is turned on. This type of extinguisher is right for class A fires (wood, paper), which need to be cooled and splashed with water. Carry the extinguisher to the fire, squeeze the handle, and spray the water over the fire.

Soda–acid.   In this type of extinguisher, baking soda and acid are released together. They cool and put out class A fires. To use, carry the extinguisher to the fire and turn bottom up. Point the stream at the base of the fire.

Foam.   A chemical foam extinguisher puts out both class A and B fires.
Note: Since foam contains water, it should never be used on class C or electrical fires. If you use the wrong extinguisher on a fire, it could cause injury to you.

Carbon dioxide.   The chemical carbon dioxide does not support combustion. It is the right type of extinguisher to use on class B and C fires. This type of extinguisher does not produce water. Carry the extinguisher to the fire, pull the ring pin, release the spray horn, and hold the insulated handle. Squeeze the handle

The improper use of fire extinguishers could injure you. Be sure to use the right type of extinguisher for the type of fire.

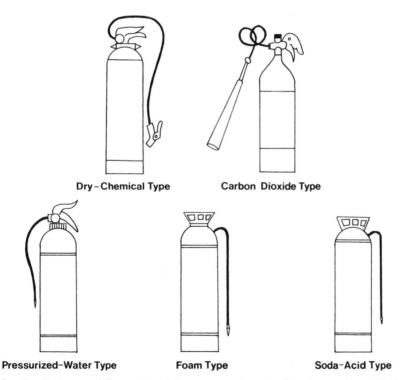

Dry – Chemical Type   Carbon Dioxide Type

Pressurized–Water Type   Foam Type   Soda–Acid Type

The five basic types of fire extinguishers are pressurized water, soda–acid, foam, carbon dioxide, and dry chemical.

and point the horn at the base of the fire. The range is only 6–8 feet.

Multipurpose dry chemical. The chemical ingredient in the multipurpose extinguisher puts out class A, B, and C fires. This is the most common type of extinguisher, and it is found in many foodservice operations. Carry it to the fire, squeeze the handle, and direct the chemical toward the base of the flames.

How to Prevent Fires. The objective of fire prevention measures is to prevent the loss of life, property, and business. Good fire safety begins with safe building construction. Fireproof building materials will reduce the risk of fire. In any kind of a building, follow these guidelines to keep fires from starting:

1. Report any fire to a supervisor at once.
2. Know where the fire extinguishers are and how to use them.
3. Inspect them every year.
4. Maintain equipment in the foodservice area. Repair bad cords.
5. Keep grease from collecting on hoods and filters.
6. Control hot fat. Never add water to fat. Keep it from splattering.
7. Control smoking materials. Keep matches in closed containers.
8. Smoke in designated areas only.
9. Control gas stoves. Report any leaks to the supervisor. Light matches before turning on gas. Turn off gas fires when not in use.

How to Control Fires. Once fires have started, follow these rules:

1. Notify a supervisor if you can.
2. Call the fire department.
3. Use a fire extinguisher until the fire department arrives.
4. Cut off the air supply. Close windows that may give more air.

Grease fires can get out of control easily. Put out a small grease fire by putting the lid on the pan at once. This will cut off the supply of oxygen.

Storage Safety. To assure safety in the foodservice area, arrange the storage area correctly and store supplies the right way.

Safe Storeroom Characteristics. The safe storeroom includes shelves that are strong and wide enough to hold supplies. It should include separate areas for cleaning supplies. The aisles should be wide enough for people to move through without bumping into supplies. Floors should be well lighted and clean and dry.

Safe Storage Procedures. Before storing supplies, remove all nails and staples from boxes or barrels. Use the right tools. Be careful not to get splinters in your hands when opening wood cartons. Throw out all empty boxes right away. Do not leave them around for people to trip on. When placing items on high shelves, use a sturdy, well-braced ladder. Store cleaning materials and insecticides away from food. Keep storage area clean and neat so fires do not get started. Never store supplies in front of fire extinguishers. Store supplies in places where a minimum of lifting is required. Place heavy items on lower shelves but never on the floor.

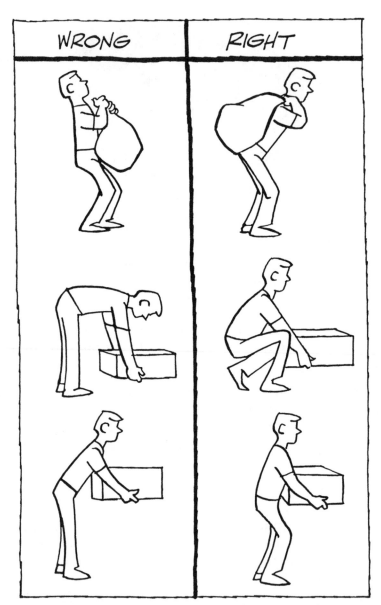

To lift a load correctly, squat in front of it and lift using your leg, not your back muscles. Carry the object close to the body so that you can see and so that the correct muscles carry the load.

Safe Lifting and Carrying.   Back injuries can be a lifelong problem. How much you can lift without injury depends on your fitness, the size and weight of the object you are lifting, and the distance you carry the load. Test the weight by lifting a corner. If it is too heavy, get help or get moving equipment. If possible, divide the load in two parts. Use a cart or hand truck. Some loads can be dragged or rolled. If it must be lifted, avoid back injuries by lifting the correct way.

Correct Lifting Technique.   Place your feet about 1 foot apart. This will give you good balance. Squat in front of the load and keep your back straight. Grab the load and push your body up with the leg muscles, not the lower back muscles. Keep the load close to your body as you rise steadily. Do not hold the load out in front of you. Do not twist or turn the body during the lift or before carrying to another place. Change directions by moving the feet slowly. Use the leg muscles and knees to lower the body to set the load down. Let go of the load only when it is firmly in place.

Correct Carrying Technique.   Be sure the object is not too heavy for you. Keep the load close to your body. Be sure you can see where you are going.

Correct Reaching, Twisting, Pushing and Pulling.   To reach, stretch out arms and legs slowly. Do not try to do the job with the back muscles.

Arrange your work so that you do not have to twist, especially when lifting. Turn the whole body, not just the upper part. Turn with little steps, pivoting with the feet.

If you must push an object, stand close to it. Bend your elbows and put your hands on the load to push with your whole body. Push close to the object's center of gravity. Do not try to push with your arms or shoulders only.

To pull, keep your feet apart, one behind the other. Straighten your legs and keep your back straight. Let your leg muscles do the work as you walk backward slowly in a semicrouching position. Be sure the path is clear before starting to pull.

Kitchen Equipment Safety. Most accidents that involve equipment are usually due to human error. Everyone in the food-service department should try to prevent equipment accidents from happening.

Care of Equipment. Be sure you know how to use equipment before you start. Report faulty equipment so that it can be repaired at once. If there are safety guards or other features, be sure they work. Be sure cutting utensils are sharp and use them the right way. Wash and store knives separately from other hand equipment to avoid cuts. Be sure all grinders, slicers, choppers, and mixers have safety guards and emergency stops. Always turn off switches and pull plugs before cleaning equipment.

Burn Prevention. Use dry hot pads or towels to hold hot pans. Never use a wet cloth or an apron in place of hot pads. When opening steamers and ovens stand to the side. Lift covers of hot utensils away from you. Turn pot handles into range top and out of aisles. Keep handles away from flames. Fill utensils only to the right level. Never overfill. If you must move a hot pan, get help and decide in advance where you will be moving it. Warn others if you place a hot pan near them. Do not drop watery food into hot fat. Ease it in with a fryer basket.

Use cooking equipment correctly to prevent burns. Open steamer door or kettle lid away from you so that steam does not burn you.

Report frayed cords to supervisors at once. Never pull the cord to unplug an appliance. Grasp the plug instead.

Electrical Shock Prevention. Report any frayed cords, loose plugs, or other defects in electrical equipment. Plug cords only in grounded outlets. Do not have water on counter or floor near electrical equipment. Be sure your hands are dry before using equipment. Always unplug equipment before cleaning. Unplug by grasping plug. Do not pull the cord.

Cut Prevention. Use safety guards on cutting and slicing equipment. Keep your fingers out of the danger zone and away from moving parts. When you clean equipment, put all pieces back together right away. Hold knives and cleavers by the handles and push on the back of the blade. Make sure knives are sharp. The job will be easier and you will be less likely to be cut. However, if you are cut, the wound will be worse if caused by a dull knife. Never try to catch a falling knife. Just let it fall. Keep your fingers away from grater surfaces. Be very careful with glass and pottery. If a glass or dish breaks, pick up the pieces with a damp wad of paper towels. Throw out all broken glass or cracked dishes in a separate container. If a glass breaks in dish water, do not reach in to remove it. Strain off water then remove with paper towels. Use a good can opener, not one with chips or nicks in the blade. Watch out for the edges on opened cans.

Clothing Safety. Wear the right kind of uniform and shoes for maximum safety in the workplace.

Shoes should be low with broad rubber heels so you will not

Pick up broken glass immediately. Use a dust pan and broom for large pieces. Then wipe up small bits and splinters with damp paper towels. Never use bare hands.

slip. Be sure the toes are closed and if possible have safety steel inside. Keep shoelaces tied.

Wear the basic uniform required for the work place. Keep apron ties short and secure so that they do not get caught in equipment. Do not wear pins, necklaces, or bracelets that could get caught in equipment or drop in food. Never wear rings around hazardous electrical equipment. In fact, the only pieces of jewelry that are recommended to be worn in the foodservice area are watches and wedding rings.

Review of Accidents and Prevention

Table 6.1 summarizes the kinds of accidents that take place in the foodservice area. It also lists steps to avoid them.

No matter how careful we are, accidents may sometimes happen. Be sure to use first aid when they do.

First Aid

First aid is just what it says: aid that we give to an accident victim first. It is not complete care. A doctor must do that. Instead, first aid is quick action to keep the injury from getting worse or to keep the victim alive until professional help comes. Standard first

Table 6.1: Accidents and How to Avoid Them

Type of accident	How to avoid it
1. Cuts	Use and store knives correctly
	Pick up broken glass correctly
	Throw out chipped glass
2. Burns	Consider every pan hot
	Handle pots and lids carefully
	Open oven doors slowly
	Get help to handle large hot pots
	Keep handles away from aisles
3. Falls	Wipe up spills at once
	Keep floors and aisles clear
	Climb only on safe ladders
	Be sure you see where going
4. Back injuries	Do not carry too much
	Lift properly, with legs
	Do not twist while lifting

aid procedures are well known. They cover wounds and bleeding, shock, stoppage of breathing, choking, and burns.

General First Aid.   Steps to follow in any accident situation are important.

Bleeding and Breathing Problems First.   If there is a mass injury such as an explosion, first treat those who are bleeding or not breathing.

Keep Lying Down.   If the victim stays lying down, he or she has less chance of further injury or shock.

Check Injuries.   Once the victim is lying down, check for all injuries.

Plan.   Decide what procedures are needed.

Go Ahead.   Carry out first aid steps necessary.

First Aid for Simple Wounds and Bleeding.   Your objective is to stop the bleeding and prevent infection. To be effective at first aid, it is almost necessary to take an approved Red Cross first aid course. In such a course you will learn to stop bleeding by applying direct pressure to the wound or the blood vessel that supplies the wound.

Keep less serious wounds from getting infected by first washing your hands with soap and warm water and then washing the wound with soap and warm water. Cover the wound with a sterile bandage.

First Aid for Shock. Shock is the state of trauma that often results from serious accidents. Shock can come after minor injuries, too. To prevent or reduce shock, keep the victim lying down. Help to keep body temperature normal by covering with blankets if cold. Give the victim a little water if he or she is thirsty. Give first aid for the injuries that caused shock.

First Aid for Breathing Stoppage. If a person stops breathing, we call this condition *asphyxia*. We know that drowning can cause a person to stop breathing, but asphyxia can also be caused by electrocution, gas inhalation, or even a heart attack. Proper care of a person who has stopped breathing requires specialized training in cardiopulmonary resuscitation (CPR.) A person not trained in CPR can help by making the victim more comfortable and by loosening clothing around the neck.

For choking on food or objects, use the standard procedure to get food out of the airway. Usually you can tell if choking is caused by food, because the victim cannot breath or speak and is grasping the throat. He or she may also turn blue and collapse. It is important to act fast because a person can die in just 4 minutes. If the person definitely cannot breathe, first try to dislodge the food with a few quick blows to the back. Then grip the victim above the waist and squeeze with quick upward thrusts. Repeat several times if necessary. Probe the mouth to remove food when it is pushed out.

First Aid for Simple Burns. Burns can come from hot liquids, chemicals, or even the sun. If the burn is mild (no break in the skin and no blisters) hold the burned area under cold water or put into ice water until pain goes away. You can apply petroleum jelly or burn ointment and a bandage. For burns with broken skin or blisters, send for a doctor at once. Apply sterile compresses. Do not try to clean out burn or break blisters. Keep the victim quiet.

If a worker suffers from heat exhaustion, treat the person the same as you would for shock.

To make your food service emergency plan even better, have safety training with first aid and CPR included.

Occupational Safety and Health Administration. OSHA is an agency of the federal government that sets up rules and standards for procedures in the workplace. The purpose of the rules is to assure that people working in any business "affecting commerce" have a safe work environment. Be sure that the requirements are observed in your workplace.

7
Nutrition

What does nutrition have to do with the food service industry, you may ask? You may think that nutrition is the business of the nutritionist, the doctor, or the dietitian.

The truth is, nutrition is a part of food production. We eat food to be nourished, which means that we provide our bodies with nutrients necessary to grow, to be healthy, and to do work. Good food preparation is essential for good nutrition. A glass of orange juice that has been stored at room temperature for a day does not have as much vitamin C as it had when it was fresh. Food that is overcooked lacks the characteristics of a good-quality product. Overcooking not only results in poor taste, texture, and color but can decrease nutrients as well.

The goal of everyone from the owner or manager down to the pantry worker, waiter, or waitress should be the same. They should all do their best to prepare, store, and serve food in ways that will maintain quality and nutrients. In this chapter we shall present the basics of nutrition. You are not expected to become experts in nutrition. However, it is important that you have a working knowledge of how nutrition fits into today's society, not only as a food service worker and future manager, but also as a nutrition consumer yourself.

Objectives and Terms

Objectives. This section should help you:

- Define nutrition.
- List the five food groups named in the daily food guide.

- List the six major nutrient groups.
- Describe the functions of protein, carbohydrate, and fat.
- Describe the functions of vitamins A and C.
- Describe the functions of the minerals calcium and iron.

Terms to Know

Nutrients. Chemicals in food that the body needs for health.

Diet. The food and drink we consume every day.

Carbohydrate. Nutrient that comes from plants and provides energy.

Starch. Carbohydrate found mostly in grains, vegetables, and some fruits.

Sugar. Carbohydrate found in fruits, sugar cane, sugar beets, and some vegetables. It is usually sweet in taste.

Fiber. Indigestible roughage necessary for good elimination.

Fat. Nutrient that comes from animal fat and vegetable oils and provides energy.

Cholesterol. A waxy, fatty substance present in our bodies and in animal foods.

Protein. Nutrient that builds and repairs body tissues.

Amino Acids. The chemical building blocks of protein.

Essential Amino Acids. Amino acids our bodies cannot make and must get from food.

Vitamins. Nutrients we need in small amounts to regulate body processes. All have different functions.

Fat-Soluble Vitamins. Vitamins dissolved in fat in foods. They are not easily destroyed.

Water-Soluble Vitamins. Vitamins dissolved in water in foods. They are easily destroyed.

Minerals. Nutrients we need in small amounts to help build certain tissues and regulate some body processes.

What Is Nutrition?

Nutrition is the food you eat and how your body uses it. It includes all of these processes:

- Taking food into the body.
- Breaking food down into chemicals called nutrients.

Table 7.1: Nutrients Groups and Functions

Nutrient group	Functions
Water	Carries all nutrients
	Major part of body
	Basis of body fluids
	Regulates body functions
Carbohydrates	Give us energy for all activity
Fats	Give us energy in a concentrated form
Proteins (amino acids)	Build and repair body tissue
	Give us energy
Vitamins	Help to regulate body processes
Minerals	In small amounts, make up some tissues
	Also help regulate some processes

- Absorbing nutrients.
- Making use of nutrients for a variety of body functions.

We humans need over 40 nutrients. Some nutrients give us energy to do work. Others build and repair our bodies. Still others help to regulate the processes of making energy and body tissues from food. We need all of the nutrients all our lives. The best way to get all of the nutrients we need every day is to eat a variety of food.

Nutrients belong to six major groups. Table 7.1 lists the major nutrient groups and some of their functions.

How Much Do We Need? We need enough of all of those nutrients to keep us healthy and to help us grow. Scientists have used both animal and human studies to decide how much of each nutrient is necessary. They put their recommendations into a form known as the Recommended Dietary Allowances or the RDA (Table 7.2).

You can see that the RDA table lists a specific recommended level for many nutrients. Those are considered key nutrients. If we get enough of them, chances are we shall be getting enough of the other nutrients as well. But how do we use the RDA table? To be accurate, we would need to use a table of food values. Then we would have to add up the amounts of nutrients provided by all the food we eat each day. We could compare the total with the amount listed in the RDA table for each nutrient to see if we are meeting our goal.

Does it sound time consuming? It is.

The Daily Food Guide.   Because it would take so much time to calculate the right foods to give us all 40 nutrients each day, nutritionists have given us the daily food guide. The guide simplifies food selection advice by lumping foods into five food groups. All foods in each group give similar nutrients in similar amounts. The groups are as follows:

Bread/Cereal Group.   Foods that come from grains such as wheat, rice, corn, barley, rye, and oats make up the bread and cereal group. This group is our best source of the carbohydrate we call starch. Carbohydrates give us energy. Breads and cereals are also good sources of some B vitamins and minerals.

Fruit/Vegetable Group.   Vegetables and fruits belong to this group. We need this group to get enough vitamins A and C. Fruits provide sugars and vegetables provide starch. These foods contain other vitamins and minerals as well.

Milk Group.   The milk group includes milk, yogurt, cheese, ice cream, and other foods made from milk (excluding butter, which is made only with milk fat). Dairy group foods are very good sources of the minerals calcium and phosphorous, which are important for growth and development of bones and teeth. The dairy group is also a good source of protein. Whole milk products contain fat, too.

Meat and Meat Alternatives Group.   Beef, pork, lamb, poultry, fish shellfish, eggs, dried beans and peas, peanuts, seeds, and nuts make up this group. Foods in this group are especially important for protein. They also contain some vitamins and good amounts of minerals, particularly iron.

"Other Foods" Group.   Foods in this group are high in fat or carbohydrate but low in other nutrients. They include fats, oils, sugars, sweets, alcoholic drinks, and other similar foods.

Table 7.2: Food and Nutrition Board, National
Recommended Daily Dietary

	Age (years)	Weight (kg)	Weight (lb)	Height (cm)	Height (in.)	Protein (g)	Fat-soluble vitamins Vita-min A (µg RE)[b]	Fat-soluble vitamins Vita-min D (µg)[c]	Fat-soluble vitamins Vita-min E (mg α-TE)[d]
Infants	0.0–0.5	6	13	60	24	kg × 2.2	420	10	3
	0.5–1.0	9	20	71	28	kg × 2.0	400	10	4
Children	1–3	13	29	90	35	23	400	10	5
	4–6	20	44	112	44	30	500	10	6
	7–10	28	62	132	52	34	700	10	7
Males	11–14	45	99	157	62	45	1000	10	8
	15–18	66	145	176	69	56	1000	10	10
	19–22	70	154	177	70	56	1000	7.5	10
	23–50	70	154	178	70	56	1000	5	10
	51+	70	154	178	70	56	1000	5	10
Females	11–14	46	101	157	62	46	800	10	8
	15–18	55	120	163	64	46	800	10	8
	19–22	55	120	163	64	44	800	7.5	8
	23–50	55	120	163	64	44	800	5	8
	51+	55	120	163	64	44	800	5	8
Pregnant						+30	+200	+5	+2
Lactating						+20	+400	+5	+3

[a]The allowances are intended to provide for individual variations among most normal persons as they live in the United States under usual environmental stresses. Diets should be based on a variety of common foods in order to provide other nutrients for which human requirements have been less well defined. See text for detailed discussion of allowances and of nutrients not tabulated.

[b]Retinol equivalents: 1 RE = 1 µg retinol or 6 µg β carotene.

[c]As cholecalciferol. 10 µg cholecalciferol = 400 IU of vitamin D.

[d]α-Tocopherol equivalents. 1 mg d-α-tocopherol = 1 α-TE.

[e]Niacin equivalents. 1 NE = 1 mg niacin or 60 mg dietary tryptophan.

[f]The folacin allowances refer to dietary sources as determined by *Lactobacillus casei* assay after treatment with enzymes (conjugases) to make polyglutamyl forms of the

We all need to choose foods from the first four food groups each day. Since foods from the fifth group give us mostly energy or calories, we can add those foods if we can afford to have extra calories. The number of servings each person needs each day depends on several factors. Your sex and age are the most important considerations. Notice on the daily food guide chart that teenagers need more servings from the milk group than adults.

cademy of Sciences—National Research Council:
llowances, Revised 1980[a]

	Water-soluble vitamins						Minerals					
'ita- in C (mg)	Thia- min (mg)	Ribo- flavin (mg)	Niacin (mg NE)[e]	Vita- min B_6 (mg)	Fola- cin[f] (µg)	Vitamin B_{12} (µg)	Cal- cium (mg)	Phos- phorus (mg)	Mag- nesium (mg)	Iron (mg)	Zinc (mg)	Io- dine (µg)
35	0.3	0.4	6	0.3	30	0.5[g]	360	240	50	10	3	40
35	0.5	0.6	8	0.6	45	1.5	540	360	70	15	5	50
45	0.7	0.8	9	0.9	100	2.0	800	800	150	15	10	70
45	0.9	1.0	11	1.3	200	2.5	800	800	200	10	10	90
45	1.2	1.4	16	1.6	300	3.0	800	800	250	10	10	120
50	1.4	1.6	18	1.8	400	3.0	1200	1200	350	18	15	150
60	1.4	1.7	18	2.0	400	3.0	1200	1200	400	18	15	150
60	1.5	1.7	19	2.2	400	3.0	800	800	350	10	15	150
60	1.4	1.6	18	2.2	400	3.0	800	800	350	10	15	150
60	1.2	1.4	16	2.2	400	3.0	800	800	350	10	15	150
50	1.1	1.3	15	1.8	400	3.0	1200	1200	300	18	15	150
60	1.1	1.3	14	2.0	400	3.0	1200	1200	300	18	15	150
60	1.1	1.3	14	2.0	400	3.0	800	800	300	18	15	150
60	1.0	1.2	13	2.0	400	3.0	800	800	300	18	15	150
60	1.0	1.2	13	2.0	400	3.0	800	800	300	10	15	150
+20	+0.4	+0.3	+2	+0.6	+400	+1.0	+400	+400	+150	[h]	+5	+25
+40	+0.5	+0.5	+5	+0.5	+100	+1.0	+400	+400	+150	[h]	+10	+50

vitamin available to the test organism.

[g]The recommended dietary allowance for vitamin B_{12} in infants is based on average concentration of the vitamin in human milk. The allowances after weaning are based on energy intake (as recommended by the American Academy of Pediatrics) and consideration of other factors, such as intestinal absorption.

[h]The increased requirement during pregnancy cannot be met by the iron content of habitual American diets nor by the existing iron stores of many women; therefore the use of 30–60 mg of supplemental iron is recommended. Iron needs during lactation are not substantially different from those of nonpregnant women, but continued supplementation of the mother for 2–3 months after parturition is advisable in order to replenish stores depleted by pregnancy.

That is because teenagers are growing rapidly. Milk gives us the mineral calcium, which is essential for fast-growing bones.

Key Nutrients. Protein, carbohydrates, fats, and some vitamins and minerals are key nutrients.

Protein and Amino Acids. As we said earlier, we need protein to build and repair body tissue. Since every cell in our bodies

The daily food guide. The suggested number of servings from each group is as follows. Milk group: adults, 2; children, 3; teenagers, 4; pregnant women, 3. Meat group: 2. Fruits and vegetables: 4. Breads and cereals: 4 or more. Other foods: no suggested number of servings.

is made of protein, that is a very important role. Protein is made up of chemicals called amino acids. Our bodies need about 22 different amino acids to build body proteins. We can make some amino acids from others. There are, however, eight amino acids that we cannot do without. We must get them from our food. We call them the essential amino acids.

Food proteins that contain all eight essential amino acids are called complete protein foods. Meat, fish, poultry, eggs, and milk products are complete protein foods. Dried peas and beans, nuts, grains, and vegetables contain some, but not all eight essential amino acids. We call these foods incomplete protein foods. It is possible to combine incomplete protein foods so that the meal provides all eight essential amino acids. One common combination is to include dried beans and grains in the same meal. Tortillas (from corn) and refried beans (pinto beans) is an example. The tortillas provide the amino acids missing in the beans, and the beans provide the amino acids missing in the tortillas. We call them "complementary proteins" because one food complements the other.

A Word about Energy and Calories.   As we said earlier, three nutrient groups provide energy. They are carbohydrates, fat, and protein. We measure the energy a food produces in the body in calories. A calorie is a unit of heat energy. The total number of calories provided by a serving of food depends on the amount of carbohydrate, fat, and protein in the food. You can calculate calories if you know how much of each a serving of food contains.

Water- and Fat-Soluble Vitamins.   It is important to know a little more about vitamins. The reason is that some foods will lose the vitamins they contain if they are not handled correctly. Since we are in the foodservice business, it is our responsibility to understand how to preserve nutrients, especially vitamins.

Some vitamins are dissolved in the water in food. Other vitamins are dissolved in fat in food. Since water evaporates easily, that means it is easy to lose the water-soluble vitamins in food. If we cook foods in too much water or leave the pan uncovered, water-soluble vitamins can go up in steam or out in the cooking water. Table 7.3 lists fat- and water-soluble vitamins, their functions, and food sources. In the food preparation chapters we shall talk more about how to preserve vitamins and other nutrients in food preparation.

Minerals.   Minerals perform many functions in our bodies. Some, like calcium, are major components of body parts (bones and teeth). Others are involved in delicate jobs like building brain cells or helping to produce energy from food. Table 7.4 lists important sources and functions of some minerals.

Some other minerals that we need in small amounts are molybdenum, copper, sulfur, selenium, cobalt, and chromium.

You may also hear about minerals such as potassium and so-

Table 7.3: Vitamins, Functions, and Sources

	Functions	*Sources*
	Fat-soluble vitamins	
Vitamin A	Helps in growth; helps maintain healthy cells that line breathing passage and digestive tract; helps eyes adjust to dim light	Dark green, leafy, yellow vegetables; some fruits
Vitamin D	Helps bone and teeth make use of calcium and phosphorus	Fortified milk
Vitamin E	Helps keep some nutrients from breaking down	Oils, whole grains
Vitamin K	Helps clot the blood when necessary	Leafy vegetables
	Water-soluble vitamins	
Thiamine (B_1)	Helps body use carbohydrate for energy; helps maintain nerve cells	Meat, dried beans
Riboflavin (B_2)	Helps body make energy from food	Dairy foods, meat, fish
Niacin (B_3)	Helps body use carbohydrates, fat, and protein	Poultry, meat, cereals, dry beans, peas
Vitamin B_6	Helps body use amino acids in proteins	Vegetables, muscle meats
Vitamin B_{12}	Helps the body make new cells of many kinds	Animal foods
Folic acid	Helps the body make new red blood cells and other important body chemicals	Green plant parts
Vitamin C (ascorbic acid)	Helps form collagen, the "cement" that holds together cells in many parts of the body; helps the body to heal and to resist infections	Citrus fruit, many other fruits, vegetables

dium. Sodium in particular is frequently in the news today. It is one of the nutrients that helps to maintain the right balance of water and other chemicals in our cells. It is present in many foods. Foods with a salty taste are usually high in sodium. Many health experts are concerned that we Americans eat too many high-

Table 7.4: Minerals, Functions, and Sources

Mineral	Functions	Sources
Calcium	Gives hardness to bones and teeth; helps clot blood; helps muscles contract	Milk, dairy foods
Phosphorus	Helps with many reactions in making energy and carrying fats and other substances in the blood	Milk group, meat group, other foods
Magnesium	Helps the body make energy and helps carry nerve impulses	Dairy foods, dry beans, flour, cereal
Iron	Makes hemoglobin, a main chemical in red blood cells; hemoglobin carries oxygen from the lungs to all parts of the body	Lean meats, whole grain and enriched cereals, greens
Iodine	Makes thyroglobulin, a thyroid hormone that regulates the rate at which many body processes take place (metabolism); metabolism involves such things as circulation, respiration, and growth	Iodized salt, seafood
Fluorine	Helps keep teeth hard so that it is difficult for cavities to form	Fluoridated water, eggs, milk, fish
Zinc	Helps the body make proteins and produce energy	Animal foods

sodium foods. High-sodium intakes may be connected with diseases such as high blood pressure.

Dietary Guidelines. Some years ago a panel of experts came up with some day-to-day guidelines for Americans to follow in selecting foods. They are called the dietary guidelines. They include the following:

- Eat a variety of foods.
- Maintain ideal weight.
- Avoid too much fat, saturated fat, and cholesterol.
- Eat foods with adequate starch and fiber.
- Avoid too much sugar.
- Avoid too much salt.

Nutrition and the Menu.   Using the basic nutrition information above, you should be able to plan simple, nutritious menus. They should follow these precepts:

- Use the basic food groups as a guide.
- Include foods both high and low in fat so that the customer can have a choice.
- Include a variety of fruits and vegetables, with different preparation methods. A customer who is concerned about salt may not want to choose canned vegetables, but may instead select fresh vegetables.
- Include some high-fiber foods.
- Use some foods high in nutritional value.
- Include a variety of preparation methods. (Avoid having all fried foods.)
- You may want to offer some special low-calorie items.

How to Preserve Nutrients in Food.   In the food chapters we shall discuss correct methods for handling, storing, and preparing different foods to preserve nutrients.

8
Recipes, Measurements, and Methods

Your grandmother is probably famous for her pot roast or fried chicken. Everyone in the family looks forward to the time when she serves her specialty. And she may never even use a recipe! How does she do it?

Grandma's dish turns out every time. That is probably because she has had years of practice. But what would happen if you would try to produce 50 servings of her pot roast without a recipe? You might add a pinch of this and a pinch of that as she does, but the results may be less than perfect. For the same results every time, you must follow a recipe. It is also important to measure ingredients the right way and follow the accepted procedures.

Objectives and Terms

Objectives. This section should help you:

- Describe a standardized recipe.
- List steps in following a recipe.
- Identify equipment used to weigh and measure ingredients.
- Measure liquid and dry ingredients correctly.
- Increase or decrease the quantity of a standardized recipe.
- Use correct food preparation terms.

Terms to Know

Recipe. A set of written directions for preparing a food product.

Standardized Recipe. A recipe that has been tested and used many times with the same results.

Ingredients. Individual foods used to produce a food product.

As Purchased. A recipe notation that indicates the weight of an ingredient to use, before any preparation is done.

Edible Portion. The weight of a food as it is prepared, ready to eat.

English System. A system of weights and measures traditionally used in England and the United States. It uses the pound, cup, and degrees Fahrenheit.

Metric System. A system of weights and measures used around the world. It is based on the gram, liter, and degrees Celsius (centigrade).

Conduction. The movement of heat from a source through a medium to a food.

Convection. The spread of heat by the flow of air, steam, or liquid.

Radiation. The movement of heat waves to a food.

Other Terms. The glossary at the end of this chapter lists many food preparation terms.

Recipes

A recipe is a set of written directions. It tells exactly how much of each ingredient to use. It also tells how to put them together and how to cook the product.

A recipe is not everything, however—it is only the beginning, a tool of food preparation. The cook's knowledge and experience play a big role in making a good final product.

Standardized Recipes. After a recipe has been tested and used many times with the same results, it becomes a standardized recipe for that operation. Standardized recipes give the same number of servings and a product of the same quality time after time. In food production, there are many opportunities for human error. By using standardized recipes, we keep errors to a minimum.

Name———

Yield:———
Portion:———

Temp:———
Time:———

Ingredients	Weights	Measures	Procedure

Notes:

Standardized recipe card. The card lists the name of the recipe, yield and portion size, cooking time and temperature, ingredients, and procedure for putting the ingredients together.

The type of standardized recipe should be especially designed for the foodservice that uses it. It should have that operation's appropriate yield and portion size.

Why Use Standardized Recipes? Besides producing the same product every time, a standardized recipe helps eliminate guesswork for the employee. It makes it easier to train employees and avoids too much dependence on one experienced cook. It also helps in ordering the right amounts of ingredients.

Procedures for Writing Standardized Recipes. Follow these steps to be sure recipes are standardized.

Heading of the Card. List the name of the product on top of the card. Write the yield or number of servings on the left under the name. Write portion size (weight or measure) under the yield. Write cooking temperature (degrees F) on the right-hand corner with baking time just below it.

Ingredients List. List ingredients in order of their use. Give both weights and measures, if possible. [*Note:* Weights are more accurate than measurements, except for small quantities, less than a tablespoon.]

Use only weights and measurements for which there are exact measuring tools. Use standard abbreviations in recipes.

Procedure. Use the right terms for the preparation steps. Terms such as cream, fold, blend, and beat have specific meanings. If a preparation term is listed in the ingredients (½ cup onions, diced) be sure to repeat the term in the preparation steps.

List as few steps as possible. Leave space between steps and number them. Be sure to list preliminary steps at the beginning. Steps such as "Preheat oven to 350°F" and "Grease pan" are obviously best done first. Repeat temperature and time of baking in the steps. Describe serving size or portion size in ounces, or ladle or scoop size. Give examples of garnishes or accompaniments.

How to Follow a Recipe. Before starting to prepare a recipe read it carefully and thoroughly. Review terms and abbreviations. If you are not familiar with a term, look it up before continuing.

Check the yield of the recipe. Make adjustments if you need more or less of the product than the recipe yields.

Gather all ingredients and tools. Be sure you have the necessary large equipment. If the product must be baked, preheat the oven. Start the preparation at the right time so that the product comes out of the oven when you want to serve it.

Weigh and measure all ingredients before putting ingredients together. Follow the steps given in the recipe.

Measurements

There is more to measuring ingredients than simply putting food in a measuring cup. It is important to have the right equipment and tools. A cook should also know about container sizes and how to make substitutions and conversions in recipes.

Measuring Equipment. Tools for correct measuring include scales and volume measures.

Scales. The two most common scales used in food production are the baker's scale (used in the bake shop) and the portion scale (used in the kitchen.)

Common tools for correct measurement are scales, measuring cups, and measuring spoons.

Baker's scale.   The baker's scale is a balance scale. It weighs ingredients up to 4 pounds. All ingredients must be weighed when baking. Weighing is more accurate than volume measuring and it is essential when baking. To use it, set the scale scoop on one side and a counterweight (the desired weight) on the other side of the scale. Set the ounce weight on the horizontal bar to the correct spot. Add ingredients to the scoop until the two sides balance.

Portion scale.   In addition to the baker's or balance scale, food operators use a portion scale. This is usually a smaller scale that weighs up to 5 pounds. There are, however, large portion scales that weigh from 5 to 25 pounds. The portion scale is mostly used for portioning items of 2 pounds or less. Adjust the knob to zero, and then place food on the scale. The pointer will indicate the weight of the portion.

Scales usually measure in ounces or pounds. However, some operations use metric measures (grams and kilograms.) Keep in mind that recipes may call for ingredients in two forms, AP (as purchased) or EP (edible portion.) AP means the weight of the ingredient in its purchased form, before any preparation takes place. EP is the weight of the ingredient after appropriate preparation has taken place. For example, a recipe calls for 4 pounds of onions. In the preparation section, it tells you to clean, peel, and slice the onions. This tells you that the 4 pounds is an AP weight. If the recipe calls for 4 pounds of peeled and sliced onions, it means EP weight.

Volume Measures.   Cups and spoons are volume measures. We use them to measure wet ingredients, some fruits and vegetables, and small amounts of dry ingredients.

Measuring spoons.   Use spoons to measure very small amounts of dry or liquid ingredients. They come in sizes of ⅛, ¼, ⅓, ½, and 1 teaspoon, and 1 tablespoon. To be accurate, level off ingredients by scraping the flat edge of a knife across the bowl of the spoon for dry ingredients.

Measuring cups.   Use cups for liquid or dry measuring. They come in sizes of ¼, ⅓, ½, and 1 cup, and larger. Glass measuring

Table 8.1: Abbreviations for Weights and Measures

	Abbreviations
Weights	
Ounce	oz
Pound	lb or #
Measures	
Teaspoon	tsp or t
Tablespoon	Tbsp or T
Cup	C or c
Pint	pt
Quart	qt
Gallon	gal

cups are most common in 1, 2, and 4 cup sizes. Metal measures are larger—1 cup, 1 pint, 1 quart, and 1 gallon.

Note: Always use the largest appropriate measure. It can be more accurate and is more efficient than filling a smaller cup two or more times.

Table 8.1 lists weights and measures used in food preparation and abbreviations. Table 8.2 lists equivalents of common measures.

Note: One cup of different foods has different weights. One cup of flour weighs about 4 oz and 1 C of sugar weighs about 8 oz. In some cases, recipes will call for ingredients that come in cans. It is

Table 8.2: Equivalents of Weights and Measures

Basic measure	Equivalent
1 Tbsp	3 tsp
1 C	16 T
1 pt	2 C
1 qt	2 pt or 4 C
1 gal	4 qt
1 lb	16 oz
1 cup	8 fl oz

Table 8.3: Can Sizes
and Approximate Volume

Can number	Volume (cups)
303	2
2	2½
2½	3½
3	5¾
10	12

important to know the volume a can contains in order to follow the recipe. Table 8.3 lists volumes contained in standard can sizes.

Accurate Measuring. Use the right techniques for wet and dry measuring. Correct measurements help control quality and quantity (the right yield).

Measuring Dry Ingredients. Heap ingredients into the measure. Level with the straight edge of a knife or flat spatula. Always sift flour before measuring. Always pack brown sugar in measure before leveling.

Measuring Wet Ingredients. Place the measure on a level, flat surface. Pour in liquid to the desired mark on the measure. Check the amount at eye level. Use the largest appropriate measure. This will assure accuracy.

To measure dry ingredients accurately, heap the ingredients into a measuring cup, and then level with the back of a knife or flat spatula.

Adjusting Recipes.   It is sometimes necessary to change a recipe before preparing food: You may want to prepare a quantity other than that listed on the recipe; you may want to substitute ingredients for those listed; or you may want to convert a recipe from measures to weights or vice versa.

Increasing or Decreasing the Quantity.   To increase or decrease a recipe, decide on a conversion factor. Suppose the recipe as written yields 50 servings but you want to prepare only 20 servings. Calculate the percentage of decrease (20/50 is equal to 40/100, or 40%, of the recipe yield). The conversion factor is therefore 0.40. Now calculate 0.40 of every ingredient listed.

First, convert all recipe measurements to equivalents in ounces or tablespoons. If the original recipe called for 3 lb of flour, change it to ounces (3 × 16 = 48 oz).

Then multiply the weight in ounces of that ingredient in the original recipe times the conversion factor (48 × 0.40 = 19.2 oz flour). Continue changing each ingredient in this way. A calculator will simplify this job. It is a good idea to have a conversion table posted in every kitchen area. Most quantity recipe books include conversion tables.

Making Recipe Substitutions.   It may happen that you do not have on hand one ingredient necessary in a recipe. In that case, it may be a good idea to substitute another food. Be sure that the substitute ingredient will give good results. Check a list of substitutions usually available in cookbooks.

Another reason for making substitutions is to use up surplus food. Suppose your purchasing agent got a very good price on nonfat dry milk. Your operation has a good recipe for macaroni and cheese that calls for whole milk. Your responsibility as a cook is to substitute nonfat dry milk for whole milk.

Sometimes managers decide to make substitutions in order to increase food value. This is especially important in health care foodservice or school lunch operations, where menus must meet a nutritional standard. Dark leafy greens contain more vitamin A than lettuce. Therefore, the cook may substitute some spinach for lettuce in a salad recipe.

Checking Recipe Calculations. Before preparing food from an adjusted recipe, check calculations a second time. It is very easy to make an error when converting a recipe. One little error can ruin a large batch of food. That becomes an expensive waste of manpower, food, and money.

Metric Measurements. Over the past 20 years, there has been a gradual introduction of the metric system in the United States. Before that, we used the English system for everything but scientific research and science education. When we say "metric system," we mean metric weights and volumes, and Celsius temperature measurements.

The foodservice industry has been very slow to adopt the metric system. One reason is that it would require a changeover to new measuring equipment and even some large equipment. If your operation uses metric recipes, you will find it very easy to adapt. Just follow the recipes and use correct metric measures.

Table 8.4: English and Metric Weights and Measures
(Approximate Equivalents)[a]

Unit	English	Metric
Weights	1 oz	28.3 g
	1 lb	453.6 g
	2.2 lb	1 kg
Volume	¼ tsp	1 ml
	1 tsp	5 ml
	1 Tbsp	15 ml
	½ C	125 ml
	1 C	250 ml
	1 qt	about 1000 ml or 1 l
	33.8 fl oz	about 1 l
Temperature	212°F	100°C
	300°F	150°C
	350°F	180°C
	400°F	200°C
	500°F	260°C

[a]Note: 1000 milligrams (mg) = 1 gram (g); 1000 grams (g) = 1 kilogram (kg); 1000 milliliters (ml) = 1 liter (l).

Table 8.5: Converting Temperatures

Fahrenheit to Celsius	Celsius to Fahrenheit
$°C = \frac{5}{9} \times (°F - 32)$	$°F = (\frac{9}{5} \times °C) + 32$

For your information, Table 8.4 lists approximate metric equivalents of standard English system weight and volume measures. Because they are only approximate, it is not a good idea to use metric conversions. Instead use a recipe that was tested as a metric recipe. Table 8.5 gives the formulas for converting Celsius and Fahrenheit temperatures.

If you find a recipe written in English measures and you want to convert it to metric, just use a conversion table. The same is true if you wish to convert a metric recipe to English measures. Table 8.6 is a metric and English conversion table.

Methods, Terms, and Concepts

Words stand for ideas. We use them to communicate those ideas. We speak English and everyone who speaks the language understands what we mean. Or do they?

Some words have more than one meaning. That makes communicating a bit more difficult. To make the matter even more confusing, words have special meanings in the kitchen.

Table 8.6: Converting Dry and Liquid Measures from English to Metric, and from Metric to English

Dry weights	Multiply by	Liquid measures	Multiply by
ounces to grams	28.35	ounces to milliliters	29.573
pounds to grams	454	pints to liters	0.473
pounds to kilograms	0.454	quarts to liters	0.946
grams to ounces	0.035	gallons to liters	3.785
grams to pounds	0.002	milliliters to ounces	0.034
kilograms to pounds	2.2	liters to pints	2.1
		liters to quarts	1.056
		liters to gallons	0.264

It is important for anyone who works in a kitchen to understand the meaning of kitchen words and terms. We call it the vocabulary of the kitchen. The most important terms in the kitchen vocabulary describe cooking methods.

Cooking Concepts.   Cooking is applying heat to a food for a period of time, resulting in a change in the food. Many kinds of changes occur because of cooking. Food becomes more palatable or more tender. In the case of eggs and other protein foods, the food gets firmer. Flavors of foods blend together in cooking, and cooking destroys some bacteria in food.

Heat Application Methods.   Heat is applied to food in three ways: by conduction, by convection, and by radiation.

Conduction.   In conduction, heat moves from a heat source through a medium to a food. A metal pan conducts heat from the gas burner to the food in the pan. Some materials conduct heat more quickly than others. Copper and aluminum pans conduct heat quickly. Stainless steel conducts heat slowly but steadily.

Convection.   In convection, heat is spread by a flow of air, steam, or liquid. This occurs naturally or by the use of a mechanical device to move air. A pan of water on a gas burner is an example of convection. The water at the bottom of the pan closest to the heat source heats up first. As it gets hot, it moves to the top of the pan and cooler water moves to the bottom. This causes natural circulation of water until it all reaches the boiling point.

In a convection oven, an electric fan moves hot air around to cook food quickly.

Radiation.   Radiation means that heat is transferred by energy waves coming from a heat source to the food. The waves themselves are not heat energy, but they change to heat energy when they reach the food. There are two types of radiation: infrared and microwave. Broiling is an example of infrared heating. A microwave oven also cooks food by radiation. Radiation goes into the food, which has some liquid. Then the rapid movement of food molecules produces heat. In microwave cooking food cooks from the inside out. That is one reason why microwave cooked food does not brown.

Convection is one heat application method. In this example, the water at the pan's bottom is closest to the heat source and heats first. As the bottom water gets hot, it moves to the top and the cooler top water circulates to the bottom to be heated.

Cooking Methods.   Cooking methods are different, depending on the food. Refer to the food production chapters for specific descriptions of cooking methods.

Commonly Used Terms for Food Preparation

Food-Cooking Terms

AP.   The "as purchased" weight of a food, before trimming and preparation.

Au gratin.   Dishes made with white sauce, topped with cheese and crumbs, and browned.

Au jus.   Food served with natural juices.

Bake.   To cook by dry heat in an oven.

Barbecue.   To cook by direct heat source; food may be basted with a sauce or drippings.

Baste.   To ladle liquid or drippings over food as it cooks.

Batter.   A semiliquid mixture of such ingredients as flour, shortening, sugar, and eggs.

Blend.   To mix ingredients well.

Blanch.   To dip into boiling water and cook briefly.

Braise.   To cook slowly in a small amount of liquid in a covered pan.

Bread.   To roll in bread, cereal, or cracker crumbs.

Broil.   To cook by direct heat from an electric or gas element or coals.

Caramelize.   To turn sugar brown by heating.

Deep Fry.   To cook food submerged in hot, deep fat.

EP.   The "edible portion" weight of a food, after trimming and preparation.

Fry.   To cook in hot fat.

Grill.   To cook or pan broil on a solid, flat, heated surface such as a griddle.

Grease.   To coat lightly with fat.

Marinate.   To soak food in a flavorful sauce or liquid.

Pan Broil.   To cook uncovered on a hot ungreased surface, pouring off drippings as they accumulate.

Pan Fry.   To cook in a small amount of fat.

Parboil.   To simmer until partly cooked.

Poach.   To cook gently in hot liquid, popular for eggs and fish.

Reconstitute.   To restore concentrated foods to original state by adding water.

Reduce.   To cook by simmering until the amount of liquid is decreased.

Render.   To cook the grease out of animal fat tissue.

Roast.   To cook in an uncovered pan in an oven.

Sauté.   To brown quickly in a small amount of fat, turning often.

Scald.   To heat milk below the boiling point until a thin scum forms.

Scallops.   Thin slices of food layered with flour, salt, cheese, or other foods and liquid, and then baked.

Sear.   To brown the surface of meat by heating at a high temperature for a short time.

Soufflé.   Baked mixture of stiffly beaten egg whites and other foods.

Simmer.   To cook in a liquid at a temperature of about 185°F; bubbles form slowly and break below surface.

Smother.   To cover with sauces or vegetables.

Steam.   To cook in steam, with or without pressure.

Steep.   To let stand in liquid below boiling point to bring out flavor.

Stew.   To cook meat and vegetables in liquid just below the boiling point.

Thicken.   To make a food firmer by adding starch, eggs, or other products and cooking together.

Food-Cutting Terms

Chop.   To cut into small pieces with a knife or other sharp tool.

Cube.   To cut into squares about ½ inch wide.

Cut.   To divide food into small unevenly shaped pieces.

Dice.   To cut into very small cubes.

Grate.   To form shreds or flakes of food by rubbing across a grater.

Grind.   To cut food into small particles by cutting fine or crushing.

Julienne.   To cut foods into long thin pieces.

Mince.   To cut or chop into very small irregular pieces.

Pare.   To cut off the outside covering with a knife or other tool.

Puree.   To force cooked foods through a strainer or run them through a blender to make a thick, smooth pulp.

Score.   To make thin parallel cuts on the surface of food.

Food-Baking Terms

Beat.   To mix with a circular motion using a spoon, rotary beater, or electric mixer.

Blend.   To mix two or more ingredients until all are thoroughly creamed.

Cream.   To work one or more foods until soft and creamy by beating or rubbing against the side of the bowl.

Cut In.   To chop fat into small particles and blend with dry ingredients using two knives or a pastry blender.

Dust.   To sprinkle lightly, usually with flour or sugar.

Fold In.   To blend ingredients by repeatedly cutting down through the mixture and across the bottom of the bowl, and then turning the mixture over with a spoon or spatula.

Knead.   To press, stretch, and fold dough such as in breads.

Mix.   To combine ingredients.

Preheat.   To heat an oven to the temperature needed before putting in the product.

Proof.   To let yeast dough rise by setting in a warm moist place (85°F).

Sift.   To put dry ingredients through a sifter or fine sieve.

Wash.   To brush a liquid such as eggs or milk over the top of a product before baking, or to brush the top of a baked product with syrup.

9
Equipment

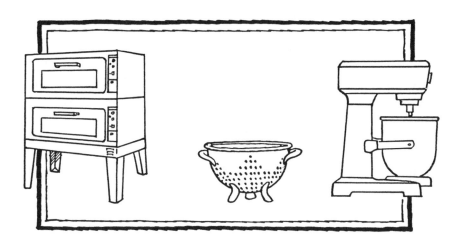

The term *equipment* in the foodservice industry means large machinery, tools, and utensils used for food production. The kind of equipment in a foodservice operation depends on the type of food purchased. If an operator uses a lot of convenience foods, he or she will need little preparation equipment. On the other hand, different equipment is needed if the operator makes everything from scratch.

Today's equipment is designed to save labor and therefore reduce labor cost. Location of equipment is also important for efficient operation. That means there should be a common-sense arrangement of people, food, and machines.

Whatever the choice in equipment, it should work quickly and safely. It should have built-in safety features that are easy to use. It should also be possible for workers to clean and maintain equipment correctly. To protect the life of all equipment, operators should be trained carefully. Remember, equipment can be hazardous. Never use a piece of equipment unless you have been thoroughly trained.

Objectives and Terms

Objectives. This section should help you:

- Follow safe procedures when using equipment.
- Identify common cooking and baking equipment.

- Identify common processing equipment.
- Identify common serving equipment.
- Identify common cleaning equipment.
- Identify common cutlery and describe uses.
- Describe correct techniques for caring for knives.
- Identify common tools and utensils used for cooking and baking.

Terms to Know

Equipment.   Usually large machines or devices used to do work in the kitchen.

Range.   Flat surface equipment with several heating elements set in or under the surface.

Griddle.   Flat surface with even heat source under the entire surface.

Broiler.   Equipment with a gas or electric heating element that gets hot and cooks food placed close to the heat source.

Grill.   A type of broiler in which the heat source is under a grate on which food is placed.

Convection Oven.   An oven that includes a fan to move heated air around food.

Revolving Oven.   An oven with moving shelves.

Microwave Oven.   Oven in which electrical waves heat moisture in food from the inside out.

Fryer.   Equipment that is filled with fat and used for frying food.

Steam-Jacketed Kettle.   Bowllike equipment in which steam, trapped in an outer layer, cooks food inside bowl.

Steam Cooker.   Equipment in which food cooks by direct contact with steam.

Blender.   Processing equipment that can combine, stir, shake, and puree foods.

Buffalo Chopper.   Large bowl with electrically powered revolving knives that cut food.

Vertical Cutter/Mixer (VCM).   A powerful, high-speed blender with whirling blades in an enclosed bowl.

Mixer.   Equipment used to mix doughs, batters, and other foods; attachments include beaters and dough hooks.

Steam Table.   A stainless steel counter with pans of hot water beneath food pans.

Bain Marie (Water Bath).   A piece of equipment in which hot water in the bottom keeps food in the top insert pans warm.

Waste Disposer.   Equipment that grinds and flushes pulverized food waste into the sewage system with water.

Flight Unit.   Very large dishwashing equipment that prewashes, washes, and rinses up to 12,000 plates per hour.

Cutlery.   Tools used to cut food.

Serrated.   Knife grind with toothlike edge.

Tool.   A small piece of equipment, used in the hand, found in both home and commercial kitchens.

Utensils.   Pans or containers used to cook, mix, combine, or store food.

Large Equipment

Large pieces include equipment for cooking and baking, food processing, serving, and cleaning. Most pieces involve electricity or dangerous moving parts. Before looking at individual pieces, consider these general safety rules.

Safe Operating Procedures.   Before operating any equipment a worker should be trained. Training should cover setup, safety features, correct operating steps, and cleaning procedure. Whoever trains a worker should demonstrate the correct use of equipment before asking the worker to use the equipment. Then the trained worker should be able to satisfy the supervisor that he or she knows how to use the equipment. Here are the ABCs or basic rules for equipment operators to follow.

A. *Before Using Machine*

1. Dress appropriately. Do not wear loose clothing. Be sure apron strings are tied short and are out of the way. Do not wear rings around electrical equipment—metal conducts electricity and can result in electrocution if the equipment malfunctions.

2. Unplug the machine before attaching or removing parts. Grasp the plug. Do not pull it out by the cord. Be sure parts are in the right place and that work area is clear.
3. Just before using, sanitize any parts that will contact food. Keep a sanitizer spray bottle near equipment.

B. While Operating Machine: Follow manufacturer's operating instructions. Turn off the switch before changing speeds or adjusting machine. Use safety features such as safety guards on cutting equipment. Never leave while the machine is running.

C. After Using Machine: Always unplug machine before cleaning. Clean and sanitize parts according to manufacturer's directions. Put the machine back together the right way.

Report to Supervisor. Call the supervisor if the machine is not running correctly or if any parts are missing or in the wrong place.

Cooking/Baking Equipment. Broilers, ranges, ovens, griddles, fryers, and steamers make up this category.

Broiler. The American consumer likes food prepared on a broiler. A broiler consists of an electric or gas heat source that gets very hot and cooks food that is placed close to it. It is the usual choice for cooking meat or fish in its own juices, without the addition of fat. Some operators advertise broiling as a low-fat alternative to frying.

Overhead (horizontal) broiler. The overhead or horizontal broiler is popular for fish and vegetables and for browning. Control the cooking temperature by raising or lowering racks on which food is placed. The salamander is a small broiler used to brown the top of food products.

Char-grill or underfired broiler. The char-grill broiler is popular for steaks, chops, poultry, and burgers. The operator needs skill in controlling the heat source, which may be charcoal briquettes or radiant rocks. Some of the popular, smoky flavor comes from meat drippings falling on hot coals.

The overhead electric boiler is popular for cooking vegetables and fish and for browning many foods.
Courtesy: Vulcan-Hart Corp.

Griddle.   The griddle is a favorite piece of equipment for breakfast items, hamburgers, steaks, and grilled sandwiches. It is a flat, smooth metal surface and is quick and efficient. Sometimes a griddle is part of a larger piece of equipment that includes a range, griddle and ovens. In that case it is called a range top (see

The char-grill or underfired broiler is used for steaks, chops, hamburgers, and poultry.
Courtesy: Vulcan-Hart Corp.

The gas griddle is important for preparing breakfast items, burgers, grilled sandwiches, and steaks.
Courtesy: Vulcan-Hart Corp.

illustration on p. 128). The cook fries food directly on the griddle.
It is important to season a griddle to prevent sticking and rusting.
Season with a griddlestone or griddle cloth and oil. Clean the
griddle after every use.

Range. The range is the backbone of the kitchen. A cook can
prepare most basic menu items using the right pans and a range.
It can be used to pan broil, stew, simmer, fry, or boil. There are
two types of range tops: An open range has visible gas or electric
coil burners, a flat-top (hot-top) range has continuous metal plates
across the top. They are heated from underneath. Since the development of steam kettles and tilting skillets the range is used
mostly for cooking small items.

Ovens. Ovens are used for various dry-heat cookery methods
such as baking, oven frying, oven broiling, and roasting. There
are four oven types with different heat sources.

Conventional oven. In a conventional oven, the heat source is
on the bottom or in the sides of the oven. Heat radiates from the
source and cooks food from the outside in. Conventional ovens
can be stacked several layers high (deck ovens) or placed under a
range top.

Convection oven. In a convection oven, a fan moves heated
air around food surfaces. The temperature of the food gradually
rises until cooked to doneness. Food cooks 30% more quickly
than in a conventional oven, and convection ovens cook at temperatures 25–75°F higher than conventional ovens. The convec-

An electric restaurant range with griddle and overhead broiler. The range top is used to pan broil, stew, fry, or simmer small quantities.
Courtesy: Vulcan-Hart Corp.

tion oven can dry out foods, especially baked products if not watched carefully.

Rotary/revolving oven.　A rotary oven is a large conventional oven with shelves that move around. One door at the front opens to all shelves as they rotate past. A rotary oven is good for large quantity baking. There are no hot spots that can result in uneven baking.

Microwave oven.　In this oven electrical microwaves heat up liquid in food and cook food from the inside out. A microwave oven has some limitations. It cannot brown food, metal pans cannot be used in a microwave, and it cannot be used to cook large

The conventional bake—roast oven. The model is a deck oven.
Courtesy: Vulcan-Hart Corp.

In this gas convection oven, a fan moves heated air around to cook food more quickly than a conventional oven.
Courtesy: Vulcan-Hart Corp.

quantities. However, food cooks very quickly in a microwave. The microwave oven is used mostly for defrosting, reheating, or reconstituting food. There is no thermostat to set and doneness is determined by the time in the oven.

Tips for Oven Cooking.   Preheat deck and rotary ovens before loading. Load them evenly so that air circulates around food. Do not open oven doors during cooking—the temperature will drop rapidly and may spoil the product. Microwave ovens only heat when the door is closed. They cannot be preheated.

Fryers.   Fryers are special deep pans used to cook food in hot fat. Fat for fryers should be the kind that does not smoke at cooking temperatures. Besides smoking, fat can break down into off-flavored products if it is not used correctly. Do not heat fat too high for frying. Be sure to filter fat regularly before reusing. Foods that contain a lot of moisture (such as potatoes) help make fat break down quickly. Salt also breaks down fat. Never salt food

The conventional electric fryer has a thermostat to control the temperature of the fat.
Courtesy: Vulcan-Hart Corp.

before frying or shake salt over a fryer. Change fat after a certain number of uses—old fat breaks down easily.

The most popular deep-fried foods are French fries, fish, seafood, chicken, and doughnuts. Three common types of fryers are automatic, pressure, and conventional.

Conventional fryer. This fryer has an open top and thermostat to control the temperature.

Pressure fryer. A pressure fryer has a tight-fitting lid that holds in moisture but still makes food crisp. It cooks food faster and at a lower temperature than a conventional fryer.

Automatic fryer. Automatic fryers have a timer and a mechanism to lower a basket of food into fat. After the correct cooking time, food is raised out of the fat for draining.

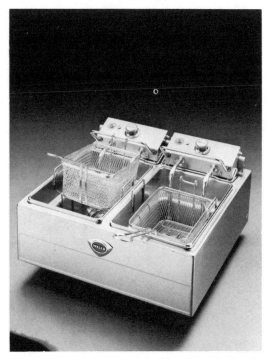

An automatic fryer has a timer and automatically raises the basket of food from the cooking fat when done.
Courtesy: Wells Commercial Cooking

Tilting Skillet. The tilting skillet is a large frypan used for frying, braising, stewing, steaming, browning, and grilling large quantities. Because it tilts on an axis, liquid products can be poured directly into pan.

Steam Equipment. Steam-cooking equipment has added a new dimension to the quantity kitchen. It reduces cooking time and cooks without burning or drying out food. Steam heat stays at a constant temperature throughout. Remember that steam equipment can be dangerous if a worker is not careful to follow directions. Steam burns are very bad.

Steam-jacketed kettle. Kettles come in sizes from 2 to 100 gal. Steam does not contact food. It is trapped between two layers of metal that form the bowl and jacket of the kettle. Food in the bowl is cooked as if in a double boiler. A deep steam-jacketed kettle is the choice for cooking vegetables, rice, noodles, or pudding. A shallow kettle is better for braising veal and poultry and for roasting pork, lamb, or ham. Cooks use a trunion or tilting steam-jacketed kettle for soups, sauces, pie fillings, and some meat mixtures.

Steam cooker or steamer. In a steamer, steam comes into direct contact with food. Steamers cook vegetables with little loss of nutrients since the vegetables sit on a rack instead of in water.

In a gas-heated steam-jacketed kettle, food is cooked by steam trapped in the wall or jacket of the kettle.
Courtesy: Vulcan-Hart Corp.

(Top) The food steamer cooks many foods with little loss of nutrients. The food is cooked under pressure. (Bottom) The smaller counter steamer cooks smaller quantities by convection.
Courtesy: Vulcan-Hart Corp.

High-pressure steam cookers cook food at 15 pounds per square inch of pressure (psi). They cook small batches of food very quickly and are excellent for defrosting or reheating food. Compartment steamers are better for large batches of food and take longer to cook. They cook at 5–7 psi. Counter steamers cook small quantities of food to order.

Equipment for Processing. Blenders, slicers, choppers, and mixers are the main types of processing equipment used in the commercial kitchen.

Blender. When blenders first appeared in the market, it seemed that they could replace many kitchen appliances. However, they do have limitations. While a blender can combine, stir, and shake foods, it cannot whip eggs or cream. It chops nuts and blends batters, but it cannot grind meat in quantities large enough to be practical. It can puree cooked food or liquify fruits. Still, it does not extract juice from fruit or vegetables. It does not knead dough in large amounts.

Slicer. Foodservice workers use the slicer to slice cheese, vegetables, fruit, and meat. The slicer cuts even, neat, standard portions. Thickness can be changed just by changing a setting with a knob.

A slicer can be a very dangerous piece of equipment, however, it is important to line up the cutting edge with the plate when not in use. Always unplug the slicer before cleaning or adjusting knobs.

Food Choppers or Cutters. Choppers and cutters cut food into small pieces. There are three types.

Meat grinder. Meat grinders chop meat into small bits. The size of the pieces depends on the size of the holes in the plate.

Food cutter/buffalo chopper. The food cutter consists of a large bowl with revolving knives that cut food. It can be used for vegetables, fruit, crackers, bread crumbs, and even meat. The pieces are coarse or fine depending on how long they are left in the bowl. Special attachments are a food grinder, dicer, and slicer/shredder.

Vertical cutter/mixer (VCM). The VCM is a large, powerful, high-speed blender, with whirling knives in an enclosed bowl. It can be used to cut, mix, blend, emulsify, or puree food. It comes in 15- to 80-qt sizes.

Mixers. Mixers mix dough and other foods. They come in 5- to 140-qt sizes, with attachments similar to those of a food cutter. The whip can make foams and light batters. A paddle is used to cream mixtures. The dough hook kneads bread dough. Mixers are used mostly in the bakery of a food production unit.

Serving Equipment. Serving equipment is designed to help serve both hot and cold food.

Hot-Food Equipment. Special equipment for hot food must keep food hot—between 140 and 180°F. That is the temperature range necessary to keep bacteria from multiplying rapidly.

Steam table. The steam table looks like a long stainless steel counter. Pans of water are heated to make steam. Rectangular pans of food are placed over the steam.

The mixer is an indispensable piece of equipment, especially in the bakery.
Courtesy: Vulcan-Hart Corp.

Pass-through.   A pass-through is a special holding unit located between the kitchen and serving area.

Warming units.   Under-the-counter warming units are used to keep bread and buns warm.

Bain marie.   The bain marie is a special hot-water bath used to hold soups and sauces on the serving line. The food is contained in a pan placed above the hot water. It prevents scalding.

Heat lamps.   Heat lamps and heating plates keep food crisp. However, they dry out most foods except French fries.

Cold-Food Serving Equipment.   Equipment for holding cold food must hold it at below 45°F. If not, undesirable microorganisms will grow quickly. Pieces include the cold pass-through between the kitchen and dining area and refrigerated display cases for salads and desserts.

Cleaning Equipment.   Cleaning equipment includes waste disposers and dish-cleaning machines.

Waste Disposers.   Waste disposer units grind and flush away pulverized food waste. Never use it for rags, paper, towels, metal, china, or any nonfood items. Before starting a disposer, move hands out of the way. Never put hands in a moving disposer.

Dishwashers.   Cleaning and sanitizing equipment is very important to the efficient foodservice operation. Dishwashers clean and sanitize dishes and come in several styles.

Single-tank type.   The wash and rinse cycles both take place in the same tank in this type of machine.

Single-tank conveyor.   Racks pass through the wash unit and then the rinse unit automatically.

Double-tank conveyor.   This machine features a power wash unit, a power rinse unit, and a final rinse unit. A prewash unit can be added to the conveyor type.

Flight unit.   These are large units with a capacity to hold 5000–12,000 plates per hour. They include prewash, wash, rinse, and final rinse cycles.

A single-tank type of dishwasher handles both the wash and rinse cycles in the same tank.
Courtesy: Vulcan-Hart Corp.

Tools and Utensils

The term *tool* generally means something a worker uses in the hand to prepare food. *Utensil* generally means pans or containers used to mix, cook, and store food.

Knives or Hand Cutlery.   The most important tool in the kitchen is the knife. Professional knives are used to cut food in pieces of a desired size. They are useful tools but can be dangerous if improperly used. Most knives are made from carbon steel or stainless steel.

Carbon Steel.   Some knives are made from carbon steel because it is easy to sharpen the edge. Carbon steel knives also require less sharpening over time than stainless steel knives. However, blades stain and they tend to turn fruit and vegetables

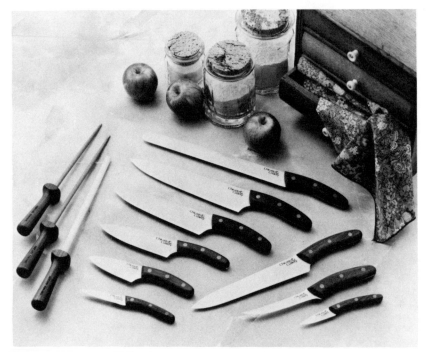

Knives are the most important tools in the professional kitchen.
Courtesy: Chicago Cutlery

brown. Carbon steel knives may also leave a metallic taste in food.

Stainless Steel. Stainless steel knives contain some carbon steel. However, they are more expensive and must be sharpened more often. Stainless steel does not discolor food.

Parts of the Knife. Every knife has a point, tip, back, shank, heel, rivets, handle, and cutting edge.

Types of Knives. Table 9.1 lists types of knives and their characteristics.

Sharpening Tools. The steel and stone are commonly used to keep knives sharp.

Sharpening Stone. This special stone is sometimes called a whetstone. It sharpens the blade of a knife.

Table 9.1: Knives shown on p. 140 and Their Characteristics

Name	*Characteristics*
a. Bread knife	Serrated edge, 9 inches long, used to slice bread, cake
b. Boning knife	Narrow blade, used to remove bones from meat
c. Butcher knife	Heavy knife, 10 to 12 inches long, used to cut all kinds of meat
d. Cleaver	Squarish blade, 3½ to 6 inches wide, used to cut bone and cartilage and dress poultry
e. French knife	6 to 14 inches long, used to slice, cut, shred, dice, chop, and mince fruits and vegetables, and slice meat
f. Utility knife	Medium-size knife used to core lettuce and pare and section fruit
g. Slicer	Long knife used to slice meats, tomatoes, lettuce wedges and sandwiches
h. Paring knife	Small knife with 3 to 4½ inch blade, used to peel, pare, cut, clean, and slice fruits and vegetables

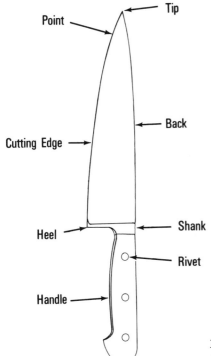

Parts of a knife.
Courtesy: Mid-America Vocational Curriculum Consortium.

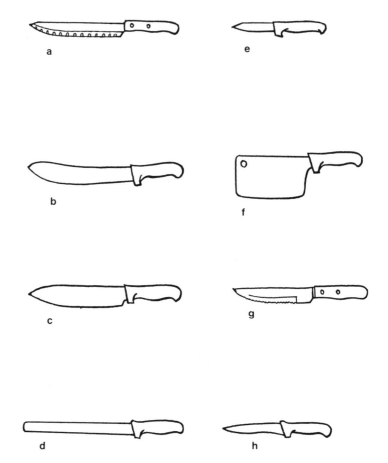

Common types of knives: a. bread knife; b. boning knife; c. butcher knife; d. cleaver; e. French knife; f. utility knife; g. slicer; h. paring knife. Refer to Table 9.1 for descriptions.

Steel. The steel is a round, swordlike piece of steel with a handle and a rough surface on the metal. By properly striking against a knife blade, the steel will hone or finely sharpen the cutting edge.

Care and Storage of Knives. Use extreme care whenever you handle knives.

Using knives safely. A sharp knife is safter than a dull knife. Be sure to use the right knife for the job you are doing. Then follow these safe handling steps:

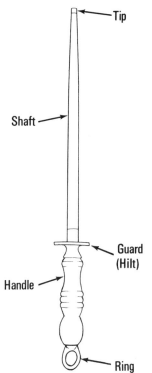

Tip

Shaft

Guard
(Hilt)

Handle

Ring

Parts of a steel.
Courtesy: Mid-America Vocational Curriculum Consortium.

1. Do not use a knife as a can opener.
2. Always use a cutting board.
3. Be sure the knife handle is free of grease so that it does not slip from your hand.
4. Cut away from your body and do not cut food in your hand.
5. If you drop a knife, do not try to catch it.
6. Keep your eyes on your work.

Cleaning and storing safely. Always wash knives by themselves, not with other utensils. Never leave knives lying in soapy water—you could cut your hand when you reach in later. Dry each knife separately and store in a knife rack or a special holder in a drawer. Never leave knives unattended.

Other Tools and Utensils. Utensils such as pans are made from many materials. Mixing utensils can be made of plastic or ceramic, but cooking utensils are usually metal.

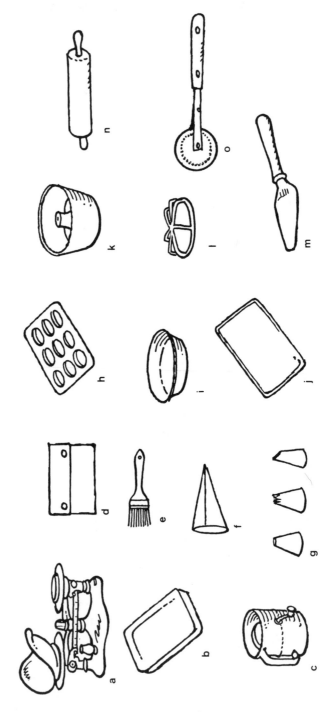

Baking tools and utensils: a. baker's scale; b. baking pan; c. sifter; d. dough cutter; e. pastry brush; f. pastry bag; g. pastry tips; h. muffin tin; i. pie tin; j. bun or sheet pan; k. tube cake pan; l. pie or cake pan; m. pie or cake marker; n. rolling pin; o. pastry wheel. Refer to Table 9.2 for use of tools and utensils.

Table 9.2: The Baking Tools and Utensils Shown on p. 142 and Their Uses

Tool/utensil	Uses
a. Scales (baker's)	Accurate weighing of ingredients
b. Pan	Baking food
c. Sifter	Sifting dry ingredients
d. Dough cutter	Cutting dough, scraping
e. Pastry brush	Brushing on liquid
f,g. Pastry bag and tip	Holds icing and makes icing designs
h. Muffin tin	Baking muffins
i. Pie pan	Baking pie or pie crust
j. Sheet pan	Baking large flat sheet cake, cookies, pastry, breads
k. Tube cake pan	Baking tube cakes such as angelfood
l. Pie or cake marker	Marking cutting lines for equal cutting of pies or cakes
m. Pie or cake knife	Cutting and serving pies or cakes
n. Rolling pin	Rolling dough to desired thickness
o. Pastry wheel	Trimming pastry

Steel is cheap and a good conductor of heat. However, pans made of steel tend to rust. Aluminum is a common metal for pans—it is light and does not rust. Copper pans conduct heat well but they are expensive. Cast iron utensils are heavy and give uniform heating. They do rust but are good for frying. Stainless steel utensils are most common even though they do not conduct heat well. Steel comes in many gauges (thicknesses) and is very

Table 9.3: The Cooking Tools and Utensils Shown on p. 144 and Their Uses

Tools/utensils	Uses
a. Sauce pan	Cooking small amount of food on range
b. Sauce pot, stock pot	Cooking large amount of food on range
c. Sauté pan, brazier pan	Cooking small amount of food on range with little fat
d. Double boiler, bain marie pans	Cooking food below boiling to prevent scorching; storing food
e. Steam table pans (counter, hotel pans)	Cooking and holding food for service
f. Roasting pan	Roasting meats

Cooking tools and utensils: a. sauce pan; b. sauce pot; c. sauté pan; d. double boiler; e. steam table pan; f. roasting pan. Refer to Table 9.3 for use of tools and utensils.

durable. All utensils should: do the job, be safe and durable, be priced reasonably, and save labor.

Baking Tools and Utensils.   Table 9.2 lists common tools and utensils used in baking.

Cooking Tools and Utensils.   Table 9.3 lists common cooking tools and utensils and their uses.

Food Preparation Tools and Utensils.   Table 9.4 lists tools and utensils used for general food preparation.

Table 9.4: The Food Preparation Tools and Utensils Shown on p. 145 and Their Uses

Tool/utensil	Uses
a,b. Wire whip (French, piano whip)	Incorporating air into liquid products
c. Grater	Grating, shredding small amounts
d. Colander, strainer	Straining liquids from food
e. China cap	Straining fine particles from liquid
f. Meat mallet	Tenderizing meat
g. Meat thermometer	Determining internal temperature
h. Peeler	Scraping or peeling fruits and vegetables
i. Melon baller	Cutting soft fruit or vegetables into ball shapes
j. Skewer	Holding food together

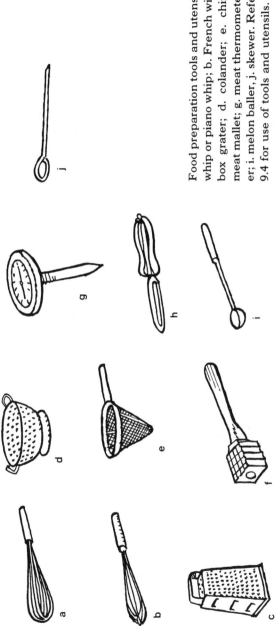

Food preparation tools and utensils: a. wire whip or piano whip; b. French wire whip; c. box grater; d. colander; e. china cap; f. meat mallet; g. meat thermometer; h. peeler; i. melon baller, j. skewer. Refer to Table 9.4 for use of tools and utensils.

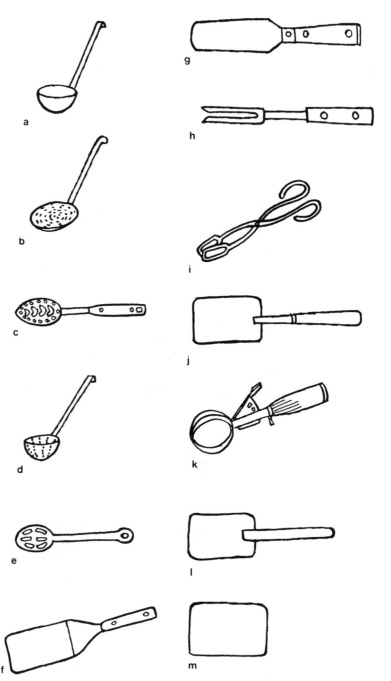

Food-serving and food-handling tools and utensils: a. ladle; b. skimmer; c. perforated spoon; d. perforated ladle; e. slotted spoon; f. offset spatula; g. flat spatula; h. fork; i. tongs; j. hotcake turner; k. disher or scoop; l. rubber scraper; m. plastic scraper. Refer to Table 9.5 for use of tools and utensils.

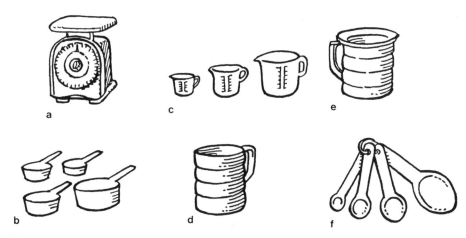

Tools and utensils for measuring and weighing: a. portion scales, b. graduated cups for dry measuring; c. graduated liquid measures; d. dry measures for large amounts; e. liquid measures for large amounts; f. measuring spoons. Refer to Table 9.6 for use of tools and utensils.

Food-Serving and Food-Handling Tools and Utensils.
Table 9.5 lists common handling—serving tools and utensils and their uses.

Tools and Utensils for Measuring and Weighing.
Table 9.6 lists tools and utensils for weighing and measuring ingredients.

Table 9.5: The Food-Handling and Food-Serving Tools and Utensils Shown on p. 146 and Their Uses

Tools/utensils	Uses
a. Ladle	Stirring, mixing, serving liquids
b. Skimmer	Removing particles that rise to the top
c,d. Perforated spoon, ladle	Serving small-cut vegetables
e. Slotted spoon, spoon	Serving large-cut vegetables
f. Spatula, offset	Mixing, spreading, scraping
g. Spatula, flat	Icing cakes
h. Fork	Turning or holding meat
i. Tongs	General food handling
j. Hotcake turner	Turning food
k. Scoop, disher (1, 2, 3, 4, 8 oz)	Portioning and serving
l. Rubber scraper	Removing food from containers
m. Plastic scraper	Scraping bowls

Table 9.6: The Tools and Utensils for Measuring and Weighing
Shown on p. 147 and Their Uses

Tools/utensils	*Uses*
a. Scales (portion)	Weighing ingredients or foods for portion control and accuracy
b,d. Dry measures, graduated	Measuring volume of dry foods (small amounts in cups or milliliters; large amounts in pints and quarts or liters)
c,e. Liquid measures, graduated	Measuring volume of liquids (small amounts in cups or millilters; large amounts in quarts and gallons or liters)
f. Measuring spoons	Measuring small amounts of liquid or dry ingredients (teaspoons and tablespoons or milliliters)

10
Appetizers
and Garnishes

Many fine restaurants offer a full line of appetizers to start the meal. Their purpose, as their name suggests, is to spark or stimulate the appetite. They are bite-sized pieces of food and are often spicy and colorful. Some appetizers take a lot of labor to prepare. Because they are small, they can reach room temperature quickly. Therefore it is important to give special attention to sanitation.

Appetizers are sometimes served even when there is no meal. Dips, snacks, and relish trays are popular for informal occasions. For more formal dining, appetizers may be cocktails, hors d'oeuvres, and canapés.

Objectives and Terms

Objectives. This section should help you:

- Define appetizers.
- List appetizers served on informal occasions.
- List two appetizers served for formal dining.
- Describe guidelines for preparing appetizers.
- Define garnishes.
- List important points in preparing garnishes.

Terms to Know

Appetizer. Bite-sized pieces of food that stimulate the appetite.

Canapés.   Appetizers made of bread, a filling, and a garnish.

Hors d'Oeuvres.   Appetizers that do not include bread but whose major ingredient is served whole or eaten with a toothpick.

Cocktails.   Bite-sized pieces of shellfish, meat, or fruit served with a flavorful sauce or topping.

Dips.   Informal appetizers made with softened dairy or vegetable products and used to dip chips or vegetables.

Garnish.   A colorful, appealing topping for food.

Appetizers

Canapés.   Canapés are bite-sized finger foods. They may be small, open-faced sandwiches cut into fancy shapes. The base for a canapé can be bread (rye, pumpernickel, white), toast, crackers, puffs, or pastry shells.

Canapé spreads or fillings may be simple or elaborate. Popular spreads are butters, cream cheese, meat (liver paté, deviled ham), and fish or poultry (shrimp, tuna, or chicken salad.)

To make the canapé look truly appetizing, add a garnish such as sliced vegetable (radish or cucumber slices, asparagus tips, mushroom, or cherry tomato), relish (olive, pickle, pimiento), fish (shrimp, herring piece, smoked fish), cheese, egg slice, or parsley.

A good-quality canapé will have fresh, pleasing flavor and an attractive appearance with the topping and garnish arranged neatly.

Cocktails.   Cocktails are bite-sized pieces of shellfish, meat, fish, or fruit served with a flavored sauce or topping. They should be ready to eat when served. Popular cocktails include:

- Seafood (shrimp, crab, clams, oysters) and a special sauce.
- Herring or fish balls.
- Tiny meat balls.
- Fruit cup with sherbet.

Dips, Dippers, and Spreads.   A dip or a spread is a softened or pureed food or mixture served with a crisp food, the dipper.

Shrimp cocktail is a popular appetizer in many restaurants. It is usually served with a tangy sauce.

There is no limit to the types of dips and spreads. Common bases are sour cream, yogurt, cheese, avocado, mashed beans, and mayonnaise. Flavoring ingredients can range from shrimp to onion to bacon. Some dips are hot (fondues) and some are cold (chip dips). The consistency should always be smooth and creamy—not too thick or too thin.

A good-quality dip or spread has no lumps, has good flavor, and—if cold—is chilled to 40°F.

Favorite dippers include chips, crackers, and crisp vegetables such as carrots, celery, cauliflower, broccoli flowerets, and pepper strips.

Hors d'Oeuvres. While they are similar to canapés, hors d'oeuvres are different in three ways. Table 10.1 compares cana-

A cheese ball is an example of an appetizer. The semisoft cheese mixture is spread on crackers.

Table 10.1: Comparison of Canapés and Hors d'Oeuvres

Canapés	Hors d'oeuvres
On bread	Not on bread
Finger food	On fork or toothpick
Pureed ingredient	Main ingredient whole

pés and hors d'oeuvres. Hors d'oeuvres are not served on bread. They are not finger foods but are eaten with tooth picks or small forks. The major ingredient of the hors d'oeuvre is served whole, not mashed or pureed. It is a good idea to have contrast in flavor and appearance in hors d'oeuvres. Some popular hot and cold hors d'oeuvres are listed in Table 10.2.

Snacks, Relishes, and Juices.   These appetizers are favorites for informal occasions. They involve little cooking and preparation.

Snacks include popcorn, potato chips, pretzels, and corn chips. They are especially popular in the bar business where they are part of the sales program.

Relishes are cut raw vegetables or pickled foods that are usually served on a small platter with ice. Vegetables can be prepared as radish roses, carrot curls, or celery hearts. In those cases, more labor is involved. Popular pickles include watermelon rin, beets, stuffed olives, spiced apples, and, of course, a variety of cucumber pickles.

Most of us only think of tomato juice when we think of juice appetizers. However, an appetizer can be any cold, tangy vegetable or fruit juice. It whets the appetite at the beginning of a meal.

Table 10.2: Hot and Cold Hors d'Oeuvres

Hot	Cold
Meatballs	Cheese cubes
Kebabs of meat, grilled fruit	Deviled eggs
	Cheese balls
Puffs	Ham rolls
	Cold kebabs
	Melon balls

Hors d'oeuvres are appetizers that may be served with toothpicks or small forks. Main ingredients are usually whole or distinct. Deviled eggs, tiny meat balls, and stuffed celery are examples.

Guidelines for Preparing Appetizers

Serving Time. Prepare appetizers as close as possible to serving time. Appetizers do not hold up well for a long time. Keep moist ingredients moist and dry ingredients dry until serving time.

Right Combinations. Select foods that complement each other.

Quality Ingredients. Use the freshest ingredients. If the appetizer you are preparing incorporates leftovers, be sure that you have stored them correctly.

Keep It Simple. One colorful garnish is more appealing than a fancy, complicated topping.

Control Temperature. Keep cold foods cold and hot foods hot to prevent bacteria from multiplying. Your appetizers will look and taste better, too.

Arrange Attractively. Take the time to prepare appetizers attractively. They will invite customers to enjoy what follows and they will want to come back again.

Table 10.3: Common Groups of Garnishes and Their Usual Forms

Group	Garnishes	Forms	Group	Garnishes	Forms
Vegetables	Carrots	Curls, strips	Fruits	Apples	Wedges, rings
	Celery	Hearts, sticks		Grapefruit	Sections
	Chives	Chopped		Grapes	Fresh, sugared
	Cucumbers	Twists, fluted slices		Citrus fruit	Slices, wedges, twists
	Mushrooms	Caps		Kiwifruit	Slices
	Olives	Sliced, whole		Melons	Slices, wedges, balls
	Parsley	Sprig, chopped		Peaches	Halves, slices
	Peppers, green	Rings, strips		Pineapples	Wedges, fingers
	Pickles	Spears, slices, fans		Strawberries	Whole, slices
	Pimentos	Strips	Other foods	Cheese	Strips, cubes, shredded
	Radishes	Roses, slices, fans		Croutons	Plain
	Tomatoes	Whole, wedges, slices		Eggs	Quarters, slices, chopped
				Nuts	Chopped
				Paprika	Plain
				Sweet chocolate	Grated, curls
				Whipped cream	Plain

Table 10.4: Menu Items and Traditional Garnishes

Menu item	*Garnishes*
Appetizers	Cucumbers, green peppers, eggs, olives, pickles
Soups	Cheese, croutons, paprika, parsley flakes, sour cream
Salads	
Fruit	Cherries, kiwifruit, strawberries, grapes
Meat, seafood	Carrots, cucumbers, eggs, green peppers, olives, radishes, tomatoes
Vegetable	Chives, eggs, green peppers, parsley, pimentos
Sandwiches	Carrots, celery, cucumbers, olives, radishes, pickles, tomatoes
Entrees	Citrus fruits, parsley, peaches, tomatoes
Desserts	Candies, coconut, fruits, nuts, whipped cream
Beverages	Berries, citrus fruits

Garnishes

A garnish is a food that makes another food look better or taste better. A garnish adds color, texture, shape, and flavor. The garnish may be part of the dish or just a decoration. Either way, it should be edible.

Most garnishes are made from fruits or vegetables. They are almost always prepared in the cold-food section of the kitchen. However, there are some traditional hot garnishes such as small potatoes and broiled tomatoes. Table 10.3 lists common garnishes in groups.

Garnishes are used in many ways. Each item on the menu may be decorated with a garnish. No single garnish can be used with all foods. Many foods have specific recommended garnishes. For example, fish is almost always served with a lemon wedge. Table 10.4 lists some specific foods and traditional garnishes.

Some important points to consider in preparing garnishes are:

1. Relate the size of the garnish to the size of the food. Do not serve a large garnish on a small serving of food—it will look silly.

2. The type of garnish should fit the cost of the meal. Use an elaborate garnish for an expensive entree. It is worth it.

3. Choose garnishes to add natural color to the food. The garnish should complement the food.

4. The garnish can contrast with the food.

5. Use the freshest ingredients for garnishes.

6. Remember, garnishes should be edible, whether the customer will eat them or not.

11
Beverages

The beverage is an important part of the meal. A cup of coffee seems like a simple thing, yet your entire foodservice operation can depend on the quality of that cup of coffee. Coffee is the thing some customers most remember about a meal.

In the same way, some people judge a restaurant on its hot or iced tea. These two beverages are very important parts of every operation, and you should know how to prepare them correctly.

Objectives and Terms

Objectives.   This section should help you:

- Explain the importance of coffee in the foodservice operation.
- List the two major types of coffee-making equipment.
- Describe characteristics of good coffee products for your operation.
- Describe elements in correct coffee-making procedure.
- List quality characteristics of prepared coffee.
- List three types of tea.
- Describe quality characteristics of tea.
- List market forms of tea.

Terms to Know

Coffee.   Brewed beverage made from ground, roasted coffee beans.

Brew. The process of producing coffee beverage from ground coffee beans and water.

Urn. A large coffee maker in which water drips through a basket of grounds.

Drip Coffeemaker. A machine that produces a small amount of coffee at a time (8 to 12 C) by water dripping through grounds into the pot below.

Decaffeinated Coffee. Coffee from which caffeine is removed.

Instant Coffee. Powdered coffee that is mixed with hot water to make coffee beverage.

Espresso Coffee. A specialty coffee that is made in a special machine that extracts coffee flavor from grounds with steam.

Tea. Beverage prepared by steeping tea in hot water.

Black Tea. Fermented tea that is dark in color.

Oolong Tea. A partly fermented tea that is between green and black in color and flavor.

Green Tea. Unfermented tea that is light in color and weak in flavor.

Steeping. The process of making tea beverage by letting tea leaves stand in hot water for the correct length of time.

Coffee

From the first cup in the morning to the last cup at night, coffee may be what your guests remember most about your operation. For that reason, it may not be a good idea to give the coffee-making responsibility to the least experienced person on the staff. True, the procedure is simple—just pass hot water through coffee—but the results are not always the same.

A good cup of coffee is hot, is rich in color, and has a characteristic coffee aroma and flavor. To be sure you get that kind of a product every time, you must use the right equipment, coffee, and procedure.

Equipment. Use the correct size coffee maker for your operation and care for it properly to prevent off-flavors. Whether it is a

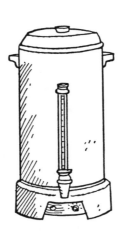 

Popular commercial coffee-making equipment includes urns for large quantities and automatic drip or vacuum systems for making 8–12 C at a time.

drip system or a large urn, the coffee maker should be made of glass, porcelain, or stainless steel. Aluminum or copper brewers can impart an unusual, unpleasant metallic flavor to the coffee.

Urn. Large production units may use a coffee urn. Water drips through a large basket of coffee to produce gallons of coffee at a time.

Drip Makers. The most common coffee makers are drip or vacuum systems for producing 8–12 C at a time.

Product. There are many varieties of coffee available from around the world. Most commercial brands are blends of different coffees. The coffee beans are first roasted to develop the natural flavor. Coffee flavor varies depending on whether the beans are roasted to the light, medium, or dark stage. Guests usually have definite ideas about how coffee should taste. Choice can be based on flavor and price.

In addition to regular, brewed coffee, a foodservice operator may offer the following:

Instant. Instant coffee is powdered coffee that mixes instantly with hot water. Most foodservice operations do not use instant.

Decaffeinated.   The caffeine is removed from regular coffee. Many operators offer decaffeinated coffee to guests. It is often served in instant form.

Espresso.   A variety of strong dark coffees can be offered as specialty items. They are brewed in special machines.

Procedure.   Many factors contribute to making good coffee:

Coffee Quality.   Coffee should be freshly ground or vacuum sealed. Once the package is opened, quality goes down quickly. Be sure to protect packages from heat, moisture, and air. Select the right grind for the equipment.

Proportion.   Use the right proportion of coffee to water. One pound of coffee is about right for 2 to 2½ gal of water.

Brewing Time for Grind.   Different grinds need different brewing times. Brew the right length of time.

Fine.   For vacuum-brewed coffee, brew 2–3 minutes

Drip.   Drip coffee in urns or smaller pots takes 4–6 minutes.

Regular.   Regular coffee percolates in 6–8 minutes.

Fresh Water.   Use only cold tap water for brewing coffee. Do not start with hot water. It will not speed the brewing process. Instead, it may result in stale-tasting coffee because the hot water has been sitting in a boiler.

Water Temperature.   Brew coffee to between 195 and 205°F. If water does not get that hot, it will not extract flavor oils from ground coffee. If water gets too hot, it will extract bitter flavors from coffee.

Brewing Directions.   Follow the exact directions for your coffee maker. Do not overbrew. Coffee should brew in 4–6 minutes. It should not take under 4 minutes or over 8 minutes with an automatic drip machine. Flavor is best from a full coffee maker. Use the right coffee maker for the amount of coffee you need.

Holding Temperature.   Hold coffee at 185 to 195°F. It is best to hold coffee for 30 minutes or less. Never hold it for over 1½ hours. Coffee will lose flavor and aroma.

Clean Equipment. Clean coffee-making equipment daily, following the manufacturer's directions to be sure all parts are clean. If some parts are not cleaned, they collect residue that turns bitter. Use good cloth or paper filters, the right kind for your machine.

Standards of Quality.   Good coffee has these characteristics:

1. Flavor should be fresh, not stale or bitter.
2. Aroma should be pleasant and right for that blend of coffee.
3. Coffee should be medium brown in color for the right strength.
4. There should be no visible particles or oiliness.
5. Temperature should be hot when served.

Merchandising Coffee.   A good cup of coffee will make its own reputation. Beyond that, you can add to its distinctiveness in these ways:

Service.   Preheat coffee cups by rinsing with hot water. When serving, fill three-fourths full. When the guest's cup is one-third empty, ask if you can refill. To draw special attention to your good coffee, serve it from silver service poured into good china at the table.

Coffee Drinks.   Offer specialty coffee drinks such as:

- Cappucino—espresso combined with milk that has been aerated with steam.
- Demitasse—any strong coffee served in little cups.
- Cafe au Lait—espresso or other strong coffee combined with scalded milk.
- Viennese coffee—demitasse topped with whipped cream.

Tea

For a long time we thought of the United States as a coffee-drinking country, but in recent years, tea has become very popular. It is served both iced and hot for good reasons:

Tea is usually made by steeping loose tea or tea bags in a teapot filled with boiling water. Some operations use instant tea.

- It is easy to make.
- Not much equipment is needed.
- It is cheaper than coffee.

Tea Varieties.   Most teas come from India and Sri Lanka.* There are many varieties and most commercial teas are blends of one or more of the following:

Black Tea.   The most popular teas in this country are fermented black teas. One type of black tea is Orange Pekoe, which is not orange at all. The name simply tells us that it is a leaf size of black tea. It has a strong flavor.

Oolong.   Oolong tea is partially fermented to a greenish-brown color. It has a flavor halfway between green and black tea.

Green.   Green tea is not fermented. It has a weak flavor and is popular in oriental restaurants.

*Ceylon, an island nation south of India, changed its name to Sri Lanka some years ago, but the tea it produces is still referred to as Ceylon tea.

Preparing Good Tea.   Follow these simple steps to make delicious tea. Be sure to start with good-quality tea.

1.   Prepare tea using fresh water.
2.   Measure accurately and use the right proportion of tea to water: 1 oz of tea to 1 gal of water, or 1 tsp of tea to 1 C of water.
3.   Use boiling water. Pour water over leaves or tea bags. Then remove from heat to steep.
4.   Do not overbrew. Tea will become bitter and dark if you steep it for more than 5 minutes.
5.   Use glass, pottery, china, or stainless steel equipment. Other metals will give tea a metallic taste.
6.   If you are preparing iced tea, add ice to room temperature strong tea just before serving. The tea will become cloudy if you refrigerate it. Clear cloudiness by adding a small amount of boiling water.

Standards of Quality for Tea.   Good tea has these characteristics:

- A slightly tart taste.
- A fragrant, fruity aroma.
- A clear appearance with no oiliness.
- Light-brown, golden color for black and oolong teas.
- The right temperature (hot tea is hot, iced tea is cold).

Market Forms of Tea.   Tea comes in several market forms:

Loose Tea.   Chopped tea leaves are sold by the pound and measured by the spoon. Once the tea is steeped, the leaves are filtered out when serving.

Tea Bags.   Fine filter bags contain measured amounts of tea. Bags come in individual (1–2 tsp) or institutional sizes (1, 2, or 3 oz).

Instant.   Instant tea powder is prepared just by adding water. It is popular for preparing iced tea and comes in unsweetened or sweetened form.

Special Flavors.   Both loose and tea bag teas come in special flavors such as mint, orange, spice, and apple.

The commercial operation usually serves a variety of soft drinks, fruit juices, milk, and hot chocolate (in season.) Workers should be familiar with their preparation, service, and equipment maintenance.

12
Salads and Dressings

In traditional restaurants, a salad was the first course of a meal. Today the salad has broken that tradition in many ways. The traditional main ingredient of the salad was a leafy green vegetable. However, today we use other vegetables, meat, fish, poultry, eggs, cheese, fruit, and even grains in salads. It can still be the first course, but it can also be a main course, a side dish, or even a dessert. Salads can be simple or elaborate.

Many kinds of salads are perfect for the health- conscious consumer. They are usually high in nutrients and may be low in calories. Properly prepared salads can add color, flavor, variety, and crispness to a meal.

Objectives and Terms

Objectives. This section should help you:

- List the parts of a salad.
- Classify salads according to their function in the meal.
- Describe steps in preparing salads.
- List ways to serve and merchandise salads.
- List three different types of salad dressings and give an example of each.

Terms to Know

Salad. A dish made of raw or cooked foods usually flavored with dressing.

Underliner.   The background for the main part of the salad.

Gelatin.   A powdered substance made from animal hooves and hides, used to make gelled food products.

Gel.   A semisolid jellylike substance.

Aspic.   A gelatin mixture, usually prepared with stock or vegetable juice.

Salad Bar.   An arrangement of salad ingredients and dressings from which a customer makes his or her own salad.

Salad Buffet.   Part of a food buffet that includes a large variety of prepared salads.

Salad Dressing.   Liquid used to bring out the flavor and appearance of salads.

Suspension.   A liquid mixture in which oil, water, and other ingredients are temporarily blended.

French Dressing.   Salad dressing made from oil, vinegar, and seasonings.

Emulsion.   A mixture in which oil and water or other liquid stay blended through the addition of a certain ingredient.

Mayonnaise.   A semisolid dressing made from vinegar and oil emulsified with egg yolks.

Cooked Dressing.   Dressing made by thickening liquid with starch or egg, but without oil.

The Parts of a Salad

It is difficult to define a salad because there are so many types. The only common characteristics are the parts of a salad.

Base or Underliner.   The underliner is a background for the main part of the salad. It adds color and texture and also provides a border on the salad plate. The underliner should always be neat and never hang off the edge of the plate.

Some underliners are prepared in the form of a cup. This gives shape and height to the plate and makes the salad more interesting. An example is an iceberg lettuce cup. Other popular bases are plain iceberg lettuce leaves and broken or shredded lettuce. Besides iceberg, other good bases include curly endive, Romaine lettuce, and leaf lettuce.

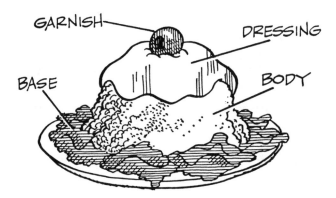

Salads consist of four parts: the base, the body (the part for which the salad is named), dressing, and garnish.

The Body.   The body is the main part of the salad and usually gives the salad its name. It can include one food or several foods. The body is arranged neatly on the underliner, so that the customer should be able to see the major ingredient. Potato salad, for example, should have firm cubed potatoes, not mashed potatoes.

The Garnish.   The garnish is not as important as the body, but it sets off the body or underliner and adds interest to the salad. In

Not all salads are served cold. Hot potato salad is a tangy favorite on some menus.
Courtesy: Oscar Mayer & Co.

some cases, a garnish can add texture, flavor, eye appeal, and contrast. The garnishes for a chef's salad are julienne strips of ham, turkey, and cheese, and maybe sliced egg. These toppings not only add color, but a lot of flavor as well. All garnishes should be simple and should not dominate the salad. They should also be edible.

Dressings.   Dressings are liquids that add flavor, moisture, and color to a salad. As a rule, use a tart dressing with green salads and a sweet dressing with fruit salads. Be careful to use the dressing to enhance flavors—it should never take over the salad. Later in this chapter we shall discuss types of dressings.

Types of Salads

Salads can be described in two ways: by their ingredients (greens, vegetable, fruit, gelatin, etc.) and by their function in the meal (appetizer, accompaniment, main dish, dessert.)

Appetizers.   Like the traditional first course, the appetizer salad stimulates the appetite. It is best to serve a small quantity and make it light. Because you do not want to give the customer a bad first impression, be sure the salad includes high-quality ingredients and a colorful garnish. Examples are seafood salad, fresh fruit, marinated mushrooms, assorted relishes, and sliced fresh tomatoes.

Accompaniment.   The most common type of salad is the side salad. It can be served with dinner or as a separate course. The portion is moderate, and it contrasts in texture, color, and flavor with other menu items. Serve a light salad if the entree is heavy; if the entree is light, the salad can be heavier. Potato salad is heavy and goes well with a light entree such as soup or a sandwich. With heavier main dishes, choose mixed-green salad, fruit and cottage cheese, pickled beets, or a molded salad. A side salad may take the place of a vegetable, especially at a luncheon meal.

A main dish salad may be the whole meal. Ham salad is a popular main dish for warm weather.
Courtesy: Oscar Mayer & Co.

Main Dish.   A main dish salad can be the whole meal. As with all salads, there should be contrasting colors and flavors. In addition, be sure that the salad is large and hearty enough to be a complete meal. Some examples are chicken salad, tomato stuffed with tuna, avocado stuffed with shrimp salad, chef salad, and fruit and cheese plate. All are popular luncheon salads.

Dessert.   Dessert salads are usually sweet. They may be fresh, jellied, or frozen. Examples are gelatin salads with fruit, creams, and mousses.

Salad Preparation Rules

Always use high-quality, fresh ingredients. Make sure different ingredients look good and taste good. Keep a salad simple but do not make it look flat. Mound it up in the center. Use uniform, bite-sized pieces—they should be large enough to recognize but small enough so that they do not have to be cut.

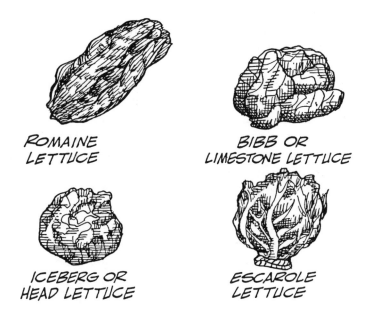

ROMAINE
LETTUCE

BIBB OR
LIMESTONE LETTUCE

ICEBERG OR
HEAD LETTUCE

ESCAROLE
LETTUCE

Iceberg or head lettuce is the most commonly used salad green. However, other types of lettuce provide a somewhat different color and texture to a salad.

Preparing Salads

Green Salad.   Clean greens carefully. Wash away all grit and dirt in cold water. To keep greens crisp, store in plastic after careful washing and draining. Too much handling and cleaning will cause greens to turn brown. Too much moisture will drown the greens.

Just before serving, cut greens into bite-sized pieces. Tearing is all right for small quantities, but cutting is recommended for large quantities. Use a stainless steel knife to prevent greens from "rusting." Treat greens with an approved antioxidant if you will be holding them for some time. Do not use bisulfite antioxidants because they have been known to cause allergic reactions in some customers. Serve salads on individual small plates or bowls, or in a large bowl for buffets.

Vegetable Salad. Cut one or more raw vegetables into bite-sized, uniform shapes. Clean and refrigerate until salad-making time.

It is best to cut vegetables as close to serving time as you can since they do not hold up well for long after being cut. Some vegetables such as peas and beets are not suitable in the raw state. However, they can be used cooked and cooled or marinated. Marination is a technique that gives salad vegetables flavor and prevents browning.

Dressings on vegetable salads are optional. Coleslaw, of course, needs a dressing for flavor but a marinated carrot salad, for example, is served without extra dressing. Other vegetables that are popular in salads are cucumbers, radishes, tomatoes, and celery. Cut them in a variety of shapes to add interest. Some vegetables, such as avocado, turn dark when cut. Dip in acid to prevent darkening. Always make the arrangement attractive for eye appeal.

Combination Salad.   Any salad that includes two or more kinds of ingredients is a combination salad. They are often served as main dishes.

Tossed Salad.   Use fresh seasonal vegetables and greens for a tossed salad.

Chef's Salad.   A chef's salad usually includes leafy greens with ham, turkey, cheese, and sliced eggs.

Stuffed Salad.   Popular vegetables for stuffing are tomatoes. They can be stuffed with a tuna or chicken mixture.

Salade Nicoise.   Salade Nicoise is a mixture of potato, string-beans, leafy greens, tuna, olives, eggs, tomatoes, anchovy fillets, and a French dressing.

There is no limit to the number of combinations a restaurant operator can offer. Common sense says to use compatible tastes, colors and textures. You wouldn't want to put peaches and anchovies together, for example.

Cooked Salads. A cooked food product is the main ingredient in a cooked salad. Macaroni and potato salads are two good examples. High-protein foods such as eggs, chicken, or ham are often used in these salads. The dressing is distinctive for each salad—it adds flavor and holds the salad together. Crisp ingredients such as celery, pickles, or onion may be included for texture. You may serve a cooked salad as an entree. Cooked salad is a good way to use leftovers.

Follow these tips to keep cooked salads safe and to assure quality.

Cool. Before adding cooked food to dressing, be sure all food is cooled. This will keep bacteria from growing.

Cook Whole. Cook potatoes whole to retain the most nutrients in a potato salad.

Cut Uniformly. Cut ingredients into uniform bite-sized pieces.

Marinate. Add zest to bland vegetables by marinating them first. This is common with potato salad and seafood salad.

Blend Dressing Carefully. To keep ingredients from getting mushy, add dressing very carefully and blend lightly.

Garnish. Get the customer interested in the food by garnishing attractively.

Fruit Salad. Use cut or sectioned fruit in fruit salad. Arrange one or more fruits attractively to make the most of the natural beauty of fruit. Some guidelines for preparing quality fruit salads include:

Quality Fruit. Use highest quality grades if you use canned fruit. Lower grades may not be firm and even in shape.

Avoid Browning. Add acid liquid to keep fruit from turning dark. Lemon, lime, orange, and pineapple juice are excellent for this purpose. They also improve the flavor of bland fruits such as apples, pears, and bananas. Handle fruit gently to keep it from bruising.

Wash Fruit. Do not use any blemished or overripe fruit. Wash fruit before using to remove dirt and some insecticide.

Serve at Once. Prepare raw fruit as close to serving time as possible. If you prepare it hours ahead of time, it may lose texture, color, and nutrients. In particular, strawberries and bananas do not hold up well.

Drain Fruit. Drain canned fruit before using in salads. Too much liquid will make a waterlogged salad.

Stainless Steel. Use stainless steel equipment to avoid stains and discoloration on fruit.

Gelatin Salads. Gelatin salads are popular, economical, and easy to make. You can prepare them ahead of time and there is no limit to the number of foods you can add to them. Gelatin is the base for these salads. The three types are:

Clear. A variety of ingredients are mixed with unflavored gelatin.

Fruit Flavored. One of many fruit-flavored gelatin mixtures is used. All are high in sugar. Artificial and natural flavors and colors give the gelatins their distinctive taste and colors.

Aspic. Basic unflavored gelatin is seasoned with meat stock, tomato, spices, and other foods.

In all gelatin salads, liquid is mixed with powdered gelatin, which is derived from the hides and hooves of animals. Gelatin molecules absorb liquid and swell. Then, when the mixture cools, the swollen gelatin cells get stiff or *gel*. Temperature, sugar, and acid affect the gelling of gelatin:

1.   Sugar increases the firmness of a gel, but too much sugar can interfere with gelling.
2.   Acids, such as lemon juice, and added ingredients weaken the gel structure.
3.   The right ratio of liquid to gelatin is important: too much gelatin will result in a stiff, rubbery product; too little gelatin makes a soft, sloppy product.

4.   Temperature is critical. For plain gelatin, stir in a few table-spoons of cold water before adding hot liquid. Use only hot liquid to dissolve flavored gelatin (100°F). One-half of the total liquid must be hot. The other half can be cold or even ice. Gelatin sets rapidly at cold temperatures.

5.   Gelatin that takes a long time to set can become stiff or rubbery.

6.   Some fresh fruits such as pineapple keep gelatin from gell-ing. Pineapple contains a chemical that keeps the gelatin from swelling when added to water. Cook pineapple to inactivate this substance, or use canned pineapple.

7.   Gelatin can be whippied to increase its volume. However, the gelling power of gelatin decreases when it is whipped.

8.   Drain fruits high in juice before adding to gelatin. Too much juice will weaken the gelatin.

9.   Add fruit or vegetables to gelatin when it begins to gel. If you add too early, the pieces will float.

10.   Gelatin can be molded or poured into pans. If poured in a large pan, cut it into squares for individual servings.

11.   To unmold, carefully dip the bottom of the mold into hot water for a few seconds. Do not hold the mold in the water too long or the gelatin will melt. Gelatin will unmold more easily if the mold is lightly greased before adding gelatin mixture.

How To Serve and Merchandise Salads

There are four basic ways to present salads to the customer—all help whet the appetite.

Salad Bar.   A salad bar usually contains three or four types of greens, garnishes, and dressings. Popular garnishes are onion slices, peppers, cheese, sunflower seeds, tomatoes, croutons, and bean sprouts. All ingredients should be fresh and chilled. The guest selects his or her favorite ingredients to create a custom-made salad. Imagination in ingredients adds to the success of the salad bar. It is popular in steak houses and gives customers some-thing to do while they wait for the main course. Salad bars have

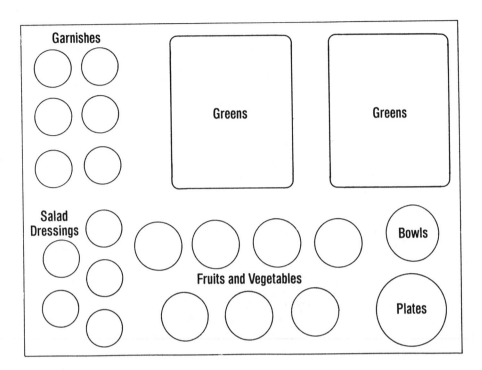

The salad bar has become a popular feature of many restaurants. The arrangement of the salad bar should make it easy for the customer to create his or her own salad.

even become standard in fast-food restaurants. Portion size may be controlled by the size of plate or bowl used.

Salad Buffet.   The buffet is similar to the salad bar. The difference is that a buffet includes salads along with other foods on the line. Some buffets are very elaborate, with salad displayed in ice bowls or carved watermelons. Variety is very important in a salad buffet. Common foods are fruit salad, potato salad, gelatin salad, macaroni salad, marinated salad, chicken salad, and seafood salad. Separate plates are usually offered for the salad portion of the buffet.

Salad Tray.   A waiter or waitress presents the customer with a tray containing four or five different types of salads. All are attractive and invite the customer to buy.

Salad Cart.   The cart is manned by a well-groomed waiter or waitress who prepares the salad tableside. Service personnel are skilled in salad-making and the use of utensils. The cart carries greens, seasonings for one or two specialty salads, and dressings. Popular tableside salads prepared from a cart are caesar salad and spinach salad.

Salad Dressings

Salad dressings are liquids used to bring out the flavor and appearance of salads. There are many kinds of dressings but they fall into three groups: French, emulsion (mayonnaise), and cooked.

French.   French dressings include oil, acid, and seasonings. The acid is usually vinegar but lemon juice may be used. A common proportion is one part acid to three parts oil. Shake the ingredients together to make a temporary blend called a "suspension." If the dressing stands for a short time, the oil and acid will separate into two layers. The dressing should be shaken just before it is poured over the salad. Consistency will be thick or thin, depending on the ratio of acid to oil, but it should always pour easily. A suspension can be made semipermanent if the chef adds

French- and mayonnaise-type salad dressings are among the most common. There are many variations of both types.

an emulsifying ingredient. Examples are sugar, spices, or tomato paste. Italian, vinegar and oil, and tomato are all examples of French dressings. These dressings do not have to be refrigerated, but the suspension will hold up longer if they are.

Emulsion Dressings.   These dressings also contain oil and an acid. The difference is that oil and acid stay permanently blended in what is called an *emulsion.* They stay blended because egg yolk is added as an emulsifying agent. It coats the droplets of oil and causes them to stay mixed with the vinegar. Mayonnaise is an example of an emulsion dressing. Emulsions are thick and must be spooned over salads. Mayonnaise is the base for other dressings such as Thousand Island, Russian, and bleu cheese. Because they contain egg yolk, it is important to keep emulsion dressings refrigerated at all times. (Remember that eggs are a good breeding ground for *salmonella* bacteria.)

Cooked or Boiled Dressing.   Cooked dressings contain liquid thickened by cooking with starch or eggs, but they are made without oil. The liquid may be milk and acid or juice. Correctly prepared, they are as thick as a medium white sauce. To prevent lumpiness or scorching while cooking, they are cooked in a double boiler. They usually contain less oil than mayonnaise. Examples of cooked dressings are those used with coleslaw or macaroni salad.

Make Your Salads and Dressings Go Together

To produce a well-dressed salad, ask yourself these simple questions before serving:

- Is the dressing the right flavor, consistency, color, and type for the body of the salad?
- Is there enough dressing to flavor the entire salad? (Too much dressing makes a salad watery.)
- Are you serving a mild dressing with distinctly flavored salads such as fish, shellfish, meat, and poultry? (Mayonnaise goes well with all types of salads.)

- Are you serving a highly seasoned dressing with a bland salad? (Fruit goes well with a combination sweet and tart dressing.)
- Will you serve dressing separately or mix with salad just before serving? (Salads such as coleslaw, potato, and meat salad are mixed with dressings.)

13
Sandwiches

A legend says that one day a British nobleman placed his slice of meat between two slices of bread and ate it. He was the Earl of Sandwich and he gave his name to the new concoction. Ever since, the sandwich has been a mealtime favorite around the world.

Today's American foodservice operator uses the sandwich in ways the Earl never imagined. Not only is the sandwich a popular luncheon item, it is also served as a snack and even for breakfast. Sandwiches may be simple or fancy, depending on the cook's imagination. The average consumer eats one out of three meals away from home, with lunch the most common meal. The sandwich is the ideal quick-service meal for that consumer. It is also a good profitmaker for the operator. Sandwiches, like salads, are traditionally prepared in the cold-food section or pantry. Hamburgers and other hot sandwiches are exceptions.

Objectives and Terms

Objectives. This section should help you:

- Define a sandwich.
- List the parts of a sandwich.
- Describe common types of hot and cold sandwiches.
- List sandwich preparation methods.
- Describe standards of quality in sandwich preparation.

186

Terms to Know

Sandwich. A food product made with bread, spread, and filling.

Spread. Creamy substance such as butter or mayonnaise that is used to coat bread in sandwiches.

Filling. The main ingredient inside a sandwich.

Open-Face Sandwich. A sandwich made with one piece of bread topped with filling.

Decker. A sandwich made with more than two pieces of bread and at least two layers of filling.

Tea Sandwiches. Small, attractively decorated cold sandwiches.

Mise en Place (meez on plahce). French term for having all ingredients in place, ready to use.

Parts of a Sandwich

Like salads, sandwiches follow no set formula. However, all sandwiches have the same parts: bread, spread, a filling, and perhaps a garnish.

Bread. A sandwich can be made with any kind of bread. Keep in mind that the bread should fit the filling. Tradition tells us to use rye for Reuben sandwiches, French bread for French dip, and pita or pocket bread for gyros.

Some other breads to choose from are whole wheat, white, Italian, pumpernickel, fruit, and nut bread. Some sandwiches call for rolls instead of bread. Typical rolls are hard and soft rolls, hamburger and hot dog buns, submarine buns, and bagels.

No matter what the type of bread, there are a few rules to follow to assure high quality:

1. Buy bread daily. Look for bread with even texture and no large holes.

2. Store bread in a dry, moisture-proof container or wrap. Follow the first in, first out (FIFO) rule.

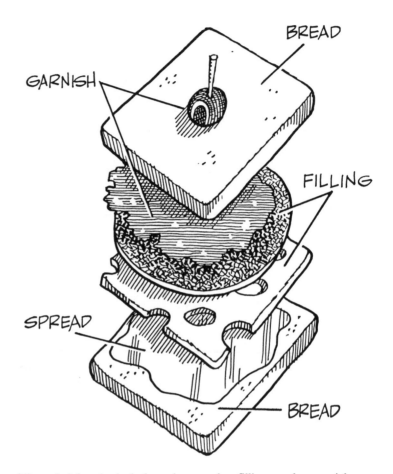

All sandwiches include bread, spread, a filling, and a garnish.

3.   Do not wrap hard breads and rolls. They will lose their characteristic hard crusts.

4.   Store breads at 70–80° F, away from heat.

Caution: Do not refrigerate bread. It is one of the few foods that will go stale fast when refrigerated. Freezing preserves freshness. Once bread gets "old" (one day), use it for toasting, for bread crumbs, or for croutons.

Spreads.   Butter, margarine, and mayonnaise are the most common sandwich spreads. They are used to keep filling from soaking into the bread and to add richness, moisture, and flavor. For large sandwich operations, it is a good idea to whip the butter or margarine so that it will spread more easily. Mayonnaise adds more flavor than butter or margarine. Cream cheese and peanut butter may also be used as spreads.

Caution: Be sure to refrigerate mayonnaise when not in use.

Fillings.   The main ingredient in any sandwich is the filling. It gives the sandwich its name. Some fillings are spreads such as peanut butter, jelly, tuna, chicken or egg salad, or deviled ham. Slices of meat, cheese, poultry, or lunch meats are also popular as fillings. Hamburgers and hot dogs are the most popular sandwiches in the United States. Vegetable sandwiches were once popular only in vegetarian restaurants. Today, however, avocado, cucumber, and sprout sandwiches can be found in full-menu restaurants too.

One system classifies sandwich fillings as either dry or moist. Table 13.1 lists some examples of dry and moist fillings. Be sure to refrigerate cold sandwich fillings. Be especially careful with moist fillings. Keep them at 45°F or lower to keep bacteria from multiplying. If acid ingredients such as lemon juice, pickles, and olives are added to moist fillings, they can help slow the growth of bacteria. They also improve flavor.

Garnishes.   As with appetizers, garnishes add eye appeal, texture, flavor, and color to sandwiches. Popular sandwich garnishes are salad greens, relishes, cheese, pickles, olives, tomato slices, and onions.

Table 13.1: Sandwich Fillings

Dry	Moist
Ground beef	Chicken salad
Cheese	Tuna salad
Cold cuts	Seafood salad

Types of Sandwiches

Although we have included sandwiches in this cold-food section of the book, sandwiches can be served cold or hot.

Hot Sandwiches. Four types of hot sandwiches are common:

Plain. Hot meat is served on bread or a roll. The hamburger and french dip sandwiches are examples.

Grilled or Toasted. Bread is buttered on the outside and the sandwich is browned on a griddle or in the oven. The grilled-cheese sandwich is an example.

Deep Fried. The sandwich is battered in egg or crumbs, then fried or baked. A Montecristo is a deep fried sandwich. Although some sandwiches are deep fat fried, the result can be greasy. Pan frying is a good alternative.

Open Faced. A piece of bread is served covered with meat and a gravy or sauce. This is actually a variation on the meat and potatoes entree. It is commonly served with mashed potatoes. A hot turkey sandwich is an example.

The Montecristo is a breaded deep-fried sandwich made with meat, cheese, and bread.
Courtesy: Oscar Mayer & Co.

A submarine sandwich is made by arranging a variety of cold cuts and other ingredients on a long roll.
Courtesy: Oscar Mayer & Co.

Cold Sandwiches. The cold-sandwich category includes regular, specialty, decker, and fancy sandwiches.

Regular. The bread or roll is filled with simple ingredients such as cheese, meat, greens, and spread.

Specialty. Specialty sandwiches may have ordinary ingredients arranged in a special way. Open-faced sandwiches are made with a single slice of bread, topped with a variety of fillings. The sandwich is arranged attractively and finished with a garnish, like a canapé. There are other specialty sandwiches known as combination sandwiches. Examples include the submarine, hoagie, or hero.

Decker. In the decker, more than two slices of bread are layered with several ingredients. The traditional club sandwich is the most common decker. It contains turkey, bacon, tomato, lettuce, mayonnaise, and three slices of bread. It is served cut into triangle-shaped quarters.

Fancy, Tea. Crusts of bread are trimmed off and the soft white part is filled with fancy light ingredients to make a tea

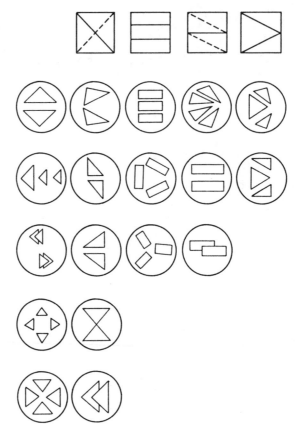

Basic sandwich cutting styles are pictured at top. Once cut in these shapes, sandwiches can be attractively arranged on plates as shown below.

sandwich. Deviled ham is one of the flavorful fillings used in fancy sandwiches. Sandwiches are often cut or rolled in decorative shapes.

Sandwich Preparation

Tools and Equipment. Standard equipment in a sandwich preparation area includes a grill, broiler, slicer, and microwave oven. Necessary tools are knives, fork, tongs, scoops, spreaders, and spatulas.

Individual Production.   To prepare sandwiches individually to order, arrange the sandwich area for efficiency.

Sanitation.   Refrigerate perishable foods such as mayonnaise, meat, and spreads.

Prepare Ingredients.   Have ingredients ready to use. The French use the expression *mise en place,* which means everything set up and ready to go.

Arrange for Efficiency.   Set up the area so that you can use both hands for maximum reach. Work from left to right, unless you are left-handed.

Control Portions.   Measure ingredients by count, slices, weights, or scoop sizes. Handle bread and sandwich filling as little as possible. Always use plastic gloves.

Quantity Production.   Arrange the area differently for large-scale production of sandwiches.

Assemble Ingredients and Tools.   Arrange everything necessary for the sandwich production line. You will be producing a lot of sandwiches at one time.

Wrap.   Use plastic wrap or waxed paper to keep prepared sandwiches fresh until serving time.

Storage.   Keep prepared, wrapped sandwiches in the refrigerator. They should be on racks for good air circulation.

Caution: If you are going to hold sandwiches over 12 hours, freeze them. Do not stack sandwiches. This will cause the bread to become mashed and soaked with filling.

Standards of Quality for Sandwiches

Appearance.   Arrange sandwich ingredients neatly and attractively. Cut all sandwiches (except hamburgers and hot dogs) before serving. Halves or quarters are easier to handle and look more appealing.

The Zorba pocket sandwich features pita or pocket bread with cold cuts and vegetables as the filling.
Courtesy: Oscar Mayer & Co.

Flavor.   Flavors should be well blended and ingredients should taste fresh.

Texture.   Bread should be firm but not porous. The customer should be able to identify the main ingredients in the filling, and it should be spread to the edges of the bread.

Temperature.   Serve hot sandwiches hot, and cold sandwiches cold.

Combination of Ingredients.   Select ingredients that go well together and are appealing.

Merchandising Sandwiches

Use the menu to describe sandwiches in detail. Be clever and give sandwiches names that follow a theme. If your operation has a movie theme, for example, name sandwiches after famous films or stars. Offer guests the ET Chili Dog, Towering Inferno Triple Decker, or the Han Solo Roast Beef sandwich. As with other foods, be sure to garnish attractively. Train all help to explain how sandwiches are prepared.

14
Stocks, Soups, Sauces

Stocks

The basis for all good soups and sauces is a good stock. Stock is the key ingredient in many traditional dishes. It is the starting point for soups, sauces, and gravies.

Objectives and Terms

Objectives.   In this section you will:

- List basic ingredients in all stocks.
- Identify the four basic types of stock.
- Identify steps in preparing a good stock.
- List characteristics of a quality stock.
- Describe advantages and disadvantages of convenience stock products.

Terms to Know

Stock.   A liquid in which vegetables and meat are cooked to extract flavor.

White Stock.   Stock prepared with beef bones that are not browned.

Brown Stock.   Stock prepared with bones that are browned.

Mirepoix (meer-ah-pwah).   A combination of vegetables including carrots, onions, and celery.

Bouquet Garni (boo-'kay gar-'nee). Mixture of seasoning spices such as parsley, peppercorns, bay leaf, and cloves.

Fumet (foo-'may). The French name for fish stock.

What is a stock? A stock is a liquid in which meat and vegetables are cooked. Meat can be the flesh or bones of red meat, poultry, or fish. The basic ingredients of all stocks are:

1. Meat or bones.
2. A combination of vegetables, known as a *mirepoix,* including carrots, onions, and celery.
3. Seasoning spices, known as a *bouquet garni.* The usual ingredients are parsley, peppercorns, bayleaf, cloves, thyme, and any of the other leafy herbs. These ingredients are used in all four basic types of stock.

Types of Stocks. There are four basic stocks.

Brown Stock. Brown stock is prepared from browned beef bones, *mirepoix, bouquet garni* and sometimes a veal knuckle. Cooking time is 3–6 hours.

White Stock. White stock uses the same ingredients that are in a brown stock, but the bones are not browned first. Cooking time is 3–6 hours.

Chicken Stock. Chicken stock includes chicken bones, mirepoix, and bouquet garni. It is cooked 2–4 hours.

Fish Stock: Fish bones, mirepoix, and bouquet garni are the ingredients in fish stock. It cooks in about 1 hour. Another name for fish stock is *fumet.*

Some chefs consider only two types of stock, white and brown. They put chicken, fish, and unbrowned veal together in the white stock category. Brown stock is made from browned beef or veal bones.

Preparing Stocks. The object in preparing stock is to extract flavor from meat and vegetables. This is quite different from preparing other foods where the object is to retain flavor in the ingredients.

To prepare white stock, cover bones and meat with cold water. Do not use hot water—it will make the stock cloudy. Bring the mixture just to the simmer point. Lift off scum and foam with a skimmer. Simmer stock for 1–2 hours. Then add the mirepoix and bouquet garni. Bring to the boiling point. Remove from heat and skim again. Then return to heat and simmer for another 1–2 hours. Keep water above the bones. Add more water if necessary. Do not boil. When the stock has cooked for the right length of time, strain out vegetables through a china cap.

Use the same preparation technique for meat, chicken, and fish stock. Cooking times will be different for each one.

For brown stock, brown bones first. Roast them in the oven at about 375°F for 1 hour before starting stock. Then proceed as you would for white stock.

Cool all stock quickly after preparing. Place the stock pot in a larger pot or sink partly filled with cold running water. Stir to speed up the cooling process. Refrigerate at 35–40°F.

Characteristics of a Quality Stock. Cook stock with the stock pot uncovered. Some of the liquid will evaporate and flavors will become concentrated.

Cook stock slowly, on simmer—never boil it.

Do not add salt to stock. There is some natural sodium in the meat and a salty flavor will develop as stock evaporates.

Skim off foam constantly.

To keep stock clear, strain through a china cap covered with cheesecloth.

Cool quickly after cooking if you will not use the stock immediately. If stock cools slowly, bacteria can grow and cause off or sour flavors to develop.

Leave fat on the stock. It will seal in flavor and help seal out bacteria as stock cools in the refrigerator. You can skim off the fat when you are ready to use stock, if you wish.

Cover the stock in the refrigerator. The maximum holding time in the refrigerator is three days. Freeze stock for up to three months.

Judging Your Stock. If you follow the correct steps, you should produce a fine, high-quality stock. These are the characteristics to check for:

- Fat free (except for the fat layer on top when chilled).
- Clear of solid particles.
- Pleasant to smell and taste.
- Reasonably bland or neutral in flavor.

Convenience Stock Products. Many concentrated stock-flavoring products are available on the market. They come in powdered, cubed, or paste form. They all must be mixed with water (rehydrated.) Some products are high in fat while others are almost fat free. Read the labels for instructions on how to store and prepare stock concentrates. Many of these products are high in salt. That is one reason why it is important to taste as you prepare them.

Should you make stock from scratch or from a concentrate? Here are some things to consider in making that decision.

Bones. Do you have a source of meat bones?

Labor. Do you have enough labor to prepare stock from scratch?

Quality. Does the quality of convenience stock meet your specifications (quality standards?)

Cost. Convenience products can be expensive. But does the product cost more than labor and energy?

Soups

Restaurant menus feature hundreds of different soups. Soup may be served as an appetizer, an accompaniment, or even a main dish. There are two main types: clear (thin) soups and thick soups. Soup is popular with guests because it is filling yet light, it is inexpensive, and it makes a meal seem more complete. The

Clam chowder—base, cup, and bowl.
Courtesy: L. J. Minor Food Corp.

foodservice operator likes soup on the menu because it is inexpensive, a good way to use leftovers, easy to prepare, and adds variety. Soup also lets the cook use his or her imagination.

Objectives and Terms

Objectives.   In this section you will:

- Identify two thin soups.
- Identify three thick soups.

- Identify three specialty soups.
- Describe correct procedure for holding and storing soups.
- List characteristics of a well-prepared soup.
- Identify two forms of convenience soups.

Terms to Know

Soup.   A liquid food with meat, vegetables, or seafood as a base.

Thin Soup.   Clear rich liquid prepared without a thickener.

Thick Soup.   Soup that becomes thick because of the products added to the liquid.

Broth.   Soup that contains meat, vegetables, or other food that is cooked but not strained.

Bouillon.   Clear, concentrated meat stock, usually made from beef or chicken.

Consommé.   Soup that is made perfectly clear by adding protein food.

Clarify.   To make stock or soup clear by adding protein food that attracts particles in stock.

Vichyssoise.   Cold potato soup.

Types of Soups.   Soups fall into two categories: clear and thick.

Thin (Clear) Soups.   White, brown, or chicken stock is the main ingredient in a clear soup. It is almost transparent and includes these familiar examples:

Broth.   Broth is made from a stock that is not strained through cheesecloth or clarified.

Bouillon.   Bouillon is a clear soup made from stock that is highly seasoned.

Consommé.   Consommé is perfectly clear stock that is clarified by using a protein food. The stock is brought to the simmer point. Then an egg white or other protein food is added. The protein of the egg attracts all of the particles or impurities in the stock and makes it clear.

Thick Soups.   Cream soups, purees, chowders, and bisques all belong to this group. Before taking a closer look at them, we should point out that vegetable soups usually do not belong to this group. They look thick but they are actually clear soups or broth with chunks of vegetables added.

Cream soups. If you put a penny on the bottom of the bowl, you will not be able to see it through a cream soup. All cream soups consist of a basic cream sauce with one or more flavoring ingredients added. The soup is usually named for the flavoring ingredient. Some familiar cream soups are cream of mushroom, cream of asparagus, cream of broccoli, and cream of celery. The cream base can be thin milk or cream sauce that is thickened with flour or some other thickening agent.

Puree soups. Purees are made from starchy vegetables that thicken the mixture by themselves. They are not as velvety as cream soups. Pea and potato (vichyssoise) soups are examples of these coarse, hearty soups.

Purees can be thickened by cooking the ingredients for a long time. Some recipes call for putting the ingredients through a food mill. Adding cream will make the soup smoother.

Bisques. A bisque is a kind of cream soup in which shellfish stock is the base. There are usually no vegetables. Lobster and crab bisques are popular examples.

Chowders. Almost all chowders include some form of fish or shellfish. Recently vegetable chowders have become popular, too. Examples of seafood chowders are Manhattan clam chowder (clams, tomatoes, other vegetables) and New England clam chowder (clams, milk, and vegetables.) Popular vegetable chowders are corn, lima bean, and mushroom chowders.

Specialty Soups. In addition to clear and thick soups, there are many well-known specialities. They are often associated with nationality groups.

Gumbo. Ingredients include okra, chicken, seafood, and vegetables. Gumbo is a New Orleans and Louisiana favorite sometimes considered a relative of chowder.

Gazpacho. Tomatoes and other vegetables make up this cold Spanish soup.

Minestrone.   Vegetables and pasta are the main ingredients in this Italian specialty.

Bouillabaisse.   The French gave us this seafood and vegetable chowder.

Egg Drop or Won Ton Soup.   Chicken stock is the base for these oriental soups.

Holding and Storing Soups.   Make soups fresh daily if possible. For serving hot, hold them at 150–160°F. If they are to be served cold, keep them at 40–45°F. Cover soups when not serving. Stir the pot occasionally as it stands on the line. Check thickness from time to time and add liquid if necessary. If you must store soup, cool it rapidly to room temperature and then refrigerate it, covered, at 40°F.

Characteristics of a Well-Prepared Soup.   Look for pleasing taste and texture in a well-prepared soup. Flavors should be blended and the soup should look and taste rich. Clear soups should be bright and sparkling. The right garnish will add to the appearance of the finished product.

Convenience Soup Products.   Convenience soup products may be frozen, canned, or dehydrated. Quality varies from one type to another. Generally speaking, frozen soups are higher in quality than canned soups. Follow directions to reconstitute convenience soups. To decide whether to use these products, consider cost versus time and labor, quality, and the manufacturer's reputation.

Sauces

French cookery has earned its reputation largely because of French sauces. Their names are often hard to spell and pronounce, but they are very important to a good foodservice operation.

Once sauces were used to cover gamy or even spoiled flavors in meat. That was in the days when food was prepared and kept

A flavorful sauce can dress up any dish
Courtesy: L. J. Minor Food Corp.

without refrigeration. Early sauces had strong flavors and were almost like medicine because they were so highly seasoned.

Today, sauces are the centerpiece of culinary art for most chefs. The person who prepares sauces often has many years of experience. Usually, before becoming the head of a traditional kitchen, a chef must be responsible for preparing fine sauces.

Objectives and Terms

Objectives.   In this section you will:
- Define a sauce.
- List common thickeners used in sauces.
- Identify five basic sauce types.
- List characteristics of a good warm sauce.
- Describe the correct procedure for handling, holding, and storing sauces.

Terms to Know

Sauce.   A rich, flavored thickened liquid used to complement other foods.

Roux (roo).   A mixture of equal amounts of fat and flour cooked together.

Flour Wash.   A blend of flour and cold liquid.

Espagnole Sauce.   One of the basic sauces, also known as brown sauce.

Bechamel Sauce.   One of the basic sauces, also known as white sauce.

Velouté.   One of the basic sauces made from roux and a white stock.

Hollandaise.   Sauce made by making an emulsion of cooked butter and lemon juice with egg yolk.

Gravy.   Sauce made from the natural juices and drippings of cooked meat.

Au Jus (aw joos).   A French term for serving meat with its own drippings.

Clarified Butter.   Butter that has been melted, with solids and water removed so that only the fat or oil remains.

What Is a Sauce?   A sauce is a rich-flavored, thickened liquid used to complement another food. It can accompany side dishes, appetizers, salads, entrees, and even desserts.

Cooks uses sauces for these reasons:

* To enhance flavor.
* To give contrast in texture and color.
* To provide balance for the menu.
* To add moisture or serve as a binding agent.
* To garnish food.

There are hundreds of different sauces, but they all come from five basic types—brown, white, velouté, tomato, and hollandaise. These five basic sauces are also called "mother sauces" or "lead sauces." They have two main ingredients: stock and a thickening agent. Common thickeners are roux, flour wash, and cornstarch.

Roux.   A roux is a mixture of equal amounts of shortening and flour. Margarine or butter is the usual shortening. The roux can be white, golden, or brown, depending on how long the shortening is cooked before blending with flour.

Flour Wash. Flour and a cold liquid are mixed together, and then cooked to make a flour wash.

Cornstarch. In cornstarch-thickened sauces cornstarch is mixed with cold liquid and then cooked. It makes an almost clear sauce popular in Oriental and other cooking.

Other thickening agents that may be used are arrowroot starch, breadcrumbs, egg yolk, and cream.

Basic Sauces. The five basic sauces are brown, white, velouté, tomato, and hollandaise.

Brown Sauce. Also called Espagnole (es-pah-'nyol) sauce, brown sauce is made with brown roux and brown stock.

White Sauce. White sauce is made with a white roux plus cream or milk. It is also known as Bechamel (bay-sha-'mel) sauce.

Velouté Sauce. Velouté (vel-oo-'tay) is a product of golden roux and a white stock made from chicken, veal, or fish.

Tomato Sauce. This sauce is made from tomatoes plus brown stock. It is thickened by reducing the amount of liquid through cooking for a long time. A roux is optional.

Hollandaise Sauce. Hollandaise is an emulsion (smooth blend) of cooked butter and egg yolks.

Basic sauces and some derived sauces are listed in Table 14.1.

Other Sauces, Butters. Cold sauces are made with a tomato or mayonnaise base. Examples are cocktail, tartar, dill, and remoulade sauces. They may be served as dips, salad dressings, or accompaniments for meat, poultry, or fish.

Butters can be cooked or mixed with other ingredients. Butter compounds are mixtures of butter with tarragon, lemon, anchovies, or other flavor ingredients.

Table 14.1: Basic and Derived Sauces, Major Ingredients, and Uses

Basic sauce	Derived types	Other ingredients	Use
Brown	Bordelaise	Shallots, wine	Steak
	Bogarde	Orange, lemon peel	Duck
	Chasseur (Hunter)	Wine, mushrooms	Meat, birds
	Mushroom	Sauteed mushrooms	Meat
White (Bechamel)	Cheese	Cheese	
	Mornay	Cream, cheese	
	Newberg	Sherry, paprika	Lobster
	a la King	Mushroom, pimento, pepper	Poultry
	Cardinal	Shrimp, lobster	
Velouté	Supreme	Egg yolks, cream	Fish, poultry, eggs
	Poulette	Mushrooms	Poultry
	Italian sauce	Vegetables, spices	Meat, poultry
	Barbecue	Sugar, spices, Worcestershire	Meat, poultry
	Creole	Vegetables, onion, garlic, mushrooms, green pepper	Shellfish
Hollandaise	Mousseline	Whipped cream	Vegetables, fish
	Florentine	Cooked spinach	Vegetables, fish
	Bernaise	Tarragon, peppercorn	Steaks, veal

Clarified butter is butter that has been melted, with water and fat removed. Only the cooked solids remain.

Gravies.   Gravies are sauces made from natural juices and drippings of roasted meat. The drippings are produced when the meat browns and the juice concentrates while cooking. This is often called pan gravy. It is similar to brown sauce, except that fat and liquid come from the meat instead of from shortening and brown stock. *Au jus* is a term used when meat is served with its own unthickened drippings. Gravies can be made from beef, pork, lamb, and poultry. Some cooks include a mirepoix in the roasting pan to add flavor to gravy. Cream gravy is one in which drippings are made into a sauce by adding milk or cream and thickening.

Convenience sauce products for the foodservice operation.
Courtesy: L. J. Minor Food Corp.

Characteristics of a Good Warm Sauce.   Warm sauces are light
and smooth with a velvety texture. They are fluid, not stiff. The
flavor is subtle and well blended with no raw starch taste. Sauce
enhances or contrasts with food. Appearance should be glossy,
not gooey or dull. White sauce is always snow white. There
should be no sight or taste of fat or flour. Sauce should never be
cold, set, solid, greasy, lumpy, or pasty. The color should be right
for the type (brown is brown, white is white).

Handling, Holding, and Storing Sauces.   Except for hollandaise, a food service operator will make a large batch of sauce at
one time. Then, storage is the same as for stock. Keep sauces out
of the danger zone (between 45 and140°F). Cool sauce first if you
are planning to store it. Do not refrigerate for more than a week. If
you intend to use the full batch the same day, hold it in a hot
water bath. If possible, make sauces to order in small amounts.

Special Instructions for Hollandaise. Never make more Hollandaise sauce than you will use in 1½ hours. Throw out what is left after that time. This rule holds for other egg sauces as well.

To prepare hollandaise, follow these steps:

1. Use a heavy saucepan to prevent the sauce from burning.
2. Use a wooden spoon for stirring.
3. Blend with a wire whip to remove lumps.
4. Always use quality ingredients.
5. Follow the recipe exactly. Hollandise needs close attention at all times.

Convenience Sauces. Like soups, convenience sauce products come in paste, powder, base, or frozen form. The foodservice operator should consider cost, customer acceptance, and quality in deciding whether to use convenience products.

Merchandising Sauces. To highlight special sauces, be sure to describe them on the menu. Waiters and waitresses should be trained to explain to guests how a sauce is prepared. Draw attention to sauces by garnishing attractively.

Use sauce for a background (the entree on top), as an accessory (served alongside the entree), as a coating (brushed over entree), or as a topping (to intensify the flavor of the entree).

15
Seasonings: Herbs, Spices, Flavorings, Condiments

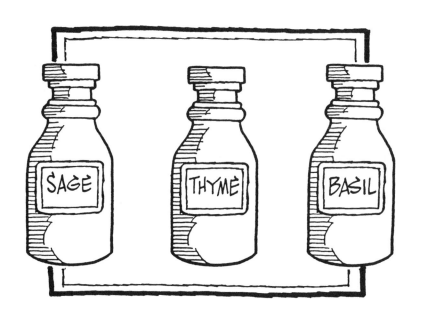

Seasonings are substances that add to the natural flavor of food. They do not cover up the flavor. They do not get lost in the food. They simply make it taste better. In other words, they enhance flavor.

Plain food can be bland. It may not have a very distinctive flavor. When we add the right seasoning, that bland food becomes much more flavorful and interesting. Seasoning brings out the flavor in the food and makes it better.

Objectives and Terms

Objectives. This section should help you:

- List common herbs and spices.
- Describe the correct method for purchasing and storing herbs and spices
- Describe basic rules for using herbs and spices.
- List common flavorings, salts, and condiments.

Terms to Know

Seasonings. Substances that add flavor to food without disguising it.

Herbs. Leafy or soft plant parts that are used whole or partly crushed to add delicate flavor.

Spices. Stronger flavoring ingredients, perhaps imported from other continents.

Flavorings. Flavors extracted from specific foods or imitations of those natural flavors.

Condiment. A very flavorful sauce that usually comes in a bottle.

Seasoned Salt. Salt to which herbs have been added.

What Are Seasonings?

Substances that we call seasonings are herbs, spices, flavorings, condiments, and mixtures such as seasoning salts. Seasonings help to make food preparation a creative experience. Because of that, it can be one of the keys to a successful restaurant. If customers notice a special flavor and remember it, they are likely to come back.

At one time, our ancestors used seasonings to preserve food, but over time the seasonings they used came to be traditional. They were the distinctive characteristics of the food. Different cultures and nationalities have their own traditionally seasoned foods. Many foods in India are seasoned with curry. Hungarian food often contains paprika. Ginger is common in some Oriental dishes. Even some American foods have traditional seasonings.

Common Herbs and Spices

The most common seasonings we use are herbs and spices. There is no clear difference between the two, but generally herbs are plant parts that have a delicate flavor. They are usually grown locally.

Spices, experts say, have stronger flavors with stronger aromas. They are often imported from faraway places. However, since there are many exceptions to these categories, we shall group herbs and spices together. Table 15.1 lists many common herbs and spices and some of their traditional uses.

Table 15.1: Common Foods with Compatible Herbs and Spices

Food	Compatible herbs and spices	Food	Compatible herbs and spices
Beef and pork	Basil	Salad dressings	Bay leaves
	Bay leaves		Basil
	Curry powder		Dill weed
	Garlic		Garlic
	Marjoram		Onion
	Onion		Marjoram
	Thyme		Mustard
Poultry, seafood	Bay leaves		Oregano
	Dill weed		Thyme
	Fennel	Potatoes	Celery seed
	Garlic		Onion
	Mustard		Paprika
	Parsley		Parsley
	Paprika	Breads	Basil
	Rosemary		Cardamom
	Sage		Dill weed
	Saffron		Garlic
	Savory		Marjoram
	Tarragon		Onion
	Thyme		Parsley
			Savory
			Thyme

Purchasing Herbs and Spices

Herbs and spices come in different forms: whole leaves or berries, ground, cracked, minced, flaked, or even whole pieces of bark, as in the case of cinnamon. Whatever form you buy, check the quality to be sure the product has good color and strong aroma.

Buy units that are small enough for quick turnover. That way, you will not have a large supply that is useless once it gets stale. Remember that whole leaves or berries will keep longer than crushed or flaked herbs and spices.

Storing Herbs and Spices

It may seem like a good idea to store herbs and spices near the range, where you will use them in cooking, but that is actually the worst place for them. Heat and moisture in the cooking area are the enemies of flavor in herbs and spices.

The best idea is to store them away from the range. It is also smart to portion out what you will need each day. Keep herbs and spices in airtight containers in a cool, dry place. Flavor oils will not evaporate and insects and rodents will not get in.

The maximum shelf life of herbs and spices is one year. A good rule of thumb is to rotate them every six months. Date the boxes when they are delivered. That way you will know if the quality starts to go down. Even if you do keep them in an airtight container, the quality will probably deteriorate after a year.

Basic Tips for Using Herbs and Spices

Recipes.   Follow the recipe and use tested recipes whenever you can. In those cases where you have no recipe, start with just a small amount of the desired herb or spice. If you are seasoning vegetables, use about 1 tsp of a mild herb to six portions of vegetables. This is recommended for basil, thyme, and other mild herbs. If you are using strong-flavored spices such as nutmeg or ginger, use just ¼ tsp of spice to six portions of food. For meat, use ¼ tsp per pound of meat or pint of liquid with most herbs. For pepper or garlic, use just ⅛ tsp per pound of meat or pint of liquid.

Moderation.   Use seasonings in moderation. Do not overwhelm food with seasonings.

Be Delicate.   Seasoning flavors should not stand out. The dominant flavor should be that of the food. The major exception to this rule is chili.

Season at the Right Time.   If food will cook for a long period of time, add the seasoning halfway through cooking. If food will cook for only a short time, add seasonings at the beginning. The heat and cooking time will help to release flavors into the food.

Whole Spices Take Longer.   If you use whole spices, allow a longer time for cooking to release the flavors. Put them in at the beginning of the cooking time. Ground spices can be added later because they will blend in more rapidly.

Blend with Fat.   Since fat absorbs flavors from seasonings, it is a good idea to blend seasonings with fat or oil. In cakes, for example, you can blend cinnamon and allspice with the shortening for richer flavor. In salad dressings, marinate herbs in oil before adding vinegar, lemon juice, or other ingredients. For vegetables or fish, add seasonings to butter and simmer.

Remove Whole Spices.   If you use whole spices, put them in a cheesecloth bag before adding to the ingredients. Then, when the product is cooked, remove the bag. That way you will avoid finding whole spices in the food.

Crush Leaves.   In the case of leaf herbs, crush them before cooking. The flavor of basil leaf, for example, will be released only when crushed.

Rehydrate Dried Seasonings.   Add water to dried seasonings before adding to the product. Just mix with a small amount of liquid first. For example, mix dried onion flakes with a small amount of water before adding to meatball mixture.

How to Get It Right

Correct use of herbs and spices does not just happen. It is an art that needs time to develop. The process is one of trial and error. The cook first seasons lightly, then tastes the food, adjusts the seasoning, and tastes again. After a few trials with the same recipe, the good cook will learn how to season that dish. Recommendations should be added to the standardized recipe.

Flavorings, condiments, salts, and herb mixtures are also important for adding flavor to foods.

Flavorings.   Flavorings are special ingredients added at the end of preparation. They are different from herbs and spices in several ways. First, we add flavors so that we can taste them. Herbs and spices, on the other hand, are delicate. They simply enhance the flavor of food. Alcoholic flavorings and flavor extracts are the most common examples of flavorings.

Alcoholic Flavorings.   Alcoholic flavorings include wine, sherry, brandy, and rum.

Flavor Extracts.   Flavor extracts are concentrated flavors extracted or taken out of certain plant foods. They may also be artificial imitations of natural flavors. They are in liquid form. Examples are vanilla, almond, peppermint, wintergreen, and lemon extract.

Extracts and alcoholic flavorings are added at the very end of the preparation. They add their distinctive tastes to foods as they are blended.

Condiments.   Condiments are liquid or semiliquid mixtures of spices or herbs with vinegar, tomato sauce, or other foods. They are usually served with the meal but are sometimes used in preparing foods. The most common examples of condiments are catsup, chili sauce, prepared mustard, soy sauce, Worcestershire sauce, tabasco, steak sauce, horseradish sauce, and seafood sauces.

Seasoned Salts and Mixtures.   Seasoned salts are mixtures of salt with one or more distinctive herbs. Examples include onion salt, garlic salt, seasoning salt, poultry seasoning, hickory smoke salt, and celery salt. Mixtures of herbs and spices are also used as seasonings. These include pumpkin pie spice, Italian herb seasoning, and soup seasoning mixtures.

Merchandising Seasonings

Seasonings are important to merchandising commercial food. As we use various herbs, spices, and other seasonings in specific foods, we shall discuss their roles in merchandising each food.

16
Meat

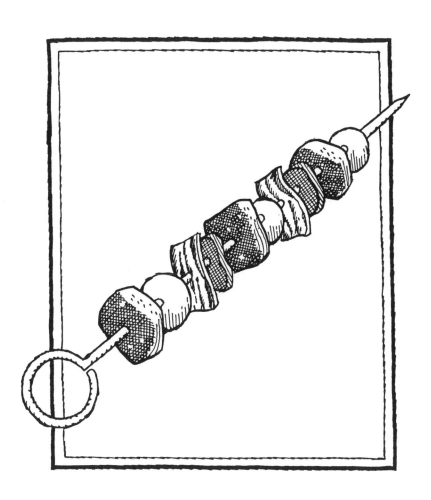

In this chapter we shall explore general information about meats. We shall discuss the nutritive value of meat, how meat is graded and inspected, how it is cut, and what market forms we shall find available. We shall discuss beef, pork, veal, and lamb.

Nutritive Value of Meat

Meat is an excellent source of many nutrients. Protein is necessary for building and repairing our body tissues. In addition to protein, meat also contains vitamins and minerals important for good health.

Most meats are a good source of the water-soluble B vitamins. Pork is among the best sources of thiamine, also known as vitamin B_1. Liver is an excellent source of riboflavin and niacin. The variety meats—liver, heart, and kidney—are rich in vitamin B_{12}. Many meats are good sources of the mineral iron. They also contain other nutrients that we need in small amounts.

Objectives and Terms

Objectives. This section should help you:
- Identify beef by class, grade, and structure.
- Identify all wholesale cuts.
- List three ways of identifying doneness of beef.
- List basic cooking methods for beef.
- Describe how to store beef.
- List techniques for merchandising beef.

- Describe grades, cuts, and cooking techniques for pork.
- Describe grades, cuts, and cooking techniques for veal.
- Describe grades, cuts, and cooking techniques for lamb.

Terms to Know

Specifications. Descriptions of meat cuts used for purchasing. Examples are IMPS and NAMPS.

Yield Grade. A grading system based on the amount of lean to fat in carcass meat.

Quality Grade. A grading system based on beef class, shape, amount of exterior and interior fat, and quality of flesh.

Marbling. Streaks of fat throughout the muscle tissue.

Prime. The beef grade that is most expensive, most tender, and highest in fat.

Choice. A high-quality beef grade that is very tender, but less tender and expensive than prime.

Collagen. In meat, the white connective tissue that is tenderized by cooking.

Elastin. In meat, the yellow, tough connective tissue that is not tenderized by cooking.

Forequarter. The front section of a side of beef.

Hindquarter. The rear section of a side of beef.

Dry-Heat Cooking. Cooking methods such as roasting and frying in which no liquid is used in cooking meat.

Moist-Heat Cooking. Cooking methods such as braising and stewing in which meat is cooked with liquid.

Trichinosis. Foodborne illness caused by a small worm parasite sometimes found in uncooked pork.

Saddle. Unsplit quarter of veal and lamb.

Rack. Unsplit rib portion of veal and lamb.

Processed Meat. Ground or chopped meat that is seasoned and shaped.

Beef

Meat is the most important item on the commercial menu and beef is the most popular of the meats. In this section you will learn why beef may be the key to a successful commercial operation.

Beef is expensive. As a matter of fact, it may cost the operation over 60% of the food budget. That is why you need to know all about beef, from the back door to the customer's plate. The more beef on the menu, the greater the chance that you could lose money by not knowing how to choose, prepare, and serve beef cuts.

Characteristics Important in Purchasing Beef. Specifications, classes, grades, structure, and beef cuts are all important considerations in purchasing beef.

Beef Specifications. We all know that beef comes from cattle, but that does not tell the whole story. There are many market forms of beef. You will see great differences in tenderness, flavor, and yield between the same cuts from different animals.

That is why a meat buyer's guide is one of the commercial foodservice operator's most valuable tools. One guide outlines over 75 major market forms of beef. The beef rib section alone has over ten different sets of descriptions, which we call *specifications*.

Each specification is written so that the sellers can know what they are selling and the buyers can know what they will get for a certain price. The specification includes the quality of meat, thickness of fat, and suggested method of preparation.

Thirty years ago there were not many specifications and they were not as long. Commercial operators had their own butchers. They bought meat as carcasses or sides and then did their own cutting or fabrication within the operation.

Today, because of rising labor costs, more and more operators are buying precut or convenience roasts and cuts. This had led to national specifications for beef. They are called Institutional Meat Purchasing Specifications (IMPS) or National Association of Meat Purveyors Specifications (NAMPS). They make it possible for a seller in Colorado to offer the same item as a seller in Chicago. This allows the buyer to know what to expect when ordering a certain item.

Each commercial food operator must decide for himself or herself which specifications give the most return for the money. For example, it would not be smart for a large operator with two butchers to buy precut meats. On the other hand, the fast-food operator would not want to buy carcasses of beef because he or she employs no butcher. Therefore, each operator must analyze his or her own situation, and think of equipment, available labor, and possible waste from different cuts. Specifications help the operator make the best decision for that business.

Classes of Beef.   The class of beef tells the buyer the sex and age of the animal. It is also an excellent guide for how to buy and prepare items for a foodservice menu. The classes are as follows:

- Steer—male cattle, castrated when young.
- Heifer—female cattle, having never calved.
- Cow—female cattle, having calved.
- Bull—male cattle, sexually mature.
- Bullock—male cattle, young mature.
- Stag—male cattle, older mature, castrated.

Grades of Beef.   Most beef is given a quality grade. Sometimes beef is graded by yield.

Quality grades are USDA prime, choice, good, standard, commercial, utility, cutter, and canner. The top three grades (shown here) are the most popular. Large cuts are stamped with a grade seal.

Yield grade. This grading system tells the buyer how much meat there is in relation to the amount of fat from the carcass. Yield grades range from 1 to 5, with 1 the meatiest.

Quality grades. The quality grade system bases grades on:

- Exterior fat.
- Class.
- Shape.
- Interior fat, marbling.
- Quality of flesh.
- Firmness of lean.

Grades are very important in deciding how to prepare meat. Normally, higher grades are more juicy and tender than lower grades. The three most important quality grades are:

1.   Prime. The highest grade. It is also the most expensive. Prime meats are high in external fat and marbling. The flesh is firm-textured. Because of the abundance of marbling, cuts are tender and juicy throughout.

2.   Choice. A high-quality grade. It contains less marbling and external fat than prime meat. But it is very acceptable to most operators. In fact, it is the most common grade used in the United States. Because there is so much choice meat on the market, it is more reasonably priced than prime.

3.   Good. A medium-quality meat. It contains less external and internal fat and is of poorer quality. It is not as tender as prime or choice. Flavor is good. The price is lower than both prime and choice.

In addition to prime, choice, and good beef, there are also standard, commercial, utility, cutter, and canner grades. They are rarely used in commercial foodservice operations but are sometimes used in institutional feeding.

When you buy beef you should know that steers, heifers, and bullocks can qualify for prime grade. Cows, bulls, and stags cannot grade above choice. As a rule, the younger the animal the better the quality, and male animals are usually more tender than female animals.

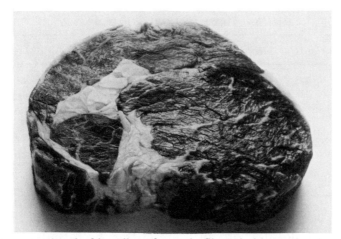

Beef cuts are composed of bundles of muscle fibers held together by connective tissue and marbled with fat. The tenderness of the cut depends on the amount of connective tissue and fat.

Courtesy: Wilson Foods Corporation.

Structure of Beef.   Meat is mostly muscle. Each muscle is a bundle of fibers held together by connective tissue. The tenderness of beef is determined by the texture of the fibers and the amount and kind of connective tissue.

Young animals (heifers and steers) have finer muscle fibers than older animals (cows, bulls, and stags). That is why the meat of younger animals is more tender.

There are two kinds of connective tissue: collagen (white in color) and elastin (yellow in color). Cooking in moist heat can tenderize the collagen in meat, but cooking will not tenderize elastin. Elastin is so tough that it must be pounded, ground, or cut away from the muscle.

Cuts of Beef.   In the past, beef was sold mostly in carcass form, but today, because of transportation cost increases, less storage, and lack of skilled labor, more and more beef is sold as ready cuts.

The best way to understand the different cuts is to break down a carcass of beef. The two main sections are the forequarter and the hindquarter. We break the quarters down into what the indus-

Table 16.1: Forequarter Wholesale and Retail Cuts

Wholesale cuts	Retail cuts
Rib (ribs 6–12)	Prime rib (most popular cut) is an oven-ready rib roast with length of ribs cut to 4 inches from the eye at the twelfth rib and 8 inches from the eye at the sixth rib
	Rib steak
Chuck (shoulder)	Pot roast, chuck roast, chuck steak, stew meat
Short plate	Short ribs, stew meat, ground meat
Brisket	Corned beef, boneless brisket
Foreshank	Stew meat, soup meat or bone, ground beef

try calls "wholesale" or "primal" cuts. The forequarter has five wholesale cuts and the hindquarter has four wholesale cuts. A wholesale cut may weigh from 25 to 50 lb. We cut retail or restaurant cuts from the wholesale cut.

Examples of retail cuts are roasts, steaks, chops, cube steaks, or ground meat. You find them packaged in the supermarket or served on a plate in a restaurant.

Forequarter.   The forequarter is the part of the side of beef from the thirteenth rib forward and from a cut made through the middle of the back bone. The forequarter is often then cut into large wholesale cuts. Table 16.1 lists major forequarter wholesale cuts and some retail cuts that come from them. The illustration on p. 227 shows where they are located.

Table 16.2: Hindquarter Wholesale and Retail Cuts

Wholesale cuts	Retail cuts
Short loin (thirteenth rib, tenderloin and attached muscles, to the front of the sirloin)	Tenderloin; club, T-bone, porterhouse, strip steaks
Sirloin (butt end of tenderloin, top and bottom sirloin)	Sirloin and hip steaks, bottom butt roast, sirloin tip
Round (rump and upper leg)	Top round and rump, bottom round, heel of round, round steaks, minute steaks, beef cutlets, ground round, cubed round
Flank (underside)	Flank steak, ground beef, flank steak rolls

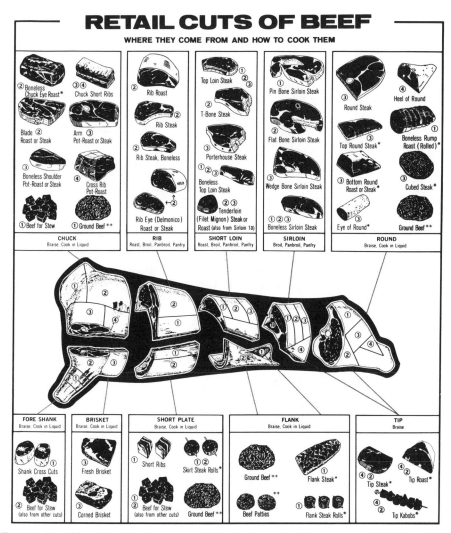

Retail cuts of beef. *, May be roasted, broiled, pan broiled, or pan fried from high-quality beef. **, May be roasted, broiled, pan broiled, or pan fried.
Courtesy: National Live Stock and Meat Board

Hindquarter.   Most of the beef entrees served in commercial restaurants come from the hindquarter. It is that part of the side including the thirteenth rib and back to the tail. Table 16.2 lists hindquarter wholesale cuts and some retail cuts.

Another popular cut often included in the wholesale category is

Table 16.3: Parts, Activity, and Features of Cuts

Part	Activity	Features of cuts
Front	Bends down to eat, chews, uses neck muscles for a lot of work, leg muscles for walking	Tough or not very tender
Rear	Hind legs and rump have walking muscles	Not very tender
Back	Muscles do not get much exercise	Most tender meat
Belly	Flat, wide, muscles that work animal's stomachs	Not tender

the tenderloin. If the tenderloin is cut away from the attached muscles, it is considered a separate wholesale cut. It is located in the short loin. Retail cuts from the tenderloin include Chateaubriand, filet mignon, tournedos of beef and tail cuts of tenderloin (often used for beef stroganoff).

Beef Cooking Methods.   To get the most for your beef dollar, choose the right cooking method for each cut of beef. To understand why this is important, look at the figure below and Table

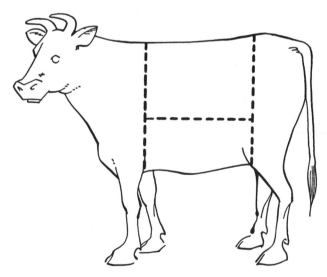

The front, rear, back, and belly of a beef animal all do different kinds and amounts of work. That influences the tenderness of cuts from each body part.

16.3. The table explains what kind of work each part of the animal does. It also describes the meat that comes from that part.

As you can see, the back contains the most tender parts. They can be cooked in dry heat. This is because they do not contain much connective tissue. They are also well marbled with fat. The rump and chuck are tougher and need moist heat to cook them. Moist heat helps break down the connective tissue, collagen. However, if a rump or chuck cut is high grade, it can be cooked in dry heat. This is because high-grade cuts have more fat throughout.

Belly cuts are very tough and need very slow, moist cooking or some method of tenderizing (such as marinating) to make them tender.

How to Know When Meat Is Done.   Because meat is expensive, it is important not to waste it. Overcooking means loss of profit; it also means loss of quality. For these reasons it is important to know when meat is done before considering cooking methods.

There are three ways to know if meat is done. The method you use depends on the meat and the circumstances.

Internal-temperature method.   This method is best for large cuts such as prime rib. The cook uses an accurate meat thermometer to measure the internal temperature of the meat. When the thermometer reaches the right temperature, the meat is cooked. Table 16.4 lists standard temperatures for different degrees of doneness.

Table 16.4: Beef Temperature, Doneness, and Color

Internal temperature (°F)	Doneness	Color
140	Rare	Red
	Medium rare	Deep pink
160	Medium	Pink
	Medium well done	Slightly pink
170	Well done	No pink

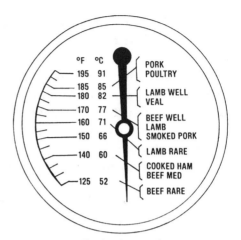

An accurate meat thermometer tells the internal temperature of a cut of meat. It is important to place the tip of the thermometer in the thickest part of the meat (but not touching any bone) for an accurate reading.

Time–weight method.   With this method, the cook figures the time based on the weight of the cut. For example, a standard timetable says to roast a prime rib of beef that weighs 20 lb for 10–12 minutes per pound at 300°F, for rare meat. To cook the same roast to the well-done stage, roast 14–16 minutes per pound. On p. 231 is a chart that lists the times for various cuts at different weights.

Feel method.   The experienced chef can tell if meat is cooked to the right point by its feel. As a rule, meat gets firmer in texture as it cooks. Table 16.5 describes the feel for different stages of doneness.

Which Method Is Best?   There is a time and place for everything, including the three methods of determining if meat is done.

Table 16.5: Doneness by the Feel Method

Doneness	Feel
Rare	Soft, little resistance to pressure; when pressed, it shows imprint
Medium	Medium firm; barely shows imprint when pressed
Well done	Firm; when pressed, springs back and shows no imprint

Cut	Approx. Weight of Single Roast (pounds)	No. of Roasts in Oven	Approx. Total Weight of Roasts (pounds)	Oven Tempera-ture	Interior Temperature of Roast when Removed from Oven	Minutes per Pound Based on One Roast	Minutes per Pound Based on Total Weight of Roasts in Oven	Approximate Total Cooking Time
Rib (7-rib)	20 to 25			250°F.	130°F. (rare) 140°F. (medium) 150°F. (well)	13 to 15 15 to 17 17 to 19		4½ to 5 hours 5 to 6 hours 6 to 6½ hours
Rib (7-rib)	20 to 25			300°F.	130°F. (rare) 140°F. (medium) 150°F. (well)	10 to 12 12 to 14 14 to 16		4 to 4½ hours 4½ to 5 hours 5 to 5½ hours
Rib (7-rib)		2	56	300°F.	130°F. (rare) 140°F. (medium) 150°F. (well)		5 to 6 6 7 to 8	5 to 5½ hours 6 hours 6 to 7 hours
Rib eye	4 to 6			350°F.	140°F. (rare) 160°F. (medium) 170°F. (well)	18 to 20 20 to 22 22 to 24		1⅓ to 1⅔ hours 1½ to 2 hours 1⅔ to 2¼ hours
Tenderloin, whole	4 to 6			425°F.	140°F. (rare)			45 to 60 minutes
Top loin (boneless)	10 to 12			325°F.	140°F. (rare)	10		1½ to 2 hours
Top sirloin butt	8			300°F.	140°F. (rare)	25		3½ hours
Rump	5 to 7			300°F.	150°F. to 170°F.	25 to 30		2 to 3 hours
Top round	10			300°F.	140°F. (rare) 150°F. (medium)	18 to 19 22 to 23		3 to 3¼ hours 3½ to 4 hours
Top round	15			300°F.	140°F. (rare) 150°F. (medium)	15 17		3½ to 4 hours 4 to 4½ hours
Round (rump and shank off)	50			250°F.	140°F. (medium) 155°F. (well)	12 14		10 hours 11 to 12 hours

Timetable for roasting beef.

Courtesy: National Live Stock and Meat Board, Meat in the Food Service Industry.

Internal-temperature (thermometer) method. Use this method for large roasts such as prime rib. It is especially good when you roast several roasts that are different sizes. The thermometer in each roast will tell you exactly when that roast reaches the right internal temperature. You may have to take some roasts out of the oven earlier than others. This method is most accurate, but be sure your thermometers work correctly.

Time–weight method. This method is fine when all the roasts are the same weight. However, you also have to be sure that the ovens you use have the same temperatures. They may need to be tested. The time–weight method is also good if you have no meat thermometers.

Feel method. Use this method for small pieces of meat. Chops and steaks are good examples. It is not as accurate as either of the

Table 16.6: Beef Cuts and Suggested Cooking Methods

Cut of beef	Suggested method	Cut of beef	Suggested method
Brisket	Moist	Rib roast	Dry
Chuck roast	Moist	Round roast	Dry or moist
Chuck steak	Moist or dry	Rump roast	Dry
Flank steak	Dry	Top round steak	Moist
Heel of round	Dry	Bottom, eye of	Dry
Plate, short	Moist	round steak	
Steaks—porterhouse,	Dry	Shanks	Moist
club, rib, sirloin,		Shoulder roast	Moist
T-bone		Short ribs	Moist
		Sirloin tip roast	Dry or moist

other methods because it depends on the experience of the cook. However, for the veteran chef who is cooking four different steaks to four different stages of doneness, the feel method is fine.

The Right Cooking Method. Dry-heat cooking can be used for tender cuts, while moist-heat cooking is best for tough cuts. However, keep in mind that there are some traditional cooking techniques that do not follow this pattern. Sauerbraten, for example, is usually a marinated, moist-cooked chuck roast, but the chef may substitute a more tender round of beef for the chuck in sauerbraten. London broil is traditionally a flank steak that is marinated, scored, and broiled. Chuck may be used in place of flank for a London broil. Still, the traditional cooking method is used.

Table 16.6 lists cooking methods suitable for various cuts. In some cases, both a dry- and moist-heat method are listed. These are cuts that may become tender even if dry-heat cooked.

Dry-Heat Methods. Broiling, pan broiling, frying or sautéing, and roasting are dry-heat methods of cooking meat.

Broiling. For tender cuts, especially chops and steaks, you may choose broiling. Broil with a gas flame, an electric heating element, or coals. The meat is placed on a rack or grid above or below the flame or element. The distance from the heat depends

Cut	Approximate Thickness	Approximate Total Cooking Time		
		Rare	Medium	Well done
		minutes	minutes	minutes
Rib, club, top loin, T-bone, Porter-house, tenderloin or individual servings of beef sirloin steak	1 inch 1½ inches 2 inches	15 25 35	20 35 50	
Beef sirloin steak	1 inch 1½ inches	20 to 25 30 to 35	30 to 35 40 to 45	
Ground beef patties	1 inch (4 oz.)	15	20	
Pork chops (rib or loin)	¾ to 1 inch			20 to 25
Pork shoulder steaks	½ to ¾ inch			20 to 22
Smoked pork chops (rib or loin)	½ to ¾ inch			15 to 20
Lamb shoulder, rib, loin and sirloin chops or leg chops (steaks)	1 inch 1½ inches 2 inches		12 to 16 17 to 20 20 to 25	
Ground lamb patties	1 inch (4 oz.)		18 to 20	
Smoked ham slice (cook-before eating)*	½ inch 1 inch			10 to 12 16 to 20
Bacon				4 to 5

Timetable for broiling. *, Allow 8–10 minutes for broiling ½-inch thick and 14–16 minutes for 1-inch thick "fully cooked" ham slice.
Courtesy: National Live Stock and Meat Board, Meat in the Food Service Industry.

on the thickness of the meat. Juices drop below the meat. Broiling is usually done at a high temperature for a short time. You can broil less tender cuts if you first treat them with tenderizer or pound them.

Pan broiling. Cook the meat in a heavy metal pan with no moisture. Use a small amount of oil or fat to keep the meat from sticking. Spoon off fat as it accumulates, so that it will not fry the meat. Use the feel method to tell if the meat is done.

Frying or sautéing. Frying is a dry-heat method that is very popular. It is slightly different from other dry-heat methds because it uses fat to enhance flavor. It is a good way to cook small cuts such as chops, steaks, and cutlets. Deep frying is frying in a large amount of fat. Sautéing is frying in a small amount of fat.

Searing is a kind of frying used before another cooking method. The meat is quickly sautéed in a hot pan. The purpose is to seal in juices and add color to meat.

Roasting. Roasting is baking meat in a shallow, open pan with no water. It is a good cooking method for large, tender cuts of meat. Use a thermometer or a time–weight chart to determine doneness. The meat needs little preparation. However, the cook can first sear the meat or roast it briefly at a high temperature. Roasting temperatures are low, usually 325–350°F. Drippings are a tasty by-product.

Moist-Heat Methods. Moist-heat cookery is best for cuts that are not very tender. Meat is tough because of the amount of connective tissue it contains. Cooking with liquid for a long period of time breaks down some of that tough connective tissue called collagen. Moist cookery works well for both thick and thin cuts, steaks, or roasts. If you wish, you can fry or broil cuts to develop color and flavor before completing the cooking with moist heat. The three most common moist-heat methods are braising, simmering/boiling, and stewing.

Braising. Cook the meat in a small amount of liquid for a long time. You can braise meat in an oven or on the range. The pan is usually covered or sealed with foil. The cooking time depends on the kind of meat and the size of the cut. Cooks usually choose braising for chucks or rounds, but briskets and short ribs can be braised, too. The meat is cooked until well done and fork tender. The internal temperature method is not a good one for determining if a braised piece of meat is done. Instead, use a table such as the timetable below for braising or use a fork to tell if the meat is done to the touch. In braising we often add vegetables and herbs for flavor. Pot roasting is a term that means braising large cuts of meat.

Simmering/boiling. In simmering, use a large quantity of liquid. The pot should be small enough that liquid covers the meat. Flavor ingredients are added and meat is cooked at just below the boiling point (190–200°F) for a long time. It is a good method for very tough meat that contains lots of collagen. Cuts such as tongue and brisket are good examples. At the beginning of the cooking process, the meat is rubbery, but as it cooks it gets more tender. When the meat is done, a fork penetrates it easily.

Boiling is a term used in some recipes. Technically, we should never boil meat, because it results in a great loss of flavor and texture. Simmering is a better choice for meat.

Cut	Average Weight or Thickness	Approximate Total Cooking Time
Pot-roast	4 to 6 pounds	3 to 4 hours
Swiss steak	1 to 2½ inches	2 to 3 hours
Round steak	½ inch (pounded)	45 minutes to 1 hour
Short ribs	pieces 2x2x2 inches	1½ to 2 hours
Lamb shanks	½ pound each	1 to 1½ hours
Lamb neck slices	½ to ¾ inch	1 to 1½ hours
Lamb riblets	¾x2½x3 inches	1½ to 2½ hours
Pork chops or steaks	¾ to 1 inch	45 minutes to 1 hour
Spareribs	2 to 3 pounds	1½ hours
Veal cutlets	½x3x5½ inches	45 minutes to 1 hour
Veal steaks or chops	½ to ¾ inch	45 minutes to 1 hour

Timetable for braising.
Courtesy: National Live Stock and Meat Board, Meat in the Food Service Industry.

Stewing. Stewing is cooking meat at simmering or low boiling temperatures. A stew is usually a combination of meat chunks and vegetables. The meat is browned before stewing. Typical stew cuts are chunks from the neck or chuck. There is usually a moderate amount of liquid (slightly thick) that can be used as a gravy or sauce.

Tenderizing Beef. A foodservice operator can tenderize beef by mechanical or chemical means as well as by moist-heat cooking.

Mechanical Means. Grinding is a mechanical process in which meat is cut into small particles. In cubing, a cubing machine cuts only surface muscle and connective tissue on both sides of a meat cut. Pounding the meat with a meat mallet also breaks down the tough surface of the meat.

Cut	Average Size or Average Weight	Approximate Cooking Time	
		minutes per pound	total hours
Fresh beef	4 to 8 pounds	40 to 50	3 to 4
Corned beef	6 to 8 pounds	40 to 50	4 to 6
Beef shank cross-cuts	¾ to 1 pound		2½ to 3½
Lamb or veal for stew	1 to 2 inch cubes		1½ to 2½
Beef for stew	1 to 2 inch cubes		2 to 3

Timetable for cooking in liquid (large cuts and stews.)
Courtesy: National Live Stock and Meat Board, Meat in the Food Service Industry.

Chemical Means.   Use a marinade or an enzyme tenderizer to make meat tender chemically. Marinating is soaking meat in an acidic liquid, which may include vinegar or wine. The meat soaks in a mixture of the acid and seasonings for up to 24–48 hours. Acid breaks down connective tissue and marinade adds flavor to the meat. Heating helps this tenderizing process to work faster.

A common enzyme tenderizer is prepared from papain, an enzyme from the papaya fruit. Commercial tenderizers are sprinkled on or injected into the meat. The enzyme also breaks down connective tissue. It acts slowly at room temperature but speeds up during cooking.

Cryo Vac.   Cryo Vac aging is a special tenderizing process that is somewhat like chemical tenderizing. Small retail cuts are vacuum packed in a small amount of moisture in moisture–vapor proof packages. These are then heated and aged. The process improves the quality of the meat.

Storing Beef.   The right method of storing meat helps the customer to be sure the meat he or she buys is wholesome. Proper storage maintains moisture, prevents spoilage, and prevents foodborne illnesses.

There are three simple rules to help prevent meat spoilage:

- Keep it clean.
- Keep it cold.
- Keep it moving.

The chart on page 237 lists the maximum time for storing different types of meat. Ideal temperatures for meat storage are

Refrigerators: 28–32°F
Freezers: 0°F or lower

Storing Fresh Beef.   Freshly cut meat should be bright red in color. Once cut, it will turn brown if it is out in the air. This is called *oxidative browning*. To avoid browning, cover the meat at once. Wrapping should be moisture–vapor proof. Cryo Vac meats are already wrapped and should stay in the wrap.

CHILLED

Solid, fresh cuts of beef, pork, lamb and veal.	2 to 4 days
Ground items and variety meats (liver, etc.)	1 to 2 days
Most cooked, processed meat items and cooked leftovers.	3 days to 1 week

FROZEN

Beef	6 to 12 months
Lamb and veal	6 to 9 months
Pork	3 to 6 months
Ground Beef	3 to 4 months
Ground lamb and veal, and variety meats.	3 to 4 months
Ground pork	1 to 3 months

Meat storage times.

Courtesy: National Live Stock and Meat Board, Meat in the Food Service Industry.

Storing Cooked Beef. Cooked meat is at the peak of quality right after it is cooked. If there are leftovers, freeze them at once. If you are planning to serve the meat later, use the cook–chill method.

For the cook–chill method, cook the meat to three-fourths done (three-fourths of the time called for). Then cool the meat, cover, and store in the cooler. Several hours before serving time, complete the cooking process.

It is important not to move a large amount of cooked meat directly from the oven to the freezer:

1.   The temperature of a large quantity of hot meat can raise the temperature of the freezer. That could lead to spoilage of all the frozen meat.

2.   The meat may not cool and freeze all the way through in a short period of time. The center could stay warm and help bacteria to grow for a while before freezing.

Therefore, meat should be cooled in the refrigerator before being moved to the freezer.

Merchandising Beef. It is not enough for the commercial operator to have tasty, well-prepared beef ready to serve. He or she must also know how to sell that beef to the customer. Three keys to good merchandising of meat are good meat, atmosphere or presentation, and good salespeople.

The Meat: Good Beef Sells.   Whatever the cut of beef, prepare it the right way. It should meet the quality standards for that menu item. If there are drippings, they should be rich and flavorful. The color should be dark but not burned. Meat and juices should not be too greasy. All meats should be tender and prepared the right way for the cut.

Atmosphere or Presentation.   A steak is a steak, but if you call it a filet, the customer notices. The menu is an important tool in creating the right atmosphere—it can set a theme, describe the food, and maybe help sell the product. Decor is also important in creating mood or atmosphere.

Most important is the way the meat is presented. In some operations, the customer can select his or her own steak from an attractive, refrigerated display wagon or case. Sometimes the customer is invited to buy by the pound or ounce. In some restaurants customers can grill their own steaks on a grill area flanked by a sign that reads, "The best cooks in the world walk through these doors."

Eye appeal is one goal in serving meat. It may be a prime rib served on a platter edged in duchess potatoes. It might be a flank steak cut on the bias and served layered on a well-garnished plate. Or, it could be juicy cubes of sirloin skewered with vegetables in a shish kabob.

Some restaurants are well known for certain beef cuts, known as "signature items." Some signature items have taken the names of the region from which they came. We have all heard of the New York strip or the Kansas City strip steak. Signature menu items do not have to be expensive cuts. Merchandising also sells less expensive cuts. A rib steak from the forequarter is less tender and cheaper than a loin steak, but marinated and embedded with whole peppercorns, it becomes a fancy "steak au poivre."

Brisket is also a marketable cut. Prepare a koshered corned beef, boiled beef dinner, or corned beef hash. All have customer

One effective merchandising technique for meat is the deli display. It can be used to show mouth watering ready-to-slice beef roasts.
Courtesy: Wilson Foods Corporation.

appeal. Table 16.7 lists many merchandising names for retail cuts. It also describes garnishes and price range.

The Waiter or Waitress: Suggestion Sells. A well-trained waiter or waitress does not just ask for the customer's order. He or she makes suggestions to the undecided guest. When a customer does not seem to have a definite idea about the entree he or she wants, the waiter or waitress suggests the specialty of the day, which may be a fancier entree than the customer might have

Table 16.7: Merchandising Names for Retail Cuts

Entree name	Wholesale cut	Garnish	Price
Roast rib of beef au jus	Rib	Parsley, popover	High
Rib eye steak	Rib	Mushrooms	Medium–high
Beef stew	Chuck	Vegetables	Low–medium
Pot roast	Chuck	Tomato soup	Low–medium
Barbecue strips of beef	Chuck	Barbecue sauce	Low–medium
New England boiled dinner	Brisket	Vegetables	Low–medium
Grilled New York cut steak	Short loin	Fried onion rings	High
Sirloin steak au poivre	Short loin	Boiled potatoes	High
Roast sirloin bordelaise	Short loin	Mushroom caps	High
London broil	Flank	Bordelaise sauce	Medium–high
Broiled hip steak	Loin end	Bernaise sauce	High
Beef kabob	Loin end	Parsley, rice	High
Swiss steak	Round	Tomato sauce	Medium
Steamship roast	Round	Spiced apple	Medium
Cube steak	Round	Mushroom sauce	Medium

ordered. The waiter may also mention appetizers or side dishes the customer might not have considered without help.

A good salesperson will never get a repeat customer if the food is not good, but if there is a good menu item, prepared well and presented well, a good salesperson can complete the sale and induce the customer to return.

Pork

In the past, people often thought that pork was a fatty meat. Now, with modern animal feeding practices, pork is a much leaner product. In many cuts, there is a high ratio of lean to fat. Even the fattier cuts now have a higher percentage of lean than they did a few years ago.

Over the past few years, pork has become an important menu item. Americans now eat over 100 lb of pork a year per person. Pork comes in three main market forms: fresh, cured and smoked, and salted. The quality of meat is consistent because of improved breeding and feeding practices.

Grades of Pork. While beef has both yield and quality grades, pork has only a yield grade. That is because pork is almost all edible. The grades range from 1 to 4 plus utility. The highest grade is US 1, which yields the highest ratio of lean to fat. Other characteristics considered in grading include conformation (meatiness), quality of finish, and exterior fat quality (it should be firm and white). Grade 2 pork is moderately meaty and the cuts are less thick and plump. Grades 3 and 4 contain lower ratios of lean to fat, and utility grade pork is least lean and meaty.

Pork Cuts. Pork cuts are not grouped by forequarter and hindquarter. Instead, the wholesale cuts include ham, loin, belly, and shoulder.

Leg or Ham. The ham is similar to the round of beef. It is the most common commercial pork cut. Fresh hams are often roasted and then carved on the serving line. The meat is similar to roast loin in flavor. Smoked cured ham is a very popular restaurant item. It is often used for ham steaks, fried ham (a breakfast item), baked ham, and seasoning in some popular vegetable dishes. Commercial hams are available with the bone in, the bone out, or canned. Retail cuts include the whole cut ham, center cut ham, or canned ham.

Loin. The pork loin weighs 10–12 lb. It includes the ribs, center, and loin sections and fat back. The loin section includes these popular retail cuts:

- Rib chops.
- Rib roast.
- Loin roast.
- Back ribs.
- Country-style ribs.

The butcher can separate the tenderloin section from the loin. It runs through the rib and loin chop area. If we smoke the tenderloin, it is called Canadian bacon.

Belly Section. The belly section includes the spareribs and bacon.

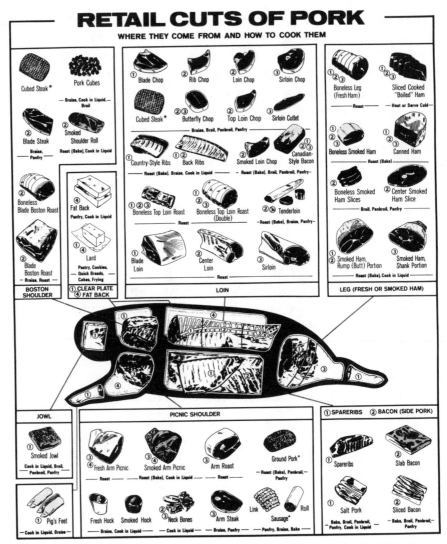

Retail cuts of pork. *, May be made from Boston shoulder, picnic shoulder, loin, or leg.

Courtesy: National Live Stock and Meat Board.

Picnic Shoulder. The picnic is the lower half of the shoulder. It is fattier than the ham (internal fat), and therefore the yield is lower. Picnic ham is the common name for the smoked picnic shoulder. The picnic shoulder may be ground.

Many pork cuts are popular on today's restaurant menu. They include roast pork loin, baked ham, pork tenderloin, and barbecued spare ribs.
Courtesy: Wilson Foods Corporation.

Boston Shoulder.   The Boston shoulder may also be called the butt. This part of the shoulder contains lots of bone. The meat is not very popular but it is cut into blade steaks and small roasts. It is more frequently ground for sausage.

Cooking Pork.   In the past cooks often overcooked pork, but they had what they thought was a good reason for doing so. When pigs were raised in unsanitary conditions, they often carried a parasite called the trichina worm. The eggs of this parasite could be embedded in pork meat and passed on to anyone who ate the meat. This caused a parasitic infection called trichinosis. Victims could become very ill. The only way to be sure the trichina eggs were not passed on was to cook the meat thoroughly. That is why it was common to overcook pork.

Now we know that it is enough to cook pork to an internal temperature of 140°F. To assure a margin of safety, we say that the internal temperature should be 165–170°F. In the past cooks

Table 16.8: Pork Cuts and Suggested Cooking Methods

Pork cut	Suggested cooking methods
Fresh	
Arm or shoulder chops or steaks	Pan fry, pan broil, braise
Ham	Roast
Hocks	Simmer
Loin or rib roast	Roast
Shoulder (picnic or Boston butt)	Roast
Spareribs	Roast or braise
Tenderloin	Pan fry, pan broil, braise
Cured	
Bacon	Broil, pan broil, pan fry
Canadian bacon	Roast, broil, fry
Ham, whole or part	Roast, simmer
Ham slices, thin	Broil, pan broil, pan fry
Ham shanks	Simmer, braise
Shoulder (picnic or Boston butt)	Roast, simmer

often cooked pork to an internal temperature of 185°F. That had the unfortunate side effect of making the meat dry and tough.

To cook pork, we use many of the same cooking methods used for beef—roasting, braising, and broiling. The color of pork is a good indicator of when it is done. When cooked, it loses its pink color and looks grayish-white. Table 16.8 lists suggested cooking methods for various cuts. If pork is to be roasted, check a standard timetable such as Table 16.9.

Storing Pork.   The ideal length of time to store pork depends on whether it is ground or in cuts, fresh or frozen:

Chilled, ground, or cuts: 2–4 days
Frozen cuts: 3–6 months
Frozen ground: 1–3 months

Merchandising Pork.   Make the most of pork menu items. Feature traditional favorites such as barbecued pork ribs with beans and cole slaw. Offer more deluxe entrees such as stuffed pork chops with applesauce, roast baked ham with pineapple, or sweet

Table 16.9: Timetable for Roasting Pork

Cut of meat	Ready to cook weight (lb)	Roasting time at 325°F (hours)	Internal temperature (°F)
Fresh			
Loin	3–5	2–3¾	165
Shoulder (picnic)	5–8	3½–5	165
	8–10	5½–7	165
Shoulder (butt)	5	3½	165
Ham, whole	10–14	5½–6	165
Ham, half	6	4	165
Spareribs	3	2	
Cured, cook before eating			
Ham, whole	12–16	3½–4½	155
Ham, half	6	2½	155
Shoulder, picnic	6	3½	155
Shoulder, butt	2–4	1½–2⅓	155
Canadian bacon	2–4	1–1¼	155
Cured, fully cooked			
Ham, whole	8–12	2¼–3	130
	12–16	3–3¾	130
Ham, half	6	1½–2	130

and sour pork with oriental accompaniments. Train the staff to promote these items as well as beef.

Veal

Veal is meat from a calf. It is usually from male calves less than 6 months of age in a dairy herd. True veal calves are 3 months old or younger. Because there are not many of these animals on the market, the price is very high.

Grades of Veal. Veal grades are prime, choice, good, standard, and utility. Since veal is very low in fat, the meat will dry out easily if it is not cooked carefully. Higher grade veal has slightly more fat than lower grades.

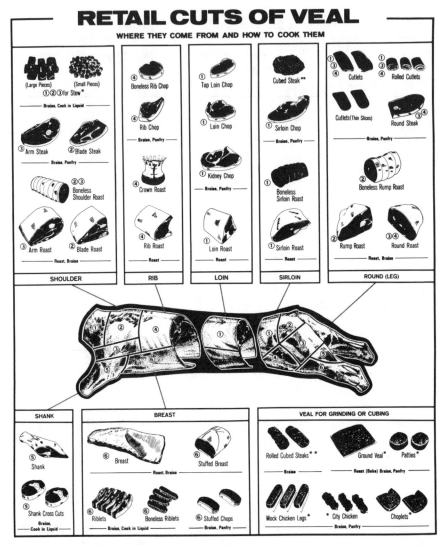

Retail cuts of veal. *, Veal for stew or grinding may come from any cut. **, Cubed steaks may be made from any thick, solid piece of boneless veal.
Courtesy: National Live Stock and Meat Board.

Veal Cuts.　The veal animal has two main parts: the foresaddle and the hindsaddle. Table 16.10 lists wholesale and retail cuts from the foresaddle and hindsaddle.

Merchandising Veal.　Veal is usually found only in expensive commercial restaurants, or in ethnic restaurants. Operators who do

Table 16.10: Veal Major Cuts and Retail Cuts

Major cut	Retail cut	Major cut	Retail cut
	Foresaddle		Hindsaddle
Rib (rack)	Rack of veal (crown roast)	Leg (round)	Veal roasts, rump, sirloin
	Veal rib roast		Veal cutlets
	Rib chops	Loin	Loin roast (saddle)
Shoulder	Veal stew meat		Veal loin chops
	Veal roasts		
Breast	Veal breast		
	Riblets		
	Cube steaks		
	Ground veal		
Shank	Shank, cross cuts		

offer veal should advertise it as a delicacy. They should use the menu to describe the delicate flavor of veal. Common veal entrees are veal marsala (thinly sliced in a marsala wine sauce), veal piccata (breaded thin slices sautéed, in a lemon and stock sauce), veal parmigiana (breaded thin slices sautéed, in a tomato sauce and cheese), and veal Oscar (breaded sautéed cutlet served over asparagus and crab meat with a bernaise sauce).

Lamb

Lamb is the meat of the young sheep. Although mutton or mature sheep is popular in some countries, Americans prefer the taste of younger animals. Most lambs are about 6 months old and weigh about 100 lb. The meat is very tender. Since there is not a great quantity of this meat on the market, the cost is fairly high.

Grades of Lamb. Lamb grades are based on quality and conformation. The grades are prime, choice, good, and commercial. Most foodservice operations use choice meat.

Lamb Cuts. The two sections of the lamb are the foresaddle and the hindsaddle. Table 16.11 lists major cuts and retail lamb cuts.

Table 16.11: Lamb Major Cuts and Retail Cuts

Major cut	Retail cut	Major cut	Retail cut
Foresaddle		Hindsaddle	
Shoulder	Shoulder roast	Loin	Loin roast
	Shoulder chops		Loin chops
	Kabobs (stew)	Leg	Leg roast
Breast, shank	Lamb riblets		Leg of lamb
	Stew meat		Leg chops
	Ground lamb		
Rib	Rack of lamb		
	Rib roast		
	Rib chops		
	Crown roast		

Lamb is very tender meat. Many cuts are popular on the restaurant menu; they include leg of lamb, lamb roast, lamb kabobs, and lamb chops.
Courtesy: American Lamb Council.

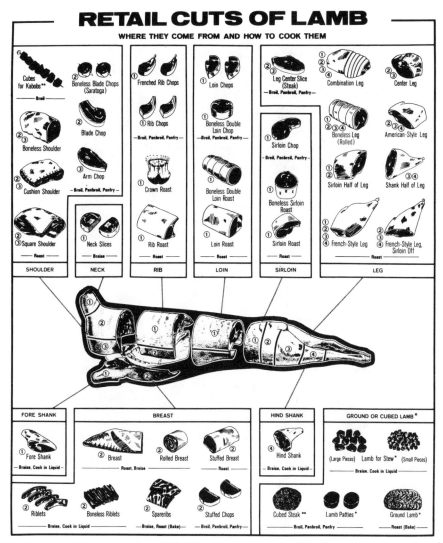

Retail cuts of lamb. *, Lamb for stew or grinding may come from any cut. **, Kabobs or cubed steak may be made from any thick, solid piece of boneless lamb. *Courtesy: National Live Stock and Meat Board.*

Merchandising Lamb. Many fine restaurants feature at least one lamb entree. To promote lamb sales, use the menu to explain lamb to the public. Since the average customer is not as familiar with lamb as he or she is with beef, describe the age, grade, tenderness, and preparation in detail. Use appealing accompani-

Lunchmeats are featured in many sandwich delis. They are a standard item in submarine-style sandwiches.
Courtesy: Oscar Mayer and Company.

ments to sell lamb. It is a good bet that the customer who tries a quality lamb entree once will become a repeat customer.

Processed Meats

Restaurants menus may list any of a number of processed meats in addition to retail cuts of beef, pork, lamb, and veal. Processed meats are ground meats that are seasoned and shaped. Most are made from pork or beef. They include such breakfast favorites as fresh pork sausage and smoked sausage. Luncheon menus feature many lunchmeats such as salami, chopped ham, liverwurst, bologna, spiced loaf, and hot dogs. Processed meats can play a major part in the operator's luncheon business. Some restaurants feature a lunchmeat display case, deli style, in the dining room. This is a very effective merchandising technique. The menu, too, can be used to help promote processed meat specialties.

17
Poultry

Southern fried chicken. Roast turkey with dressing. Those are favorite poultry menu items in the United States. However, poultry has worldwide appeal: from oriental chicken dishes to Russian chicken Kiev to coq au vin from France, poultry is a versatile favorite.

Poultry no longer comes just as whole birds. Processors are providing the operator with many simple-to-prepare, low-waste products, among them:

- Turkey parts.
- Individually quick frozen (IQF) chicken parts.
- Pressed turkey breast.
- Chicken roll.

All of these products give comparatively high yield for low cost. Poultry is usually a good buy when red meat prices are high.

Objectives and Terms

Objectives. This section should help you:

- List characteristics that are important in selecting poultry.
- List kinds of poultry and examples of classes for each kind.
- Describe correct techniques in handling and storage of poultry.
- Describe appropriate cooking methods for poultry.
- Recommend two methods for merchandising poultry.

Terms to Know

Poultry. Birds that are domestically raised as food for humans.

IQF Chicken Parts. Individually quick frozen chicken parts.

Kinds of Poultry. Species or different types of poultry, such as chicken and turkey.

Classes of Poultry. Subcategories of poultry kinds based on characteristics of sex, weight, age, and tenderness. Examples of turkey classes are toms and hens.

Broiler–Fryer. A young, tender chicken of either sex, less than 12 weeks old.

Cornish Game Hen. A very young, tender breed of chicken.

Capon. A castrated male chicken that is very large and tender.

Tom Turkey. A male turkey.

Selecting Poultry

Think about grades, brand, sex, age, processing method, class, and style when selecting poultry.

Grades. Grades are set by the Food Safety and Quality Service (FSQS) of the USDA. When they decide on grades, inspectors look at a variety of factors including conformation, fleshing, fat covering, and defects. Grades are

A   Full fleshed with good appearance
B   With some defects, such as torn skin; not as meaty
C   Carcass has parts missing and a poor appearance

Packers Brand. The poultry buyer has a good chance of getting consistently good poultry if he or she selects a brand with a good reputation. Some of the best known brands are Tyson, Perdue, Country Pride, Holly Farms, and Hillcrest. Brand names are advertised mostly to the homemaker, but brand names are also important when we buy processed poultry for commercial operations.

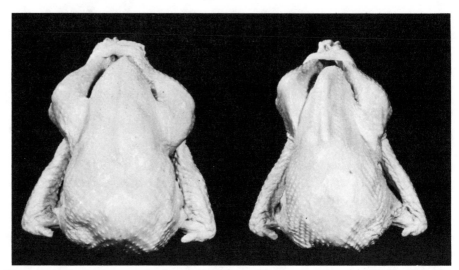

The grade A chicken at the left is fleshier and has a better appearance than the grade B chicken at the right.
Courtesy: United States Department of Agriculture.

Sex of the Bird.   It is not important whether a young bird is a male or female. For older birds, however, sex affects flavor, texture, and yield. Female birds are tastier and juicier and have a better yield of cooked meat per pound of raw meat than males.

Age.   As birds age, they become tougher but they develop more fat and flavor. You can use dry-heat cooking methods for young birds because the meat is tender. Moist-heat cooking methods will assure tenderness in older birds. Older birds are often used for chicken soup or stock because the extra fat gives more flavor. They are also larger and give a better yield of cooked meat.

Type of Processing Used.   Poultry may be sold fresh, storage or chilled, or frozen.

Fresh Killed.   Poultry that is sold within 3 days of killing and has never been frozen is called fresh killed.

Storage or Chilled.   Storage poultry is chilled for 3–30 days at 27–31°F.

Table 17.1: Poultry Kinds and Classes, Characteristics, Age, and Size

Kinds and classes	Age	Size (lb)
Chickens		
Cornish game hen: an immature chicken that is very tender; Cornish chicken cross-breed	5–6 weeks	under 2
Broiler, fryer: young, tender chicken either male or female; smooth skin, flexible breastbone cartilage	9–12 weeks	1–3½
Roaster: young, tender chicken; smooth skin, breastbone cartilage less flexible than broiler	3–5 months	3½–5
Capon: castrated male chicken that is large and tender	4–5 months	4–7
Stag: male chicken with coarse skin, somewhat tough and dark flesh	10 months	3–6
Hen: mature female chicken with meat less tender than roaster and firm breastbone	10 months or more	3–6
Cock: mature male chicken with toughened, dark meat	10 months or more	4–6
Turkeys		
Fryer–roaster: immature male or female; tender meat, smooth skin, and flexible breastbone cartilage	Under 16 weeks	4–9
Young hen: young female; tender, with smooth skin and cartilage firmer than fryer–roaster	5–7 months	8–22
Young tom: young male that is like young hen	5–7 months	8–22
Yearling: fully mature tom or hen; fairly tender meat and smooth skin	Under 15 months	10–30
Mature turkey: old male or female; coarse skin and toughened flesh	Over 15 months	10–30
Ducks		
Broiler: young male or female; tender meat and soft bill and windpipe	Under 8 weeks	2–4
Roaster: young male or female; tender meat, a bill not completely hardened; windpipe that is easily dented	Under 16 weeks	4–6
Mature: older male or female; tough flesh, hardened bill and windpipe	Over 6 months	4–10

(*continued*)

Table 17.1: (*Continued*)

Kinds and classes	Age	Size (lb)
Goose		
Young goose: young male or female; tender flesh, windpipe that is easily dented	Under 6 months	6–10
Mature goose: older male or female; tough flesh, hard windpipe	Over 6 months	10–16
Guineas		
Young guinea: male or female; tender	Under 6 months	¾–1½
Mature guinea: male or female; tough flesh	6–12 months	1–2
Pigeons		
Squabs: young male or female; very tender meat	3–4 weeks	Under 1
Pigeon: mature male or female; coarse skin and tender flesh	Over 4 weeks	1–2

Fresh Frozen.   Poultry that is frozen soon after killing and is held frozen for a short time (up to 60 days).

Frozen Storage.   Poultry that is frozen and held for 60–100 days is frozen-storage poultry. To be held longer than that, poultry must be heat processed or canned.

Poultry Style.   Poultry is sold live, dressed (with the entrails out but possibly with head and feet still on), or ready to cook. Ready-to-cook forms include

- Whole carcass
- Cut up pieces
- One-half
- One-fourth
- Individual pieces: breast, thigh, drumstick, leg, wing, back, neck, and giblets (heart, gizzard, liver).

Kinds and Classes of Poultry.   The category "poultry" includes these kinds (species): chickens, turkeys, ducks, geese, and other birds. Classes are subgroups of each kind of poultry. Class is

Table 17.2: Characteristics of Poultry Parts

Parts	Characteristics
Breast, wings	Light meat, little fat, little connective tissue, cooks quickly
Thighs, drumsticks	Dark meat, more fat, more connective tissue, takes longer to cook

based on age, weight, sex, and tenderness. Table 17.1 lists kinds and classes of poultry and describes their characteristics.

Advantages of Convenience Poultry

Poultry pieces that are ready to prepare have many advantages over poultry from whole birds. They require less storage and oven space. They take less time to thaw and heat. Best of all they need less labor and they result in excellent portion control. The operator never has to worry that a chef is cutting the portions too large or small. Table 17.2 lists characteristics of poultry parts.

Guidelines for Judging Poultry upon Delivery

Fresh Birds. Judge poultry quality by the temperature, look, smell, and feel of the birds.

Chicken should be handled properly. The best temperature range for holding chicken is between 33 and 35°F. Just a few hours at 36°F will make chicken spoil fast.

Note: Chicken should look fresh, cleanly dressed, with clear, clean skin and firm flesh. The color of the fat gives few clues about freshness. Fat color relates more to the feed the chicken ate than to freshness.

Skin should feel smooth and dry to the touch. There should be no stickiness—that is a sign that the chicken is becoming old or was handled incorrectly.

There should be no bad odor on the skin or in the cavity. When cut, there should be no trace of blood, even in the joints.

**Table 17.3: Timetable
for Refrigerator Thawing Poultry**

Poultry	Weight (lb)	Time
Chickens	4 or more	1–1½ days
	Less than 4	12–16 hours
Ducks	3–7	1–1½ days
Geese	6–12	1–2 days
Turkeys	4–12	1–2 days
	12–20	2–3 days
	20–24	3–4 days

Frozen Poultry. If IQF chicken parts are held at the right temperature (below 0°F) there will be little problem with quality.

Handling and Storage of Poultry

Fresh Storage. Fresh poultry is extremely perishable. It arrives on ice and should be kept packed in ice. For best quality, use it within 24 hours. At the longest, use within 4 days. Wash poultry, equipment, and cutting surfaces before using. Poultry often carries *salmonella* bacteria. Try to avoid letting bacteria multiply to the point where they spoil quality or cause illness.

Frozen Storage. Store frozen poultry at 0°F. Thaw in the original wrapper in the refrigerator. Table 17.3 lists thawing times.

Sometimes it will be necessary to thaw poultry more quickly. In those cases it is acceptable to thaw in cold water. Place the poul-

**Table 17.4: Timetable for Cold-Water
Poultry Thawing**

Poultry	Weight (lb)	Time
Chickens	3–4	1–2 hours
Turkeys	4–12	4–6 hours
	12–20	2–3 days
	20–24	8–12 hours

try, in its original wrap or other watertight plastic bag, in cold water. Change water often and thaw until pliable. Approximate thawing times are listed in Table 17.4.

Caution: Some commercial poultry comes already stuffed. Never thaw this ready-stuffed poultry before cooking. Follow cooking directions on the package.

Cooking Poultry

Cooking poultry is like cooking meat, except that poultry is more tender than most meat. It also requires the right kind of handling, once cooked. Always serve poultry well done. Never partially cook and store it, to finish cooking later.

Like red meat, poultry will have less shrinkage if cooked at a low temperature. The bird will also look better and be more moist. Small birds such as cornish game hen and squab are exceptions to the rule. They lose a minimum of moisture if cooked for a short time at a high temperature (400°F).

Large, fatty birds need to cook a long time in moist heat. Cook to well done but do not overcook birds.

Testing for Doneness. Cook large birds to an internal temperature of 180°F. For the right thermometer reading, insert the tip into the thickest part of the thigh, taking care not to touch bone. Use the thigh because it is the last part of the bird to be thoroughly cooked.

For smaller birds, the meat is cooked when the joints are loose. The juice is also clear, not pink or red. Flesh separates easily from the breast or leg bone when meat is fully cooked. If the meat separates from the bone too easily, it is overcooked and possibly dried out. When done, small birds are also firm to the touch. Do not pierce poultry—this will cause valuable juices to be lost.

The trick in cooking poultry is to get dark meat and white meat cooked to the same doneness at the same time. Some ways to do that are as follows:

1. Roast the bird breast side down so that the breast stays moist.

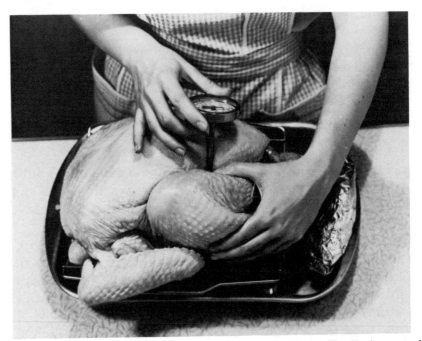

A meat thermometer inserted in the thickest part of the thigh will tell when a turkey is done (180°F).

Courtesy: United States Department of Agriculture.

2.   Baste the bird with fat, not water or stock.

3.   Cover the bird with a layer of bacon or pork fat to keep the breast from drying out.

4.   Separate the pieces and roast similar pieces the same length of time, until done.

Cooking Methods.   The methods used to cook poultry are just like those for red meat. For more details, refer to Chapter 16.

Roasting and Baking.   Before roasting, brush the inside of the cavity with fat. Truss (sew the opening to the cavity) smaller birds—this will help the bird brown and prevent drying. Add paprika for extra browning. Fill pans with roasting birds. The birds should not touch the sides of the pans.

Place large birds breast down on perforated trivet liners in

Table 17.5: Poultry Roasting Temperatures

Temperature	Result to expect
Low (about 250°F) for large birds	Tender and juicy finished product
Medium (300–350°F)	Tender and juicy finished product
Searing temperature (450°F, 15 minutes; then reduce to 250–300°F); good for ducks, geese	Melts off some fat, makes skin crisp, gives brown color
High temperature (400–425°F); for cornish game hens	Golden color, juicy

roasting pans. This will make it easy to baste the birds. Fatty birds such as ducks and geese do not need basting. Roast them breast side up. When you do baste a bird, do so every 20–30 minutes. More frequent basting will cause the oven temperature to drop too much.

Season the skin of a roast bird only if you will eat the skin. Seasoning on the skin will not penetrate into the flesh.

Roast at the temperature that will give the results you want, whether roasting whole birds or parts. Table 17.5 lists temperatures and results.

Broiling, Grilling, and Barbecueing.

These methods are similar to methods used for red meat. However, it is easy to burn poultry on the outside before the inside is cooked. That is why it is important to use slightly lower temperatures than you would for red meat.

To broil, grill, or barbecue, start cooking poultry pieces skin side down. This helps keep the juices in the meat. Then flatten the poultry with a spatula to ensure even cooking. Brush with fat or oil to add moisture, color, and flavor. Avoid basting with sauces high in sugar—these caramelize quickly and cause the outside to burn.

For large-quantity production, start poultry in the broiler or on the grill. Then finish cooking in the oven.

Sautéing, Pan Frying, and Deep Frying.

These three fat cooking methods are ideal for poultry because poultry is lean and tender.

Sautéing.   Sautéing is quick cooking in a small amount of fat. It is best for boneless pieces. For large poultry items, sautéing is used for browning. In classical cooking it is common for the cook first to sauté poultry to develop color and flavor, and then to finish cooking by simmering.

Pan frying.   Pan frying is a good way of cooking poultry pieces that are breaded first. For best results, there should be a ¼ inch layer of fat in the frying pan. Fry skin side first. This is called the "presentation side" and is turned up on the serving plate. After pan frying poultry at a high temperature, lower the heat and cook 30–45 minutes until done.

Deep frying.   Deep frying is similar to pan frying except that poultry pieces are submerged in hot fat. They are cooked throughout. This method works best for small chickens, about 2½ lb. For even cooking, fry at 325–350°F.

Simmering, Poaching, and Braising.   These cooking methods depend on water or other liquid to cook birds.

Simmering.   Simmering is a method in which poultry is cooked at just below the boiling point. It is a good method for cooking tough, older birds. To make a flavorful sauce, add salt, herbs, and mirepoix to the simmering water. Use the flavorful broth for soups, creamed dishes, salads, and casseroles. To simmer poultry, start by placing the poultry in a stock pot or steam-jacketed kettle. To produce the most flavor in the soup, start with cold water. To produce the most flavor in the meat, start with hot water. When the poultry is cooked, cool it in cold water or stock. If it cools at room temperature, the chicken will develop a dry, tough outer surface.

Poaching.   Poaching results in greater yield, moisture, flavor, and tenderness than roasting. This is especially true for large birds. Poaching takes a minimum of cooking time and space. To prepare poultry for poaching, use stock as the cooking liquid. Cover poultry when cooking and use the liquid to make a sauce after cooking. You can poach poultry in the oven or on the range. Oven poaching produces more even heat.

Braising. Braising is cooking meat in a small amount of liquid. It tenderizes tough meat and also adds flavor and moisture to poultry dishes. Favorite classical braised dishes include coq au vin, chicken chasseur, arroz con pollo, chicken fricassee, paprika chicken, and chicken cacciatore.

Storing Leftover Poultry. Separate leftover poultry, broth, stuffing, and gravy. Cover each individual container and refrigerate. Use within 1 or 2 days. Freeze for longer storage.

Tips for Serving and Merchandising Poultry. For consistency in the operation, choose traditional poultry serving portions. A common serving size for poultry is one-quarter of a 2½-lb bird. Another standard serving is one-half breast portion. This produces a serving size of about 5 oz. To be sure that all pieces are uniformly cooked, select uniform-sized pieces for cooking together.

Besides using the right seasonings and garnishes, it is important to merchandise poultry items with imagination. Try a few creative ideas for serving poultry:

- En brochette—on a skewer with fruit pieces.
- With a piecrust in a ceramic dish as a fancy pie.
- Stuffed with an exciting new stuffing.
- Marinated or curried with seasoned rice.
- Use the menu to give the customer a mouth-watering description of each poultry speciality.

18
Fish and Shellfish

In the last few years, there has been a boom in fish and shellfish sales. Even though the cost of fish is high, this surge of popularity continues. This is partly due to the increase in the number of popular fish and seafood restaurant chains in the country. It is also because consumers are willing to try more varieties of fish and shellfish. Sixty percent of all fish sold in the United States goes to commercial food service. It is available year round and in all parts of the country. It is easy and quick to prepare and easily portioned. It also comes in many varieties.

Objectives and Terms

Objectives. This section should help you:

- Define fin fish and shellfish.
- List major fat and lean fish.
- List major shellfish.
- Describe correct methods for handling and storing fish and shellfish.
- Describe correct methods for cooking fish and shellfish.
- Describe common merchandising techniques for fish and shellfish.

Terms to Know
Fin Fish. Sea and freshwater animals with fins.
Shellfish. Sea and freshwater animals with shells.

268

Mollusks.   Shellfish with two hard shells.

Crustaceans.   Shellfish with segmented thin shells.

Important Points about Fish and Shellfish

Fish generally means sea animals with fins. Shellfish, of course, have hard or soft shells. Fish and shellfish are protein foods that have delicate texture and a fragile quality. All types have very little connective tissue. That is why fish and shellfish:

- Cook quickly.
- Are naturally tender (if overcooked, protein becomes tough).
- Must be handled carefully (cooked fish will fall apart easily).

Fin Fish

Market Forms.   Fin fish comes in many different market forms. The forms have different uses (Table 18.1).

Whole or Round Fish.   The fish is intact, just as it was caught.

Drawn Fish.   The fish is eviscerated or internal organs (entrails) are taken out.

Dressed Fish.   Entrails, scales, head, and tail are usually removed. A variation is "pan dressing." For merchandising purposes, the head and tail are left on. This is a popular method for serving trout or other small fish.

Chunk Style.   This form consists of cross sections of large, dressed fish.

Fillets.   Fillets are boneless sides of fish with no skin or entrails. Butterfly fillets are both sides of the fish, still joined.

Steaks.   Steaks are cross-sectional cuts of dressed fish. Steaks are smaller than chunks. They are popular market forms for salmon, halibut, and swordfish.

Fish Sticks.   Sticks are cross-sectional slices of fillets.

Table 18.1: Piscatorial Primer—Fin Fish

Form	Definition	Preparation
Whole or round, fresh	Whole fish, just as it comes from the water	Remove scales and entrails; head, fins, and tail may be removed; cut into serving size pieces or cook whole
Drawn, fresh or frozen	Whole fish, eviscerated	Scale; head, fins and tail may be removed; cut into servings or cook whole
Dressed or pan-dressed, fresh or frozen	Ready to cook	Cut into steaks or fillets, if you wish
Steaks, fresh or frozen	Cross-sectional cuts of large fish	None
Fillets, fresh or frozen	Meaty sides of the fish	None
Butterfly fillets, fresh or frozen	Two single fillets held together by a small piece of skin	None
Breaded/battered fillets, frozen raw or cooked	Fillet with seasoned crumb coating or batter coated	None
Breaded/battered portions, frozen raw or cooked	Uniform, serving portions; cut from frozen blocks of fillets, seasoned crumb coating or batter coated	None
Fish sticks, frozen raw or cooked	Uniformly cut from frozen fillet blocks; seasoned crumb coating or batter coated	None

Source: National Fisheries Institute.

Purchase Forms of Fish.   Foodservice operators can buy fish in four forms: fresh, frozen, canned, and smoked.

Classifications of Fish.   Fish is classified by the kind of water in which it lives and by its fat content.

Water in Which Fish Is Found.   Saltwater fish comes from oceans and seas. Freshwater fish is caught in rivers and lakes.

Table 18.2: Piscatorial Primer—Freshwater Species

Species	Popular varieties	Where caught	Market forms[a]
Catfish		Pond raised commercially; U.S. lakes, inland rivers, ponds, creeks; Brazil	Whole, dressed
Lake trout		Coldwater lakes of North America	Whole, drawn, fillets, steaks
Pike	Walleye, Northern	Lakes	Whole, dressed, fillets, steaks
Rainbow trout		U.S. commercial fish farms, Denmark, Japan	Drawn, boned, fillets, frozen breaded
Smelt		North Atlantic, Pacific Coast, bays from Mexico to Canada, Great Lakes	Whole, dressed, breaded, precooked
Whitefish		Great Lakes, Canada	Whole, drawn, dressed fillets, smoked
Yellow perch	Lake perch	Great Lakes, Canada	Whole, drawn, dressed, fillets, butterfly fillets

[a]Most forms available fresh or frozen.
Source: National Fisheries Institute.

Some types of fish, such as salmon and perch, are both salt- and freshwater types (Tables 18.2 and 18.3). In addition to fish that live naturally in salt- and freshwater, there are cultivated fish. Examples are catfish and trout raised in artificially built ponds.

Fat Content of Fish.   Fish is also classified by the amount of fat it contains. It is important to be aware of fat content because it influences the cooking method. We call some fish "fat fish" and some "lean fish." Lean fish contains about 2% fat, while fat fish contains over 5% fat. Fat fish is usually darker in color than lean fish. Fish with 2–5% fat is called "medium-fat fish." Table 18.4 lists common fat and lean fish.

Control, Handling, and Storage of Fin Fish.   As we said earlier, fish is delicate. Handle it carefully and quickly to preserve

Table 18.3: Piscatorial Primer—Saltwater Species

Species	Popular varieties	Where caught	Market forms[a]
Alaska pollock		North Pacific, Bering Sea	Fillets, frozen breaded raw or cooked sticks and portions
Atlantic pollock		North Atlantic	Drawn, dressed, steaks, fillets, frozen breaded raw or cooked sticks and portions
Bluefish		New England to Gulf states	Fillets
Butterfish		Northeastern U.S.	Whole, dressed, smoked
Cod	Atlantic cod, Pacific cod, scrod (2½ lb or less)	North Atlantic, North Pacific	Drawn, dressed, steaks, fillets, frozen breaded raw or cooked sticks and portions
Croaker		Middle and South Atlantic, Gulf	Drawn, dressed, fillets
Flounder	Fluke, yellowtail, dab	Atlantic, Pacific, Gulf, Bering Sea	Drawn, dressed, fillets, frozen breaded raw or cooked fillets, sticks, and portions
Greenland turbot		North Atlantic, North Pacific	Fillets
Grouper		South Atlantic, Gulf, Pacific	Whole, steaks, fillets
Haddock	Scrod (2½ lb or less)	North Atlantic	Drawn, dressed, fillets, frozen breaded raw or cooked fillets, sticks, and portions
Halibut		North Atlantic, North Pacific	Steaks, fillets
Mackerel	Atlantic blue Spanish King	North Atlantic South Atlantic, Gulf South Atlantic, Gulf	Whole, drawn, fillets, steaks
Mahi Mahi (dolphin fish)		Tropical/subtropical waters	Fillets
Monkfish		Western Atlantic—Grand Banks to North Carolina	Fillets, tails
Mullet		South Atlantic, Gulf	Whole, fillets, smoked

272

Fish	Variety	Location	Forms available[a]
	Snapper (West Coast)	Pacific	...llets, portions
Rockfish		Pacific	Drawn, dressed, fillets
Sablefish		Pacific Coast	Whole, steaks, fillets, kippered, smoked
Salmon	Sockeye	Pacific Coast, Alaska	Dressed steaks, fillets, smoked, canned
	Chinook	Pacific Coast, Alaska	
	Silver	North Pacific	
	Pink	Pacific Coast	
	Chum	Pacific Coast	
Sculpin		Pacific	Fillets
Sea bass	Black, striped	Atlantic, Pacific	Whole, fillets, steaks
Sea trout		Middle and South Atlantic, Gulf	Whole, drawn, fillets
Shad		Coastal rivers from Maine to Florida, Washington to California	Whole, drawn, fillets, boned, smoked, canned; shad roe: fresh or frozen, canned
Shark		Atlantic, Pacific	Steaks, fillets
Snapper	Red, yellowtail	South Atlantic, Gulf, Pacific	Whole, fillets
Sole	Lemon	Atlantic Coast, Atlantic	Whole, fillets, breaded portions, stuffed, stuffed breaded
	Gray	Atlantic Coast	
	Dover	Pacific Coast	
	Petrale	Pacific Coast	
	Rex	Pacific Coast	
	Dover	English Coast	
Swordfish		Atlantic, Pacific	Fillets
Tilefish		Atlantic Coast, Gulf of Mexico	Steaks
Tuna	Albacore, yellowfin, skipjack, bluefin, little	Atlantic and Pacific Coasts, worldwide	Whole, drawn, dressed, fillets Canned
Whiting	North Atlantic	North Atlantic	Whole, drawn, dressed, fillets, frozen breaded raw or cooked sticks and portions
	South Atlantic	South Atlantic	
	South African	South Africa	
	Pacific	Pacific	

[a] Most forms available fresh or frozen.
Source: National Fisheries Institute.

273

Table 18.4: Common Fat and Lean Fish

Fat fish (5%+)	Lean fish (2%)
Mackerel	Flounder
Salmon	Sole
Swordfish	Halibut
Trout	Cod
	Haddock
	Catfish
	Perch

good quality. United States food laws do not require federal inspection of fresh fish, but processed fish goes through voluntary inspection by the U.S. Department of Commerce.

Fresh Fish.   Hold fresh fish at 30–34°F for 1–2 days. Keep fish moist by covering with crushed ice. Change the ice daily. Cover the container or store in a separate box. Do not bruise the fish. Cut pieces of fish should be wrapped, but it is not necessary to wrap whole or drawn fish. To be sure the quality of fresh fish is good:

- Fish should be odor free.
- Eyes should be clear and bright.
- Gills should be reddish pink in color.
- Flesh should be firm and elastic.
- Scales should be bright and shiny.
- Skin should be shiny.

Frozen Fish.   There should be no discoloration or freezer burn on frozen fish. Like fresh fish, it should be free of odor. It should be wrapped in moisture- and vapor-proof wrapping material. A buildup of ice crystals indicates that the fish was refrozen.

Store frozen fish at 0°F or colder. Frozen fish will stay good for 2–6 months, depending on the fat content. Remember to follow the first in, first out rule when storing fish.

Thaw frozen fish in the refrigerator—this will take 18 to 36 hours, depending on the size of the pieces. Never thaw fish at room temperature. It will help bacteria grow and will cause loss of flavor. Handle frozen fish carefully and do not refreeze. Once fish is thawed, treat it as fresh fish.

You can prepare IQF fish pieces from the frozen state to make handling easier. Small portions can be breaded while they are partially frozen.

Canned Fish. Store canned fish and seafood in a cool, dry place. Check for dents or damage to cans. Once opened, store the fish or seafood in a tightly covered container. It will keep refrigerated for 2–3 days.

Shellfish includes two broad categories: mollusks and crustaceans. Mollusks have a pair of hard shells and crustaceans are covered by many thin shells linked together (Table 18.5).

Mollusks. Oysters, clams, and scallops belong to this group. They have a two-part shell joined by a hinge.

Oysters. The shell of the oyster is dark in color and rough in texture. Table 18.6 lists oyster varieties.

Oysters come in three market forms: live in the shell, shucked or removed from the shell (either fresh or frozen), and canned.

Characteristics of good oysters are rough, irregular shells and flesh that is soft, delicate, and moist. The freshest oysters have tightly closed shells. If they are shucked, the oyster meat has a mild sweet smell.

Clams. Clams come with such names as littleneck, cherrystone, long neck, and steamer. They are either hard or soft shelled. Table 18.7 lists some clam varieties.

Market forms for clams are live, in the shell, shucked or removed from the shell (fresh or frozen), and canned. Freshness characteristics are the same as for oysters.

Store clams and oysters carefully to keep them fresh. Live clams and oysters will keep for a week if they are cold and wet. Store fresh-shucked clams and oysters at 30–34°F for up to a

Table 18.5: Piscatorial Primer—Shellfish Species

Species	Popular varieties	Where caught	Market forms
Clams	Butter	North Pacific, Alaska	Live in shell; shucked, fresh and frozen; frozen breaded, raw, and cooked; canned; clam strips
	Littleneck	Pacific Coast, Alaska	
	Cherrystones	New England, Middle and South Atlantic	
	Quahog		
	Razor	Pacific Coast, Alaska	
	Soft Shell	New England, Middle Atlantic, Pacific	
	Surf	Middle Atlantic, Alaska	
	Geoduck	Washington's Puget Sound	
	Ocean Quahog	New England, Middle Atlantic	
Crabs	Blue	Middle and South Atlantic, Gulf	Live in shell (blue and dungeness); fresh or frozen: cooked meat, sections, claw; specialties: frozen breaded, raw or cooked (cakes, patties, deviled, stuffed, etc.); canned; pasteurized (blue); softshell (blue)
	Dungeness	Pacific Coast, Alaska	
	King	Alaska	
	Stone	Florida	
	Snow	Alaska	
	Jonah	New England Coast	
	Red	New England and Middle Atlantic Coast	
Lobsters	Northern	North Atlantic	Live in shell; fresh or frozen: cooked meat, cooked whole, tails; raw; canned
	Rock	South Africa, Australia	
	Spiny	Virtually all continental shelf areas	
Mussels		New England, Middle Atlantic	Live in shell; frozen in sauces, canned
Oysters	Eastern	New England, Middle and South Atlantic, Gulf	Live in shell; shucked, fresh and frozen; frozen breaded, raw or fried; canned, smoked
	Pacific	Pacific Coast, Japan, Korea	
	Olympia	Pacific Coast	
Scallops	Bay	New England	Fresh or frozen: shucked, frozen breaded, raw or cooked, specialties
	Calico	Florida, Gulf	
	Sea	Atlantic, Pacific	
Shrimp	White, Brown and Pink	South Atlantic, Gulf, Pacific	Fresh or frozen: raw, headless, in shell, peeled (including deveined) raw or cooked, frozen breaded, raw or fried; canned; packaged, split in the shell
	Northern	North Pacific, North Atlantic	
	Bay	Virtually world-wide	
	SeaBob	Gulf	
	Royal Red	South Atlantic, Gulf	
	Rock	Gulf, South Atlantic	
	Freshwater	Hawaii, Asia	
Squid		Atlantic Coast, Pacific Coast, Gulf of Mexico	Whole, cleaned, fillets, strips, pieces, breaded products

Table 18.6: Popular Oyster Varieties and Regions

Name	Region
Eastern	Northeast, Atlantic, Gulf Coast
Pacific	Pacific Ocean, Japan
Olympia	U.S. Pacific coast

week. Keep frozen mollusks at 0°F or colder and thaw in the refrigerator.

Cook clams and oysters by heating just enough to keep them juicy. Good cooking methods are poaching, french frying, baking, and steaming. They are good in soups, stews, and chowders. Never overcook mollusks. The meat will shrink and dry out, making them tough and rubbery.

Scallops. Scallops are sold shucked only. Small bay scallops are the best type but the larger sea scallops are also good. Scallops should be white in color and sweet to the taste. They are ready to cook and require no cleaning. Store them at 30–34°F and keep them covered. Cook as you would cook any fish—carefully so that the protein does not become tough.

Crustaceans. Lobster, shrimp, and crab make up the group called crustaceans. They are characterized by many thin shells, linked together, covering the soft parts of the animal's body.

Lobsters. Lobsters are among the largest crustaceans—they range in size from a few ounces to 20 lb. Table 18.8 lists lobsters by name, region, and size.

Table 18.7: Clam Varieties

Shell type	Name
Hard	Littleneck
	Cherrystone
	Chowder
Soft	Longneck
	Steamers

Table 18.8: Lobster Types, Regions, and Size

Name	Region	Size
Northern	Maine	1–20 lb
Rock	South Africa, Australia	2–12 oz tail
Spiny	Europe, North America	Few ounces (also called crawfish, crayfish)
Langosta	Florida, Gulf of Mexico	Few ounces, like shrimp

Market forms of lobster include live in the shell, frozen cooked lobster meat, or frozen lobster in the shell. Live lobsters should be moving actively to assure freshness. Cooked lobster should have a fresh, sweet smell. Live lobsters are stored packed in seaweed or in saltwater. Cooked lobster should be stored covered and refrigerated at 30–34°F.

As with all seafood, it is important not to overcook lobsters. Cook in simmering or boiling water just until tender. Overcooking will make a tough product.

Shrimp.   Shrimp are small crustaceans that are classified by the number of shrimp per pound. Larger shrimp are more expensive than smaller shrimp. In general, 1 lb of raw shrimp yields ½ lb of cooked shrimp. Table 18.9 lists count of shrimp and names.

Table 18.9: Commercial Count/Shrimp

No. per pound	Name
Less than 10	Extracolossal
10–15	Colossal
16–20	Extrajumbo
21–25	Jumbo
26–30	Extralarge
31–35	Large
36–42	Medium-large
43–50	Medium
51–60	Small
61–70	Extrasmall
More than 70	Tiny

Table 18.10: Types of Shrimp

Name	Region	Preparation method
White	South Atlantic or Gulf of Mexico	Deep fry, whole or butterflied
Brown and pink	Atlantic, Alaska	Steam, broil, in cocktails, salads, entrees
Rock	Gulf of Mexico	Broiled or grilled (called scampi)

Shrimp comes in four major types, from different geographic areas. Table 18.10 lists the types, regions, and best preparation methods.

Market forms of shrimp include the following:

- "Green" shrimp (raw, in the shell, fresh or frozen).
- Peeled and deveined shrimp (P&D)—usually IQF. Deveined means the dark vein along the back of the shrimp has been removed.
- Peeled, deveined, and cooked shrimp (PDC).
- Canned.

To be sure that shrimp are fresh, check that they are solidly frozen and have no freezer burn. Fresh shrimp should have no fishy or iodine smell.

Store frozen shrimp at 0°F and thaw in the refrigerator. Store fresh shrimp in crushed ice or covered in the refrigerator.

Shrimp will become tough and rubbery if it is overcooked or cooked at a temperature that is too high. Cook just until tender, whether peeled before cooking or after. Shrimp can be served peeled or unpeeled, hot or cold. Butterfly shrimp are cut lengthwise. They are attractive and popular as a fried menu item.

Crab. Crabmeat is lean and sweet, similar to lobster, but it is less expensive than lobster and more common in the marketplace. Six types of crab are popular in the United States. Table 18.11 lists them by name, region, suggested use, and characteristics.

Table 18.11: Types of Crab

Name	Region	Uses and characteristics
Blue	Mid-Atlantic, Gulf of Mexico	Lumpmeat in salads, cocktails; weight: 5 oz, frozen
Dungeness	Pacific, Alaska	Whole or flakes in salads; weight: 1½–4 lb; sweet meat
King	Alaska	Live in shell, fresh or frozen, legs are served; weight: 6–20 lb; expensive
Stone	Florida, Texas	Claws are used
Snow	Pacific Coast, Alaska	Legs and claws used in soups, salads, entrees
Softshell	Atlantic	Sautéed, fried; served and eaten shell and all

Market forms of crab include the following:

- Live in the shell (best when fresh).
- Cooked in the shell, fresh or frozen (popular forms for king crab legs, Dungeness crab legs, snow and stone crab claws, softshell crabs).
- Cooked, frozen crabmeat.
- Canned.

Live crabs are packed and shipped in seaweed. Frozen crab is stored at 0°F.

To cook live crabs in the shell, boil, broil, or steam them. Keep the cooked crabmeat warm and moist. Overcooking dries and toughens the meat. Cook frozen crab as you would cook shrimp or lobster. It can be sautéed, poached, or fried.

To prepare all shellfish, cook them quickly. Shellfish are low in fat and therefore moist-heat methods are best to keep them from drying out. Serve immediately, if possible. A lemon garnish is an important part of correct fish service and adds to the flavor.

Canned Fish

We look at canned fish as a separate category since it includes both fin fish and seafood. Canned seafood makes up a very large portion of the seafood market—more than either fresh or frozen seafood. The most popular canned seafood varieties are tuna and salmon. But other canned seafood products are:

- Anchovies—fillets or paste, salt cured.
- Clams—whole or minced, in no. 3 or no. 10 cans.
- Codfish balls.
- Crab meat.
- Herring.
- Lobster.
- Sardines—four grades.
- Shrimp—small, in brine or dry pack.

Tuna.   There are 11 different kinds of tuna on the market. They have different color, form of packing, and packing medium. Solid-pack tuna comes from the loin of the fish. It contains no more than 18% small flakes. Chunk tuna is a mixture—half muscled pieces and half pieces without muscle structure. Grated or shredded tuna contains all flaked pieces.

White tuna is also called albacore. There is also light tuna and dark or blended tuna. Tuna can be packed in oil (cottonseed or olive), water, or saltwater.

Solid-pack tuna is best for salads or main course; chunk tuna is good for cooked casseroles; and flaked tuna is satisfactory for sandwich spreads.

Salmon.   There are many species of salmon, ranging in color from dark red to white. The deeper the red, the higher the oil content and the better the quality of the salmon (Table 18.12).

Table 18.12: Classes of Salmon

Type	Names and characteristics
Dark red	Red or sockeye, also called blueback; very oily, with small flakes
Chinook or king	Contains large flakes and is oily
Coho or silver	Red to pink in color; multipurpose
Pink or humpback	Yellow to pink in color; the most frequently used type
Chum or white	Least oily; pink to yellow in color

Fish and Shellfish Cookery

Remember that your goal is to cook fish and shellfish just until done. When fish flakes easily but does not fall apart, it is cooked enough. If the fish is compact and tough, it is overcooked. You want to enhance the natural flavor, and preserve moisture and texture. Do not concern yourself with tenderizing fish and shellfish—it is naturally tender and overcooking makes it tough. Since fish and shellfish have their own delicate taste, they take little seasoning.

Lean Fish.   To cook lean fish, use a little fat and moist heat to preserve the moisture in the fish. Avoid overcooking. If you use a dry-heat method, baste the fish frequently. Frying and sautéing are good methods. Serve lean fish with sauces to keep products moist.

Fat Fish.   Fat fish will tolerate some heat without getting dry and tough. Moist heat is fine for such fish as trout and salmon, but dry heat is best. Broiling and baking are good choices to minimize oiliness in the finished product. Add a small amount of fat to add color and flavor if desired.

Cooking Methods.   Broil, bake, fry, poach, or microwave fish and shellfish.

Broiling.   To broil fish, place it 5 inches or less from the broiler and cook it quickly. Fat fish presents no problems in broiling but watch lean fish carefully—it will cook in just a few minutes. To avoid drying out, coat the lean fish pieces with margarine or butter. You can also coat fish in flour to form a protective coating. When broiling, remember these important points:

- Use high heat but do not overcook.
- Small steaks or fillets are best for broiling.
- Season fish before broiling. Use salt and pepper. Add lemon if you wish.
- Place fillets or pieces on a greased pan before placing under broiler. Place skin side down.

- Broil small pieces on one side only.
- Cook only until done.
- Broil to the customer's order and serve immediately.
- Turn thick cuts such as salmon steaks once during broiling. This results in even cooking and adds colorful grill stripes to the outside.

A new restaurant variation on broiled fish is grilled fish. In this cooking method, the fish is grilled over an open pit in front of guests. Specialty woods such as mesquite may be used for the fire.

Baking. Baking is a slower method than broiling. Because it takes longer, it can dry out fish. It is a good cooking choice for fat fish and large pieces or whole fish. Small fillets or steaks may dry out when baked. For large-volume cooking, some chefs quick fry breaded fish pieces and then finish off the cooking by baking. The product has the color and flavor of fried fish, but the ease of preparation of baking.

The following are helpful tips for baking fish:

- Use whole or large pieces of fat fish.
- Season fish before baking.
- Bake at 350°F until done (flakes when touched with a fork).

Deep-Fat Frying. Frying is the most popular method of preparing fish or shellfish. It is especially good for lean fish. Perhaps this is because the batter or breading helps to retain moisture and flavor. Frying is the most common commercial method of fish cookery. Just think of the number of fried-fish restaurants that have sprung up in the past 10 years.

While frying is ideal for lean fish, it is not the best method for fat fish. This is because frying keeps in the natural fat in the fish, which can result in an oily, fishy taste.

Many forms of lean fish are available as frozen breaded pieces that can be fried without thawing.

Remember these tips when deep-fat frying fish:

- Select small, lean portions of fin fish, shrimp, scallops, clams, or fish sticks.
- Bread or batter pieces before frying.

- Fry at 350°F until golden brown.
- Fry only one fish, or a few small pieces at a time. Too many pieces can cause the temperature to drop. This will make fish greasy.
- Drain fish right after frying to remove excess oil.
- Serve at once.

Poaching.   Poaching is cooking fish in a flavorful liquid at a temperature of 160–180°F. It is a common technique for cooking lean fish, but fat fish are also good poached. Poaching cooks fish gently, at a low temperature, but quickly. Fish retain their maximum moisture and flavor when poached. In addition, the cooking liquid adds extra flavor to the fish.

Many chefs consider poaching the very best way to cook fish. The liquid may be a fumet of white wine and spices. After cooking, the liquid is used as the base for a hot fish sauce.

An interesting variation on poached fish is *court bouillon.* Whole fish is first cooked in water containing acid and seasonings. Then the cooked fish is chilled and coated with the cold liquid, to which gelatin has been added. When the coating gels, the fish is decorated and displayed before serving.

Pan Frying or Sautéing.   Pan frying is a good method for small fish, whole fish, or fillets of lean fish. The oil or butter used for frying keeps the fish moist. Usually the fish is seasoned and dredged in flour or breaded before frying on both sides until golden brown. Breading keeps the shape of the fish, prevents sticking, helps retain moisture, and gives color.

A popular sautéing method is *á la meuniere.* First, dredge the fish in flour. Then sauté it in butter, and season it with fresh lemon juice and chopped parsley. Hot brown butter may also be added. To make fish *almondine,* top with slivered almonds.

Important points to remember when pan frying or sautéing fish are:

- Coat the fish with flour or breading first.
- To improve the crust, soak fish in milk before breading.
- Use a minimum of fat.
- For small fish or pieces, use high heat; for large fish pieces or

whole fish, use low heat. (You can also sauté large fish, and then finish them in the oven.)
- Handle fish carefully to avoid breaking the fish or crust.
- Cook to order and serve at once.

Simmering and Steaming.   These are popular methods for cooking all shellfish and for some fish specialties using fin fish. Bouillabaisse is a fish soup with a well-seasoned taste. Fisherman's stew is prepared by cooking fish in a small amount of liquid.

Microwave Cooking.   Microwave cooking is better than conventional cooking methods for fish and shellfish. It maintains their natural moisture. If done properly, microwave cooking will not dry out or toughen fish.

Merchandising Fish

Dining room showmanship has become one of the most effective ways to sell seafood. Many of you have seen one or more of these merchandising concepts in action:

- Oyster bar.
- Clam bake.

Merchandise shellfish by serving in unique, attractive ways.

Table 18.13: Fish and Seafood Entrees

Entree name	Market form	Garnish	Price
Fried smelt	Drawn	Lemon wedge, paprika	Low
Trout almondine	Drawn	Lemon slice,	Medium–high
Baked flounder	Drawn	Crab stuffing	High
Broiled or baked Baley bluefish	Drawn	Celery stuffing, bacon slices	Medium–high
Broiled salmon steak maitre d'	Steak	Lemon wedge, paprika	Medium
Poached salmon	Steak	Aspic, egg slices	High
Halibut Duglere	Steak	Tomatoes	High
Halibut steak au gratin	Steak	Cheese sauce, chopped chive	High
Fried fillet of sole	Fillet	Lemon slice, parsley	Low–medium
Salmon fillet ravigote	Fillet	Aspic, caviar	High
Sole bonne femme	Fillet	Mushroom and chive cream sauce	Medium–high
Broiled whitefish	Fillet	Lemon butter	Medium
Fried fish sticks	Sticks	Tartar sauce	Low
Broiled lobster tails	In shell	Drawn butter	High
Broiled crabs	In shell	Cocktail sauce	Medium–high
Clams casino	In shell	Bacon, garlic, paprika	High
Oyster stew	Shucked	Chopped parsley	Medium–high
Fried scallops	Shucked	Lemon wedge, parsley	Low–medium
Scallops bonne femme	Shucked	Cream sauce, parsley, mushrooms	Medium–high
Scalloped oysters	Shucked	Paprika	Medium
Shrimp newberg	Headless	Sherry wine sauce	Medium–high
Shrimp creole	Headless	Celery, tomatoes, garlic, onions	High
Fried shrimp	Headless	Lemon wedge, cocktail sauce	High
Baked deviled crab	Cooked meat	Hollandaise sauce	High
Alaska crab	Cooked meat	Bread crumbs, paprika	Medium–high
Baked crabmeat Maryland	Cooked meat	Green pepper, onion, paprika	High
Tuna noodle casserole	Canned meat	Olive slices	Low
Baked salmon loaf	Canned meat	Parsley	Low
Crab imperial	Canned meat	Parsley, lemon wedge	Medium–high

- Wisconsin fish boil.
- Seafood buffet.
- Sushi bar.
- Live lobster tanks (you pick your own dinner).
- Fish fry.

In addition to these special features, fish menu items can sell themselves. Table 18.13 lists many favorite seafood entrees along with typical garnishes. Use this type of information for descriptive menus.

Selecting Fresh or Frozen Fish

Many restaurateurs would like to be able to advertise fresh fish on their menus. The words give the customer a message: "This fish was just caught." Naturally, the customer wants to try it.

However, the term "fresh" really means "not frozen." There is no indication of how long the fish has been on ice and how it has been handled since being caught. As a matter of fact, correctly handled frozen fish may offer more freshness and flavor than so-called fresh fish.

Because fresh fish requires constant attention, it is harder to handle and therefore costs 60–80 cents a pound more than frozen fish. Freezing helps preserve the quality of fish, especially the lean varieties.

19
Vegetables
and Potatoes

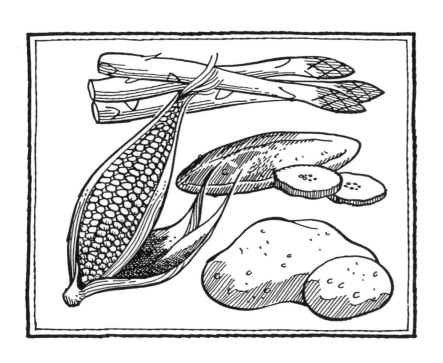

Many customers today are very health conscious: They know that vegetables are full of necessary nutrients; they look for more fiber, variety, and color in their meals; and they know that well-prepared vegetables are flavorful, appealing, and may be low in calories.

Smart foodservice operators realize that vegetables can be more than a minor part of the meal. The potato, of course, is the most common vegetable served with meals. It is a starchy vegetable that can be prepared in many different ways. Other vegetables, whether cooked tender crisp or served raw, can make menus unique. Vegetables add the color, texture, and variety the customer wants.

Objectives and Terms

Objectives. This section should help you:

- Classify vegetables by plant part, color, texture, and flavor.
- Identify the four market forms of vegetables.
- Describe correct storage and handling methods for all market forms of vegetables.
- List appropriate cooking methods for vegetables.
- Describe the two types of potatoes.

Terms to Know

Vegetables.   Plant parts that may be used for food.

Root Vegetables.   Vegetables that come from the plant part that absorbs water and nutrients from the soil.

Tuber Vegetables.   Vegetables that are starchy growths off the roots.

Acid.   A chemical characteristic of food. It usually tastes sour or tart. Lemon juice and vinegar are examples of acids.

Alkali.   A chemical characteristic of food that is the opposite of acid. It usually tastes slightly bitter. Baking soda is a common example.

Al Dente (ahl 'dentay).   Term that describes stage of doneness that is tender to the bite.

Mealy.   Characteristic of mature potatoes. They are high in starch and low in sugar and moisture.

Waxy.   Characteristic of young or new potatoes. They are low in starch and high in sugar and moisture.

All About Vegetables

Vegetables are plant parts.

Classifications.   Vegetables may be classified by the part of the plant, by color, by texture, or by flavor. Table 19.1 lists vegetables

Table 19.1: **Plant Parts of Vegetables and Examples**

Part	Examples
Bulb	Garlic, onion
Flower	Broccoli, cauliflower
Fruit	Cucumber, tomato, squash, eggplant, pepper
Leaf	Lettuce, greens, spinach, cabbage, brussels sprout
Root	Beet, carrot, radish
Seed	Bean, corn, pea
Stem	Asparagus, celery
Tuber	Potato

No plant actually looks like this. It is a composite that illustrates how many different plant parts are common vegetables.

according to plant part (as shown in the above figure); Table 19.2 lists vegetables by color; Table 19.3 lists vegetables by the texture of the vegetable; and Table 19.4 lists vegetables by their flavor.

Market Forms of Vegetables.   Vegetables come in four market forms: fresh, frozen, canned, and dried. Fresh vegetables are available year round. However, the cost may be high at some

Table 19.2: Colors of Vegetables

Color	Examples
Red	Beet, red cabbage, red bean, tomato
Green	Green bean, pea, greens, broccoli, asparagus
Yellow, orange	Corn, carrot, squash, sweet potato
White	Potato, onion, mushroom, cucumber, celery, cauliflower

Table 19.3: Vegetables by Texture

Texture	Examples
Hard	Artichoke, asparagus, green bean, beet, broccoli, carrot, cauliflower, celery, pea, pepper, winter squash
Soft	Brussels sprout, cabbage, corn, greens, cucumber, eggplant, mushroom, onion, summer squash, tomato

times of the year. This is because cost goes up when supplies are low. On the other hand, when supplies are large (at peak harvest times) costs go down. Some locations in the country have locally grown spring and summer supplies of vegetables. As you would expect, local vegetables cost less than those shipped across the country. If they are handled correctly, fresh vegetables can be the best for flavor, texture, and appearance.

Frozen vegetables are frozen at peak harvest times. Therefore, they are all available all year round, for about the same price. Before freezing, processors partially cook raw vegetables to prevent the vegetables from changing color or getting tough when they are frozen. This process is called blanching. If vegetables are quickly and correctly frozen, there will be a very small loss of nutrients. Freezing gives the foodservice operator a standard product year round. In quality, frozen vegetables are almost as good as fresh. Because they need less labor for preparation, they can be less expensive even though the frozen product may cost more than the fresh product. Vegetables that are high in liquid do not freeze well.

Canned vegetables are heat-processed at peak harvest time. Despite that, the canned product is not as attractive as fresh or frozen vegetables. Canned vegetables are also somewhat lower in

Table 19.4: Flavor of Vegetables

Flavor	Examples
Strong	Onions, cabbage
Mild	Green bean, pea
Sweet	Corn

Canned green beans and three bean salad are examples of popular canned vegetables.
Courtesy: Del Monte Corp.

water-soluble vitamins than frozen or fresh vegetables. Still,
canned vegetables are consistent in quality and they are most
convenient.

Dried vegetables can be stored for long periods of time. Seed
vegetables such as peas, beans, and corn are sometimes dried as
they are. Other vegetables can be cut and dehydrated to reduce
water content. They may come in several purchase forms: gran-
ules, flakes, slices, and diced pieces.

Handling and Storage.   Vegetables are very perishable—they
start to lose quality as soon as they are picked. That is why it is
important not to wait too long to serve fresh vegetables. When
they begin to dry out and deteriorate, they no longer look attractive to the customer. Keep vegetables refrigerated from receiving

to serving time—be sure that the refrigeration system has enough humidity and ventilation and keep the temperature at 45°F or lower (but above 32°F). Remember to follow the FIFO rule in using vegetables. Handle vegetables carefully to prevent bruising and decay.

Keep dried vegetables stored in tightly sealed containers in a cool, dry area. They should have an even bright color. If there is a loss of color, it means there is a loss of freshness. There should be no defects or foreign matter in dried products.

Hold frozen vegetables at 0°F. If the temperature should go above 0°F for any time, the vegetables may lose quality. Check for signs of freezer burn (a dried-out, whitish look on the surface) or ice crystals. Never refreeze vegetables once they have thawed.

Hold canned vegetables for up to one year in a dry, cool, well-ventilated area. If cans look dented or bulging, the food may be spoiled. Throw out those cans. Remember the basic rule of food safety: When in doubt, throw it out!

Cooking Vegetables.   The goal in cooking vegetables is not just to heat them. You want to

- Enhance the flavor.
- Preserve the natural color.
- Preserve nutrients.
- Maintain texture.

To enhance or bring out flavor, cook vegetables for a short period of time. Use the smallest amount of water possible, or steam the vegetables. Most operators cook vegetables in lightly salted water, but since many people are now salt conscious, you can cook vegetables without salt. Use herbs and other seasonings to enhance flavor. If you cook vegetables in oil, use the smallest amount possible (except when deep frying). Oil absorbs some of the natural flavors in vegetables; it also clings to the vegetables when they are drained.

To preserve color in vegetables, follow the right guidelines for each color.

Red Vegetables (Except Tomatoes).   Slightly acid cooking liquid intensifies the red color of beets and red cabbage. However, acid also makes the vegetables tough and they need a correspondingly longer cooking time. Alkaline liquid causes red vegetables to turn an undesirable purple. Water, which is usually slightly alkaline, makes red vegetables break down quickly. As a result, the best recommendation seems to be to use a short cooking time with a small amount of water and a small amount of vinegar, wine, or lemon juice added (acid). Save the cooking liquid and serve with vegetables.

Green Vegetables.   Acid changes the bright green color to dull olive green. A slightly alkaline liquid will help preserve the green color. However, the strong alkaline liquid made by adding baking soda to water is too strong. It will cause a loss of nutrients and will make vegetables mushy. The best advice is to cook green vegetables uncovered. This will let the acids in the vegetables evaporate so that they do not produce color changes. However, it may result in some loss of nutrients. Use the shortest time possible for cooking. Steam vegetables, if you can. Cook in small batches and do not hold vegetables in a steam table for a long time.

Yellow and Orange Vegetables.   Yellow and orange vegetables hold up well in both acid and alkaline cooking liquid. They do lose color if they are overcooked. You may have noticed that carrots look dull and faded after long cooking in soup or stock. Once again, the best advice is cook vegetables for a short time. It will prevent loss of color and preserve flavor, nutrients, and crispness.

White Vegetables.   Overcooking turns white vegetables gray. It also develops an unpleasant taste. Alkaline liquid causes a slight yellowing, while a slightly acid liquid keeps vegetables white. Too much acid will make them tough, however. For best results, cook white vegetables quickly and do not hold them too long.

Keeping Nutrient Losses to a Minimum.   Vegetables are good sources of many nutrients. They are especially important because they provide vitamins C and A. Vitamin A is fat soluble and fairly stable; vitamin C, on the other hand, dissolves in water and is easily destroyed by heat.

To keep losses of vitamin C to a minimum, it is important to follow these steps:

1. Cook just long enough to make vegetables tender crisp.
2. Cook as close to serving time as you can.
3. Use a small amount of liquid.
4. Keep liquid slightly acid or neutral.
5. Cook just below the boiling point.
6. Peel and cut vegetables as little as possible. This will keep the cut surface area to a minimum and will limit loss of nutrients from the cut surfaces.

Maintaining Texture in Vegetables. Vegetables include cellulose, the tough fibers that make raw vegetables stiff and crisp. The purpose of cooking vegetables is to soften those fibers, but we do not want our products to be mushy. Our goal is to have vegetables that are *al dente,* or firm to the bite. Since different vegetables have varying amounts of fiber, cooking times will be different. If the cooking liquid includes acid or sugar, those ingredients will keep the fiber firm. On the other hand, alkaline liquids soften fiber. To keep changes to a minimum, cook vegetables as close to serving time as you can.

Quality Standards for Cooked Vegetables. When they come out of the steamer or steam-jacketed kettle, cooked vegetables should be tender crisp. Some vegetables such as potatoes are supposed to be soft, however. The customer should be able to taste the distinctive flavor of the vegetable and the color should be bright. Vegetables should have a uniform appearance and the final dish should be lightly seasoned or sauced.

How to Cook Processed Vegetables. Follow these steps to cook frozen, canned, and dried vegetables.

Frozen Vegetables. Frozen vegetables need no thawing. Boil or steam them from the frozen state. The only exceptions are vegetables frozen in a solid block, such as corn on the cob or spinach. The block needs to be thawed somewhat before cooking.

Canned Vegetables.   Canned vegetables are fully cooked. Cook them by first draining part of the canning liquid. Then heat quickly to just under the boiling point.

Dried Vegetables.   Dried vegetables usually need to soak before cooking. Follow directions for the correct amount of water and soaking time. Then simmer covered until tender.

Selecting Vegetable Cooking Methods.   Favorite cooking methods for vegetables are baking, boiling, steaming, braising, frying, and sautéeing.

Baking.   Baking is a good method for vegetables high in moisture and starch (potatoes and squash.) Parboil low-moisture vegetables before baking. (Parboiling is simmering until about half-cooked). Cover low-moisture vegetables while baking to retain moisture. Baking gives vegetables an appealing brown color because they are caramelized. Baking also retains nutrients because there is no cooking water to leach out the vitamins and minerals. Bake hard vegetables at temperatures between 350 and 450°F. Bake potatoes, squash, and tomatoes in the skin. Baking is also a good technique for finishing some vegetables and casseroles containing vegetables.

Boiling.   To boil vegetables, cover the vegetable with liquid and bring the liquid just to the boiling point. Use barely enough liquid to cover vegetables. Salt lightly and cook *al dente*. Cook some vegetables covered and some uncovered. Table 19.5 lists vegetables to cook covered and uncovered. After boiling, drain vegetables well. Be careful not to overcook.

Steaming.   Steaming is a good technique for most vegetables: it reduces cooking time, but it can be easy to overcook vegetables. Be sure to follow a timing chart exactly. Pressure steamers have pressure settings of 5–15 psi. The higher the pressure, the quicker the vegetables will cook. For the best circulation of steam heat, use perforated pans in the steamer. To retain cooking liquid, use solid pans.

Table 19.5: How to Boil Vegetables

Covered	Uncovered
Fruits (except peppers)	Leaf
Roots (except turnips)	Seeds (except corn)
Tubers	Stems
	Flowers
	Bulbs
	All strong-flavored, dark greens

Caution! Before using the pressure steamer, be sure there is no steam pressure in the compartment from a previous batch. The gauge should tell you that there is no pressure. However, to be sure the gauge is not broken, open the steamer gradually before starting to cook.

Braising. To braise vegetables, cook slowly, covered, in a small amount of liquid. It is an especially good method for cooking soft vegetables such as mushrooms, potatoes, and summer squash. There are many ways to braise vegetables. Here are three steps common in braising:

1. Sauté vegetables such as celery, onions, cabbage, lettuce or peas in a small amount of fat until slightly cooked.
2. Add liquid such as stock, wine, or water. Finish cooking vegetables on the range top or in the oven.
3. Serve the flavorful cooking liquid with the vegetables.

Broiling. Broiling is a good technique for tender, moist vegetables. Broiling can also be a finishing process after using other cooking methods. For example, broil firm, dry vegetables after parboiling first. Broiling adds flavor and color to make vegetables more attractive. Examples of popular broiled items are tomatoes with bread crumb topping and vegetable casseroles topped with bread crumbs and cheese.

Deep Frying. Deep-fried vegetables are the most popular vegetable items on the commercial menu. French-fried potatoes and onion rings are the most common, but fried okra, zucchini, mushrooms, cauliflower, eggplant, and other vegetables are also gaining in popularity. The steps for deep frying vegetables are about the same as for meat and fish. Some good general rules to follow include:

- Cut vegetables into even-sized pieces so that they all cook in the same time.
- Partially cook hard vegetables before frying. Steaming and boiling are good partial cooking methods.
- If the vegetable will be breaded, add breading carefully. Pieces of breading can fall to the bottom of the fryer where they will burn.
- Bring the temperature of the fat or oil up to 325–375°F before adding vegetables.
- Fry small batches at a time. Overloading will prolong cooking time and result in a greasy, unevenly cooked product.
- Cook just to golden brown.

Pan Frying. Pan frying is a technique that is popular for many forms of potatoes. Cottage fries, hash browns, and potato pancakes are all pan fried. They are cooked in a fairly large amount of fat or oil for a long time. They can be cooked in a pan or on a griddle. Pan frying is also used for onions served with liver and mushrooms served with steak.

Sautéing. To sauté vegetables, cook small cut pieces in a small amount of fat for a short time. Many chefs toss vegetables in a pan over high heat. Stir frying is the Oriental version of sautéing. The chef stirs the vegetables quickly instead of moving the pan. A wok is the usual cooking pan. In sautéing or stir frying it is important to do a small amount of vegetables at a time. Overloading will cause the temperature to drop and the vegetables to become soggy.

Merchandising Vegetables. Take advantage of the naturally bright colors and many different shapes of vegetables on your menu. Serve them attractively and they will promote themselves. They will also make the entree more attractive. Season vegetables just enough to bring out natural flavors. Serve hot vegetables hot and cold vegetables cold. Use combinations of vegetables for maximum color, flavor, and texture variety.

Clockwise from upper left: Frozen hash browns, home fries, cottage fries, and patties are just a few of the many forms of potatoes on the commercial market. *Courtesy: J. R. Simplot.*

Potatoes.   Because we serve them in so many ways, it is possible to have potatoes every day, even at all three meals. They are high in carbohydrates, but also in vitamin C and iron if prepared in ways that do not lose these nutrients. Unpeeled potatoes are high in fiber, too. Potatoes are the most common starchy vegetable in this country.

Types of Potatoes.   There are two basic types of potatoes: mealy and waxy.

Mealy Potatoes.   Mealy potatoes are high in starch, and low in moisture and sugar. They seem dry when cooked. Varieties are 'Russets' or Idaho potatoes. They are best for French fries, mashed and baked potatoes.

Waxy Potatoes.   Waxy potatoes are lower in starch and higher in moisture and sugar than mealy potatoes. They hold their shapes well when cooked. They are the best for boiling to use for salads, soups, and hash browns. Because of their high sugar content, they are not good for deep frying. If fried, they may have poor texture and dark streaks.

Storing Potatoes.   Store potatoes in a cool, dry place (between 55 and 60°F). Store at room temperature if they will be used soon. It is not necessary to refrigerate potatoes.

Market Forms of Potatoes.   Potatoes come in four major market forms:

- Fresh.
- Frozen (precut in many shapes).
- Canned, whole.
- Dehydrated (to reconstitute as mashed, diced, flaked or sliced potatoes).

Cooking Methods for Potatoes.   Common cooking methods for potatoes are boiling, mashing, baking, pan frying, and deep frying.

Boiling.   Start potatoes in cold water and bring to a boil. This results in more even cooking and heat penetration. Do not cool potatoes in cold water. They will become soggy.

Mashing.   First, boil or steam potatoes. Then puree or beat until they are thoroughly mashed. Add butter and cream for smoothness and flavor. Good quality mashed potatoes are free of lumps, fluffy, and moist, hold their shape, and are creamy white, not gray in color. Mashed potatoes are used for whipped potatoes, duchess potatoes (with egg yolks added), and potato croquettes (deep-fried mashed potato balls).

Baked.   Select a starchy potato for this true American food. Scrub the skins and pierce so that steam can escape. You can wrap potatoes in foil to speed baking time. However, steam will not escape well and the potato can become too moist and soggy. For crisp skins, leave potatoes dry. Oil skins to make the baked skin more tender. Bake for 40–60 minutes (depending on the size of the potatoes.) The oven temperature should be around 400°F. When done, the potato will yield to pressure. The inside should be white, fluffy, steamy, and mealy (almost dry). Hold baked potatoes for no longer than 1 hour. For microwave baking, follow the instructions for the microwave you have.

Pan fried or sautéed. American Fries and home fries are examples of sautéed potatoes. They are potatoes cut into small pieces, mixed and tossed while cooking in a small amount of oil. Hash browns and potato pancakes are pan fried. They are browned in oil on both sides and served in one piece.

French fries. To prepare French fries from scratch, follow this three-step method:

1. Fry sliced potatoes at 300–325°F until slightly brown. This is called blanching in oil.
2. Remove from oil, drain, and refrigerate.
3. At serving time, fry at 350–375°F until golden brown and crisp.

For large-quantity cooking, this method is the only practical way. If an operator uses frozen French fries, the potatoes are already blanched. To serve, just do the final frying. No matter what the style or cut of French fries, the rules for quality are the same. They should be golden brown, thoroughly cooked, nongreasy, crisp on the outside, and tender on the inside.

Merchandising Potatoes. Perhaps no food merchandises itself better than the potato. Use the menu to describe a stuffed baked potato or crispy tender French fries. Garnish potatoes attractively and be sure the waiter and waitress can describe the varieties available.

20
Starches

Everyone expects to have a starch served with a main dish. Rice, pasta, and potatoes are almost as important as meat, poultry, and fish on the restaurant menu. We discussed potatoes in Chapter 19—now we shall look at rice and pasta.

Objectives and Terms

Objectives. This section should help you:

- Identify market forms of rice.
- Describe one method of cooking rice.
- List at least three types of pasta.
- Describe the preferred method of cooking pasta.

Terms to Know

Long-Grained Rice.   A variety of rice in which the kernels are long and thin. When cooked they separate easily.

Short-Grained Rice.   A variety of rice in which the kernels are short and thick. When cooked it becomes sticky and soggy.

Converted Rice.   Partly cooked or parboiled rice.

Wild Rice.   A marsh grass that looks like dark rice and is served as a starch.

Pasta.   A starch product made from durum wheat flour and water. Spaghetti, macaroni, and noodles are examples.

Rice is a popular alternative to potatoes on the typical American menu. It may be added to soups or served plain as an accompaniment for meat. It can also be an ingredient in baked dishes and desserts. However, in some parts of the world and in certain regions of this country, it is more traditional than the potato.

Market Forms of Rice.   Rice comes in many market forms:

Long-Grained Rice.   Long-grained rice makes a fluffy product. The grains separate easily. It is the best rice for entrees and side dishes.

Short-Grained Rice.   Short- or medium-grained rice is tender and moist. However, it is also sticky and soggy when cooked. The grains do not separate easily. It is best for rice puddings and molded rice dishes.

Enriched Rice.   Enriched rice is coated with vitamins and minerals. This is done to partly make up for some of the nutrients lost in the rice milling and polishing process.

A rice ring can be the base for many casserole-type dishes such as this one.
Courtesy: The Rice Council of America.

Table 20.1: Proportions of Rice and Water

Type of rice	Amount of rice	Amount of water
Regular (long-grain)	1 lb	1 qt
Parboiled	1 lb	4½ C
Short-grain	18 oz	1 qt

Converted Rice. Parboiled or converted rice is partially cooked. The grains stay firm and separate, and the rice holds well on a steam table. For this reason it is most often used in commercial foodservice. The rice has less flavor and texture than long-grain rice, but it does retain vitamins and minerals well.

Instant Rice. Instant rice is completely cooked and then dehydrated. It does not hold up well. It loses its shape and becomes mushy quickly. Although it has a very short cooking time, it is the most expensive type of rice.

Wild Rice. Wild rice is not rice at all—it is really a marsh grass from the Great Lakes region. It is hand harvested by Native Americans and is expensive. The strong, nutty flavor of wild rice goes well with wild game.

Cooking Rice. In general, never wash rice before or after cooking. It is already clean and washing will only flush away some of the nutrients. When cooked, rice increases in volume three times. Rice is always cooked in liquid, but there are three ways to do it.

Boiled Rice. Boil or steam rice on the range, in the oven, or in the steamer. The keys to success are the right proportion of rice to water and the right cooking time. Table 20.1 lists correct proportions.

Follow this procedure to boil rice on the range top or in the oven:

Recipe for boiled rice	
Rice	1 C
Salt	1 tsp
Water	2 C

To cook on top of the range add salt to the water and bring to a boil. Stir in the rice and bring the water back to the boiling point. Then lower the heat until the water is just bubbling. Cover tightly and cook gently for 20 minutes. Remove from heat and let stand for 10–15 minutes with the pan covered. Fluff the rice with a fork before serving.

For oven cooking, use the same proportions. Preheat oven to 350°F. Place the rice and salt in a casserole or pan. Pour boiling water over the rice. Stir and cover. Bake 30–35 minutes or until rice is tender.

The Pasta Method of Cooking Rice. Boil rice in a large amount of boiling water. Many nutrients are lost in the cooking water but the grains of rice stay separate and do not stick. This method is not the best but it is sometimes used for large quantities.

Pilaf Method. Sauté rice in fat or oil before adding liquid, if desired. Fat helps rice absorb the flavor ingredients and keeps grains separate. Cook rice, covered, in liquid seasoned with onions and herbs.

Pasta

There are dozens of kinds of pasta on the commercial market. Pasta is a dried, shaped mixture of wheat flour and water. Spaghetti and lasagna are varieties of pasta. Noodles include those same ingredients, plus eggs. Like rice, pasta is served as an alternative to potatoes on most menus. However, it is the standard starch in many specialty restaurants, especially Italian restaurants.

Pasta Quality. The finest pasta is made from durum wheat. It requires a longer cooking time than lower quality pasta. It absorbs more water and therefore swells in volume more than lower quality pasta. It also keeps its slightly firm texture longer.

Pasta Preparation. To prepare pasta, follow this procedure.

Boiled Pasta (4–5 cups cooked)	
Salt	1 tsp
Water	6 C
Pasta, uncooked	8 oz

1. Add salt to water. Bring water to a full boil.

2. Add pasta gradually to water so that boiling never stops. Spaghetti may stick out of the pan until it is softened enough to curl under the water.

3. Leave pan uncovered and stir occasionally to keep pasta from sticking and to keep pieces separated.

4. Cook pasta until just tender. Pasta should break cleanly and evenly when done. The Italian expression for the correct stage of doneness is *al dente,* or just slightly firm to the bite.

5. If the pasta will be held or refrigerated, rinse it in cold water. It can also be mixed with a small amount of fat or oil to keep pieces from sticking together.

Table 20.2 lists names of pasta and descriptions.

Tips for Producing Quality Pasta.   Do not overcook pasta. If it is too soft, it is not appetizing. If pasta will be mixed with other ingredients and cooked further, shorten the cooking time.

Good-quality pasta breaks easily and cleanly, is not sticky, and retains its shape.

Table 20.2: Pasta Kinds and Descriptions

Name	Description
Elbow	Tube shaped, small
Manicotti	Tube shaped, large, usually stuffed
Noodles	Wide, flat shaped
Fettucine	Narrow, flat shaped
Lasagna	Wide, flat, curly edges, layered with meat, cheese, or spinach
Spaghetti	Round, long
Linguini	Flat spaghetti
Vermicelli	Fine spaghetti

21
Eggs

Eggs may appear on the breakfast, lunch, or dinner menu. They are low in cost and always available. Since we use everything but the shell, there is very little waste.

Eggs are among our best sources of protein. You probably remember that protein is essential for building and repairing body tissue. Eggs contain high-quality, complete protein. Eggs are also a source of vitamin A, some B vitamins, fat, iron, and other minerals.

Objectives and Terms

Objectives. This section should help you:

- List ways eggs are used in food production.
- Describe eggs by size and grade.
- Tell how to store eggs correctly.
- List factors that affect coagulation of eggs.
- Describe how to make an egg foam.
- List correct methods for cooking eggs.
- Describe quality egg products.

Terms to Know

Yolk. The thick, yellow center part of the egg.

Albumin. The transparent (when raw) semiliquid part of the egg. It is also called the white because it turns white when cooked.

Egg Grades. Quality classifications of eggs based on height of the white when cracked out of the shell.

Egg Foam. A frothy, light mixture of air and beaten egg (any part.)

Coagulation. The setting or firming of protein, especially egg protein, by cooking or other means.

Poached Egg. An egg that is cooked gently in simmering water.

Omelet. A mixture of egg beaten with liquid and cooked in a thin layer.

Souffle. A mixture of an egg white foam, a sauce, and other flavor ingredients.

Custard. A combination of milk and eggs in which the protein is coagulated by heat. A custard can be liquid like a sauce (stirred) or slightly firm (baked).

All About Eggs

Composition of Eggs. The egg is made up of three parts: The yolk is yellow and thick and contains fat and protein. The white is mostly protein, called albumin. The outer shell is a fragile cover for the yolk and white. It is porous, which means it contains many holes that we cannot see. However, through these tiny holes moisture passes from the egg over time.

Egg Quality and Size. Egg grades give the buyer a good idea of the quality.

Grades. Eggs come in grades AA, A, B, and C. Grade AA is the highest. The grading system is based on the height of the white and cleanness and firmness of the yolk when broken out of a shell onto a flat surface. Grade AA has a much thicker white and firmer yolk than grades A and B. We use grade AA eggs for frying or poaching. Grade A eggs are fine for hard-cooked eggs, and grade B eggs are suitable in cooking and baking.

Size. Eggs come in sizes jumbo, extralarge, large, medium, small, and peewee.

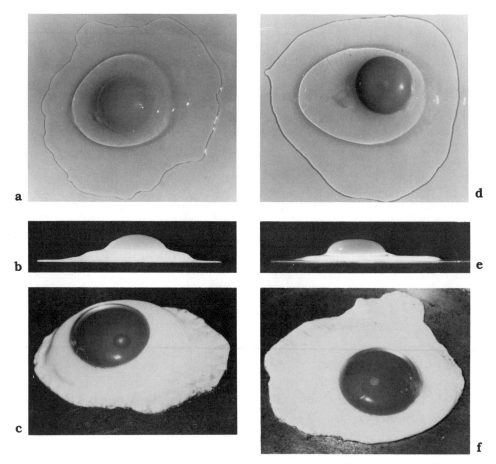

(a–c) Grade AA egg: (a) Uncooked. (b) Fried, side view. (c) Fried, top view. White is firm and stands high. Yolk is high. (d–f) Grade A egg: (d) uncooked. (e) Fried, side view. (f) Fried, top view. White is reasonably firm and stands fairly high. Yolk is high.

Courtesy: United States Department of Agriculture.

Table 21.1 shows the approximate number of whole eggs of different sizes to make a cupful. You can see that it takes more small eggs to make 1 cup of egg than large eggs. Table 21.2 is a guide for using whole eggs in recipes. It lists the volume of egg that results from eggs of different sizes. This information is useful in following recipes that call for eggs by volume.

Table 21.1: Number of Eggs Needed to Make 1 Cup

Egg size	Whole eggs	Whites	Yolks
Small	7	10	18
Medium	6	8	16
Large	5	7	14
Extralarge	4	6	12

Source: USDA Home and Garden Bulletin *103*.

Storing Eggs.   To maintain the quality of eggs, store them in containers, at temperatures of 36–40°F. If held at room temperature, eggs will lose quality. Because eggs absorb other flavors, store them away from strong-flavored foods.

Market Forms of Eggs.   In this discussion we shall be talking about fresh eggs most of the time, but there are other forms on the market:

Fresh, Frozen, and Dried Eggs.   Fresh eggs come in cases of 30 dozen. Frozen eggs come in a variety of sizes ranging from 1-pt cardboard containers to 30-lb cans. They are used in

Table 21.2: Guide for Estimating Number of Eggs
to Use in Recipes

Large	Extralarge	Medium	Small	Approximate volume
1	1	1	1	3 T
2	2	2	3	¼ C + 2 T
3	3	4	4	½ C + 2 T
4	3	5	6	¾ C + 1 T
5	4	6	7	1 C
6	5	7	8	1 C + 3 T
8	6	10	11	1½ C + 2 T
10	8	12	14	2 C
12	10	14	17	2¼ C + 2 T

Source: USDA Home and Garden Bulletin *103*.

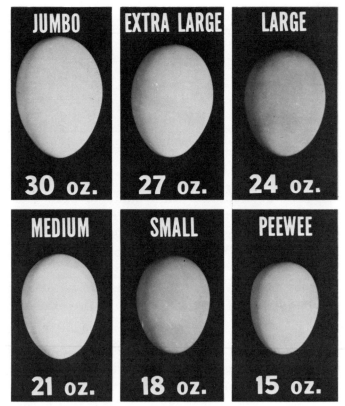

Eggs come in these six sizes.
Courtesy: United States Department of Agriculture.

scrambled eggs, omelets, and bakeries. They must be stored at 0°F or lower and are thawed under cold running water. Dried eggs come in the form of dried whole eggs, dried yolks, and dried whites. Dried eggs are used mostly in bakery products. One pound of dried eggs equals about 30–40 large eggs. When dried eggs are mixed with water, they should be used within 1 hour.

Convenience Egg Products. Food technologists are bringing us new egg products every day. Some of the varieties available are the egg roll (a long roll of cooked white and cooked yolk that can be sliced into many equal slices), boil-in-the-bag

Table 21.3: Egg Characteristics and Food Uses

Characteristic	Example
Coagulate	Cooked eggs; clarify consomme
Thicken	Custard
Bind and coat	Meatloaf; egg dip before breading
Whipped to foam	Meringue; souffle
Emulsifying agent	Hollandaise; mayonnaise

scrambled eggs, precooked omelets (frozen and ready for heating before serving), and frozen poached eggs.

Eggs in Food Preparation. Eggs have many characteristics that we use in food preparation. They coagulate, form foams, emulsify mixtures, thicken mixtures, and bind ingredients together among other things. Table 21.3 lists some uses of eggs based on these characteristics.

Egg Coagulation. Coagulation is one of the major characteristics we shall look at. Eggs contain the protein called albumin. When albumin is cooked it coagulates, which means it becomes thicker and firmer and loses its transparency. It changes from a semiliquid to a solid state and becomes white in color. The basic purpose of any kind of egg cookery is to coagulate egg without overcooking. Overcooking makes egg protein tough and rubbery. Table 21.4 lists temperatures of coagulation for eggs.

Table 21.4: Temperatures at Which Eggs Coagulate

Egg	Temperature of coagulation (°F)
Whole	156
Yolks	144–158
Whites	140–149
Custard (egg plus liquid)	175–185

Factors that affect egg coagulation.   Some procedures that we use in cooking have an effect on the coagulation of egg in products. When eggs are mixed with sugar, the coagulation temperature rises and the eggs do not cook as quickly. That is why the coagulation temperature for a custard (eggs, sugar, and milk) is higher than for eggs alone.

Adding acid to an egg mixture results in a more tender egg product. Some common food acids are cream of tartar, lemon juice, and tomato juice. Hollandaise is a smooth, creamy sauce made from egg yolks and lemon juice.

Cooking eggs at high temperatures makes them tough and develops a strange flavor.

Egg Foams.   Now we shall look at the foaming ability of eggs. When you beat an egg, you make a foam of air bubbles and egg. It can be a foam of the whole beaten egg, the beaten yolk, or the beaten white. Beaten whites make the highest foams. Remember these important principles in the foaming or beating of eggs:

1.   Egg whites will not foam to their maximum height if there is fat in the mixture. Since egg yolks contain fat, be careful not to mix any yolk in an egg white foam. Be very careful that equipment is clean and free of fat.

2.   Eggs foam best when they are slightly warm—between 75 and 110°F.

3.   Salt in the mixture helps make the foam more stable (last longer).

4.   Acid in the mixture helps to tenderize foam and make the eggs more stable. Lemon juice or cream of tartar added to an egg white foam makes it higher and makes it last longer.

5.   Sugar gives a foam stability. The foam will hold up longer than one in which there is no sugar added.

6.   Overbeating causes bubbles to dry and stretch too thin. That will make the foam break down. It is important in beating egg foams to beat just enough, but not too much.

Methods of Cooking Eggs.   The most common methods of preparing eggs as menu items are "boiling" (cooking), frying, scrambling, poaching, or using in omelets, souffles, and custards.

FOAMY WHITES   SOFT PEAKS   STIFF PEAKS

Recipes may call for egg whites beaten to the foamy stage, to soft peaks, or to stiff peaks.

"Boiled" or Cooked Eggs. We speak of boiling eggs in the shell, but we mean simmering eggs. As we have already said, overcooking damages egg protein. Boiling will make eggs tough and rubbery. To cook eggs in the shell follow one of these three different methods:

1. Let eggs stand at room temperature for a while. Cold eggs may crack if they go directly into boiling water. Bring the water to a boil and add the eggs carefully. Bring the water only to the simmering point and cook for the right length of time:

Soft cooked: 3–5 minutes
Medium cooked: 7 minutes
Hardcooked: 15–20 minutes.

Drain hot water and cover eggs with cool water. This will stop the cooking. Peel eggs from the large end—that is where the air space is. It makes peeling easier. If the egg sticks to the shell, run under cool water. Refrigerate eggs until time to use them.

2. Place eggs in cold water. Bring the water to a boil. Reduce water to a simmer and cook eggs half the time listed in method 1.

3. Place eggs in water and bring to a boil. Then remove from heat and let stand for 20 minutes.

Tip: How to tell if an egg is cooked or raw. A cooked egg will spin smoothly; a raw egg wobbles.

Quality standards for cooked eggs. The white of the egg should be evenly coagulated and not rubbery. There should be a clear, shiny color with no dark ring around the yolk. If you want to stuff or slice eggs, cook them slightly longer than the hard-cooking point. They will hold up better.

Fried Eggs.   Fried eggs are cooked in a small amount of fat in a fry pan. They are usually fried to the customer's order and served at once. For fat use butter, bacon fat, or margarine. Margarine produces the best color and the best overall results. The most common types of fried eggs are:

Over easy.   The egg is cooked almost to done on one side, then turned over to cook the top partly.

Sunnyside up.   The egg is fried on one side until cooked to the desired stage. It is not turned over.

Basted.   A true basted egg is basted with fat while frying. It is common practice to cover the fry pan and partly cook the egg in steam.

Quality standards for fried eggs.   The white of a good fried egg is shiny and uniformly set and tender, not brown and hard. The yolk is set to the customer's request. It may be runny to firm. A sunnyside-up egg yolk is barely set. It is yellow and round. Other types should have a thin layer of coagulated white over the yolk. A fried egg should stand high and be compact. It should not be thin or spread out.

Poached Eggs.   Poached eggs are cooked, unshelled, in hot water. To poach an egg, select only the freshest eggs that are grade A or AA. Special pans for poaching eggs have small compartments over the water-holding section. Grease the compartments well before using. This will help the eggs slide out easily when they are cooked. You can also use a nonstick pan.

Fill the poaching pan with water to the level indicated. If you use a plain small frypan, fill it with less than ½ inch of water. The recipe you use may call for salt or vinegar in the water. Vinegar helps to coagulate the egg. Salt will help to raise the water's boiling point a little higher—this will cook the egg faster than plain water. Bring water in the pan to a boil and remove from the heat source. Gently slide egg out of the shell into the water. If you

use a poacher with comparments, put one egg in each compartment. Return pan to heat. Keep water at the simmer point for 3–5
minutes, depending on the hardness desired.

Quality standards for poached eggs. The egg should be compact, round, tightly bunched, and not spread out. The white
should be bright white, not porous and dull looking. The yolk
should be high and slightly liquid.

Scrambled Eggs. Scrambled eggs are a mixture of eggs and
milk. They are the easiest type of eggs to prepare for very large
groups, but they are best cooked to order in small batches. If you
plan to cook a large batch to hold in a steam table pan, slightly
undercook the eggs. They will continue cooking in the steam
table. If you will be holding the eggs for longer than 30 minutes on
the line, mix a small amount of medium white sauce into eggs.
Overcooked scrambled eggs will be tough and watery. (They may
even turn slightly green when the compound iron sulfide begins
to form.) The same thing can happen if you hold them on a steam
table for too long.

Quality standards for scrambled eggs. Good scrambled eggs
should be:

- Tender and soft.
- Moist, not dry with water pooled at the pan bottom.
- Delicate in texture.

Omelets. Like scrambled eggs, omelets are made from a
basic mixture of eggs and liquid. They look quite different, however. To make a good omelet, you will need high heat and a
sloping sided pan that is well conditioned (coated with oil).

To cook a plain omelet, pour the egg mixture into a hot pan and
spread the mixture around by tipping the pan. Then cook just
until the egg sets in a solid thin sheet that is slightly browned or
tan on the bottom. The omelet should be nicely shaped so that
you can roll it, perhaps with a filling.

To make a foamy omelet, beat the yolks and whites separately,
and then fold together. Cook on the range until the bottom is set
and finish cooking the top of the omelet in the oven.

Quality standards for omelets.   An omelet should be moist, tender, and delicate in flavor. Its appearance should be light brown on the outside and moist inside.

Souffles.   A souffle can be a main dish or a dessert. There are three basic parts in every souffle:

1.   Sauce—often this is a Bechamel sauce with egg yolks added.

2.   Flavor ingredient—cheese is common but it may be a vegetable or seafood. Flavor ingredients in dessert souffles can be chocolate, strawberry, or other dessert-type flavors.

3.   Egg whites, beaten.

Quality standards of souffles.   A souffle should be slightly rounded on top. It can be cracked and should be puffy. The souffle should be delicate brown in color.

Popular breakfast items include cooked eggs (top left), scrambled eggs (top right), poached eggs (lower left), and fried eggs (lower right).
Courtesy: American Egg Board.

Custard. A custard is a combination of milk and eggs in which the protein is set by heat. There are entree custards, such as corn pudding, and sweetened dessert custards. Two basic types of custards are:

1. Stirred custard—the milk and egg mixture is stirred gently as it cooks. The custard stays semiliquid and can be poured over cakes or other foods.

2. Baked custard—after milk is mixed with eggs, the mixture is baked until it "sets."

Caution: Do not bake custard to an internal temperature higher than 185°F or it will curdle and become watery.

Quality standards for custards. A stirred custard should be smooth with no lumps. Baked custard should have a tender, tight texture, but it should not be watery. Flavor should be uniform throughout the product.

Merchandising Eggs. Since eggs are so versatile, the foodservice operator can merchandise them in many ways. Restaurants that serve breakfast often use colorful menu insert photos to show popular breakfast plates. For the luncheon menu, they use appealing terms to describe a variety of omelets.

22
Dairy Products

Objectives and Terms

Objectives. This section should help you:

- List three important nutrients contributed by milk.
- List three different types of milk or dairy products.
- List conditions that cause milk to curdle.
- Describe natural cheese.
- Describe processed cheese.
- List examples of unripened and ripened natural cheese.
- Describe the correct method for storing cheese.
- Describe correct cooking procedures for cheese.

Terms to Know

Butterfat (Milkfat). Fat in milk and milk products.

Skim Milk. Milk from which fat is removed.

Nonfat Dry Milk. Product made by removing nearly all water from skim milk.

Yogurt. A sour, semisolid product made by adding a special bacteria culture to milk.

Buttermilk. A sour, thick liquid product made by adding a special bacteria culture to milk.

Evaporated Milk. Milk with half the water evaporated.

Cream. A product of milk that contains 18–30% milkfat.

Rennet. An enzyme used in cheesemaking. Rennet comes from the lining of the stomachs of ruminant animals.

Curds.   The semisolid particles formed when milk is made into cheese.

Curdling.   The formation of semisolid particles from milk due to heat, acid, or the addition of certain bacteria or other ingredients.

Whey.   The liquid left when curds are formed from milk in cheesemaking.

Natural Cheese.   Cheese that is produced by coagulating milk. It may or may not be pressed or ripened.

Process Cheese.   A blend of natural cheeses that is heated.

Process Cheese Food.   A blend of natural cheeses that includes nonfat dry milk or whey solids and water. It contains less natural cheese than process cheese.

Coldpack Cheese.   A mixture of two or more natural cheeses blended without heating.

Milk and Cream

Milk is the first dairy product. From milk comes cream, lowfat milk, powdered milk, ice cream, and a wide variety of cheese. All of these products are important in the foodservice industry. Milk and its products are served as they are or they are used in preparing many recipes.

Nutrients in Milk.   Milk is a good source of complete protein. It contains all of the essential amino acids we need to make body protein. Milk is an excellent source of the minerals calcium and phosphorous. We need these minerals to build bones and teeth. Milk is also a good source of the water-soluble vitamin riboflavin, which is important in converting carbohydrates to energy.

Milk, as it comes from the cow, contains over 3% fat (called butterfat or milkfat.) Some milk products contain lots of fat. Butter and whipping cream are examples. Others, such as cheese, ice cream, and homogenized whole milk, also contain some fat. Milk is a fair source of the fat-soluble vitamin A, but it is common practice in the dairy business to fortify milk with standard amounts of vitamins A and D. Vitamin A is important for growth, for healthy

Milk, cheese, yogurt, ice cream, cottage cheese, cream, and butter are all dairy products. They are important in the foodservice industry.
Courtesy: American Dairy Association.

breathing and eating tracts, and for night vision. Vitamin D helps our bodies make use of calcium and phosphorus to make bone and teeth.

Milk and Its Products.   Now we shall discuss some of the types of milk and milk products.

Milk.   Whole milk is the fluid that comes from the cow. However, we do not usually drink it as it is—dairies first treat it with heat. This process, called pasteurization, kills common bacteria that can grow in milk. If dairies did not pasteurize milk, it would not keep as long as it does.

Whole milk will separate into two parts if it stands for awhile. The lighter cream or fat will float to the top and the nonfat part of the milk will go to the bottom. To make a uniform product, dairy processors homogenize milk. A special machine mixes the milk and fat so thoroughly that cream no longer floats to the top. This homogenization process keeps milk from separating even after it sits on the refrigerator shelf for several days.

Skim milk and low-fat milk. To make skim milk, the processor separates the fat or cream from milk. The remaining milk is pasteurized and packaged. Low-fat milk is made by removing about half of the fat that is naturally present in milk. Then the milk is pasteurized and homogenized before packaging. Whole milk contains about 3.25% butterfat; low-fat milk contains 0.5–2% butterfat; skim milk contains almost no fat (0.5%).

Evaporated milk. Evaporated milk is made by evaporating half of the water in whole milk. Condensed milk is a mixture of evaporated milk and sugar.

Nonfat dry milk. Nonfat dry milk is a powder made by removing nearly all the water from skim milk.

Yogurt and Buttermilk. Yogurt and buttermilk are cultured milk products, which means that a special kind of bacteria is added to milk and allowed to change the milk. Yogurt becomes sour and semisolid. Buttermilk takes on a slightly sour taste and becomes a thick liquid.

Cream. Three types of cream are common in the foodservice industry. The first is regular cream, or coffee cream. It contains 18% milkfat or butterfat. Half and half is a mixture of one-half whole milk (about 3.25% butterfat) and one-half regular cream (18% butterfat). Whipping cream contains between 30 and 40% butterfat. Besides these basic cream products, there are cultured products. Sour cream, for example, is a cultured product made from regular cream with a bacteria culture added to produce a sour flavor and thickness.

Ice Cream, Ice Milk, and Sherbet. Ice cream is a frozen dessert made from cream, milk, sweeteners, and flavorings. It contains at least 10% milkfat. Ice milk is made from milk, sweeteners, and flavorings. It contains 2–7% milkfat. Sherbet must contain 1–2% milkfat.

Purchasing Dairy Products. To help the consumer buy good milk products, the USDA has developed a set of quality grades.

Grades help the consumer to identify quality dairy products. (a) The U.S. Extra Grade shield is used on nonfat dry milk. (b) Butter and cheddar cheese of the highest quality are marked with the AA shield. (c) The Quality Approved shield appears on cottage cheese, process cheese, and sour cream that are of good quality and produced in a clean plant. *Courtesy: United States Department of Agriculture.*

They ensure that the product is packaged under wholesome conditions. Grades for cheddar cheese and butter indicate quality of flavor and texture.

What Causes Milk to Curdle? Milk separates or curdles for many reasons:

Acid. If milk is mixed with wine, lemon juice, tomato juice, or vinegar, the acid will cause the milk to curdle.

Tannins. A group of chemicals present in vegetables such as asparagus and potatoes, when mixed with milk, cause it to curdle.

Salt. Cured meat mixed with milk can cause the milk to curdle.

Heat. Overcooking milk can produce curdling, scorching, and a surface scum.

Hard water. If coffee and tea are made with hard water, milk can curdle when added to the beverages.

How to Prevent Curdling. Avoid curdling milk by following these practices:
- Cook milk mixtures over low heat.
- Add salt just before serving.
- Add acid ingredient last.
- Add starch to the milk—it will stabilize the mixture.
- Add a small amount of hot liquid to milk before blending in the rest of the milk.

How to Prevent Scorching and Surface Scum. Follow correct procedures to avoid scorching milk or forming a scum.

Scorching. Scorching is the quick coagulation of a thin layer of protein on the bottom of a pan on direct heat. Scorching produces a burned flavor and a brown to black color in the milk. To avoid scorching, cook milk mixtures in a double boiler or steam-jacketed kettle and stir constantly while cooking.

Scum or Skin. Milk can also coagulate at the surface when cooking. This thin scum or skin is also coagulated protein. It is produced by contact of heated milk with air. To prevent a skin from forming, cover the pan or add a small amount of fat.

Foams from Milk Products.   Milk and cream have the ability to foam just as eggs do. The combination of fat and protein make this foaming possible. Milk products with a high fat content foam better than low-fat milk products. The best foams come from cream with 30% or more butterfat. This is known as whipping cream.

How to Whip Cream.   For the best results, use cold ingredients and chill the whipping attachment of the mixer. Then follow these steps:

1.   Do not sweeten the cream until it is whipped almost to the point desired. Adding sugar too soon makes the foam less stable. Use powdered sugar for a fine-textured whipped cream.
2.   Do not overwhip. Whip just until soft peaks form. If stiff peaks develop, the cream will turn to butter soon.
3.   If cream is to be folded into other ingredients, underwhip slightly.
4.   Use a deep bowl to incorporate a lot of air into the foam.

Cheese

How Is Cheese Made?   Cheese is a product of milk. The milk can come from any animal, but it is usually cow's milk. Cheese is made by deliberately curdling milk. This is done by adding a bacteria culture that causes milk to curdle or by adding rennet, an enzyme that produces curdling in milk. Rennet comes from stomach linings of animals with many stomachs (ruminants).

As the curdling proceeds, milk forms solid curds and a watery substance called whey. The curd is then heated and stirred. Fresh soft curds are known as cottage cheese. If that same cheese is pressed and ripened or aged, it loses moisture. In the process, the cheese becomes heavy and dense, with a characteristic flavor. High temperatures harden the cheese.

Cheese is a popular sandwich ingredient in commercial foodservice operations. *Courtesy: American Dairy Association.*

Kinds of Cheese. The two main types of cheese are natural cheese and processed cheese.

Natural Cheese. Natural cheese is block cheese that is shaped and pressed and may be aged or ripened for a period of time. It comes in many varieties. The kind depends on the kind of bacteria culture used to curdle the milk and the conditions used in ripening. Swiss, cheddar, gouda, and edam are examples of natural cheeses. They are usually aged for several months. Table 22.1 lists natural cheeses and their characteristics.

Process Cheese. Process cheeses are pasteurized blends of fresh and aged natural cheeses. Pasteurization stops aging. Process cheeses have a mild flavor and are soft and smooth. The price is lower than the price of natural cheese. Process cheese comes packaged in slices and loaves. It keeps and melts well.

Process Cheese Food. Process cheese food is similar to process cheese. However, process cheese food contains less cheese and has nonfat dry milk or whey solids and water added. Process cheese spreads contain even more moisture and less milkfat than cheese food.

Table 22.1: Natural Cheeses and Their Characteristics

Kind/name	Flavor, age	Body, color	Uses
Soft, unripened (not aged)			
Cottage	Mild, acid	Soft, curd particles, white	Salads, dips, cheesecake
Cream	Mild, acid	Soft, smooth, white	Salads, dips, snacks, desserts
Ricotta (Italy)	Sweet, nutlike	Soft, moist/dry, white	Appetizers, salads, ravioli, lasagne, desserts
Firm, unripened (not aged)			
Mozzarella (Italy)	Delicate	Slightly firm, plastic, creamy white	Snacks, sandwiches, pizza, lasagna, casseroles
Soft, ripened			
Brie (France)	Mild to pungent, ripened 4–8 weeks	Soft, smooth when ripe, creamy yellow-white crust	Appetizers, with crackers or fruit as dessert
Camembert (France)	Mild to pungent, ripened 4–8 weeks	Soft, smooth when ripe, creamy yellow-white crust	Appetizers, with fruit as dessert
Semisoft, ripened			
Brick (U.S.)	Mild to moderately sharp, ripened 2–4 months	Medium firm, elastic, many small holes	Sandwiches, appetizers, dessert
Muenster (Germany)	Mild to mellow, ripened 1–8 weeks	Semisoft, many small holes, moist	Appetizers, sandwiches, dessert

Kind	Flavor and aging	Appearance	Uses
Firm, ripened			
Cheddar (England)	Mild to very sharp, aged 1–12 months	Firm, smooth, some openings, white to orange	Sandwiches, sauces, in hot dishes, desserts
Colby (U.S.)	Mild to mellow, aged 1–3 months	Softer than cheddar	Sandwiches, snacks
Edam (Netherlands)	Mellow, nutlike, aged 2–3 months	Semisoft to firm, creamy yellow to orange, red wax coating	Appetizers, snacks, salads, desserts
Gouda (Netherlands)	Mellow, nutlike, aged 2–6 months	Semisoft to firm, smooth small holes, yellow to orange	Appetizers, salads, snacks, seafood, sauces
Provolone (Italy)	Mellow to sharp, smoky, salty, aged 2–12 months	Firm, smooth, light creamy inside, light brown outside	Sandwiches, appetizers, can be grated if dried
Swiss	Sweet, nutlike, aged 3–9 months	Firm, smooth, large round eyes, yellow	Sandwiches, snacks, fondue, sauces
Very hard ripened			
Parmesan (Italy)	Sharp, piquant, aged 14–24 months	Very hard, granular, creamy white to light brown	Grated on pasta, vegetables, pizza
Blue-vein mold ripened			
Bleu	Tangy, peppery, aged 2–6 months	Semisoft, pasty, white with blue-vein mold	Appetizers, salads, dips, sandwich spread, dessert
Roquefort (France)	Sharp, faintly peppery, aged 2–5 months	Semisoft, pasty, white with blue-vein mold	Appetizers, snacks, dips, salads, spread, dessert

Source: Adapted from USDA H&G Bulletin 193, How to Buy Cheese.

Among the popular natural cheeses on the market are (clockwise from top left) gouda, edam, muenster, bleu, white cheddar, yellow cheddar, colby, cheddar slices, provolone, parmesan, and swiss.
Courtesy: American Dairy Association.

Coldpack Cheese. Coldpack cheese (or club cheese) is a blend of fresh and aged natural cheeses. It is different from process cheese because the blending is done mechanically, without heating the cheese. Coldpack cheese food has other ingredients added. Popular coldpack cheese foods contain pimentos, fruit, vegetables, or meats. Some have a smoked flavor.

Uses of Cheese. Cheese is a nutritious and versatile food. In main dishes it is popular as fondue, as souffle, in omelets, and on pizza. It is also a favorite in salads and salad dressings. Cheese is a popular snack food, especially when served with crackers or in spreads and dips. Favorite hot and cold sandwiches are made with cheese. Cheese desserts include cheesecake, cheese pies, and plain sliced cheese with fruit. In addition, cheese is also a garnish or an ingredient in binders, sauces, and toppings.

Handling and Storing Cheese. Refrigerate all cheese. Firmer cheese holds better than soft varieties. Soft cheese will spoil if not used within a short time. Ripened cheese keeps for a few weeks in the refrigerator. Store cheese, tightly wrapped, in the refrigerator until shortly before serving. For best flavor, serve cheese at room temperature. If there is a small amount of mold on the outside of the cheese, simply cut it off before serving.

Cooking Cheese. Natural cheese will become stringy if it is not properly cooked. To avoid this problem, cook cheese correctly:

- Use low temperatures (125°F). Never boil cheese mixtures.
- Cook cheese for a short time if possible. If you are making a sauce, add the cheese at the end of the cooking time.
- Grate cheese before cooking. It will melt evenly.
- Cook just until melted.
- Combine cheese with other ingredients such as milk or soup to help prevent stringiness.

Merchandising Cheese. Use the right cheese for the menu item. Select a flavorful natural cheese for slicing in sandwiches. Use a smooth, rich cheese in sauces. For grated cheese topping and as a salad ingredient, select a mildly tangy natural cheese. Do not settle for one processed cheese for all menu items.

Use the menu to describe cheeses used. Or feature a menu enclosure that describes all cheeses on the menu. Commodity groups such as The American Dairy Association may provide promotional material on cheese. Inform all waiters and waitresses of the kinds of cheese used so that they can inform the customer and help sell products.

23
The Bakery—Bread

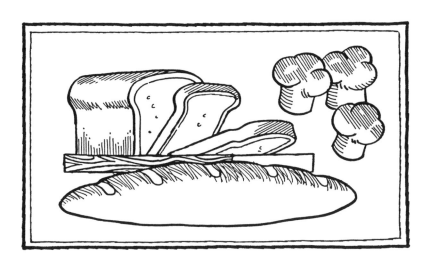

Very few foodservice operations today have a full-time baker. Most operators have turned to readymade or convenience baked goods. In this chapter, we shall review some of the basics of baking. We do not expect you to become a prize-winning baker, but it is important for a well-trained foodservice worker to understand the fundamentals. They apply to all baked products: breads or desserts.

Objectives and Terms

Objectives. This section should help you:

- List the principles of successful baking.
- Describe ingredients used in baking and their effects.
- Describe three types of wheat flour.
- Describe the functions of ingredients in bread.
- List steps in making yeast breads.
- List steps in making quickbreads.
- Describe quality characteristics of biscuits and muffins.

Terms to Know

Gluten Formation. The development of an elastic protein network from the protein in flour.

Browning. Development of brown or golden color on the surface of baked products.

340

Bread Flour.   Flour made from wheat that contains lots of wheat protein. It develops much gluten when mixed with liquid.

Cake Flour.   Flour made from wheat that contains little wheat protein. It develops little gluten when mixed with liquid.

Shortening.   Fat that is solid at room temperature. It is used in baking.

Leavening Agents.   An ingredient in baked goods that helps introduce air or gas into the mixture to raise the product.

Creaming.   Whipping fat and sugar together with air trapped in the mixture.

Baking Soda.   A chemical leavening agent that releases gas when mixed with acid ingredients.

Baking Powder.   A chemical leavening agent that does not require acid to produce gas.

Yeast.   A single-cell plant that multiplies rapidly in warmth and moisture to produce gas for raising dough.

Yeast Bread.   Bread made with yeast as the leavening agent.

Sponge Method.   A method of mixing yeast bread ingredients in which a little flour is mixed with liquid and yeast before adding the balance of flour.

Quickbreads.   Breads and other flour products made by leavening dough with chemical leavening agents.

Benching Dough.   Allowing dough to rest before shaping. This allows gluten to relax.

Proofing Dough.   Placing yeast dough in a warm place so that yeast will multiply and form gas, which causes dough to rise.

Muffin Method.   Mixing method for quickbreads in which liquid ingredients are added all at once to blended dry ingredients. There is little mixing.

Biscuit Method.   Mixing method for quickbreads in which shortening is cut into flour until the mixture is crumbly. Liquid is then added and the mixture is kneaded slightly.

Principles of Baking

Measuring.   The most important principle in baking is measuring correctly. Baked goods have so few ingredients that a slight mistake can ruin the finished product. To measure correctly, weigh ingredients. Weights are far more accurate than volume measures. Weigh everything except water, milk, and eggs. An easy rhyme that will help you remember the correct measure of liquids is "A pint a pound the world around."

Right Ingredients. It is extremely important to use the right ingredients for baked products. Do not substitute unless the recipe gives you examples of substitutions.

Gas Formation. Bakers use some type of gas-producing ingredient in all baked products. Gas bubbles give bakery products the light texture that makes people like them. Gas can come from yeast, from baking powder, even from mixing air into the batter. In some products, gas is not formed until the product bakes.

Gluten Formation. Gluten is the protein in flour. It gives structure to baked products. Cakes have very little gluten structure. Yeast breads contain a strong gluten network. The amount of moisture and the mixing method both affect how much or how little gluten is developed in a product.

Moisture. Moisture either toughens or tenderizes dough, depending on how much is added. Some baked goods require very little moisture in the recipe. Piecrust, for example, calls for just a few tablespoons of water. The resulting product is a very tender crust.

Mixing. The more the baker mixes the dough, the more gluten is developed in the dough. High amounts of gluten make a very elastic dough. Bread dough is an example. On the other hand, the baker mixes cakes and muffins very little. The goal for those products is a nonelastic tender crumb that comes from developing very little gluten.

Browning. Heat causes the typical ingredients in baked goods to change color. This color change is what gives bakery goods a characteristic brown crust. Browning also adds flavor. Sugar, starch (flour), and protein are the ingredients that cause these changes.

Heat Coagulation.   Heating coagulates gluten and egg protein. Different temperatures result in coagulation at different times. The results are different types of products. In baking cream puffs, for example, an extremely high temperature would split the crust. A low temperature would make the puffs collapse. The goal is a temperature hot enough to puff the shells without destroying them.

Ingredients and Their Effects

Baked products normally include flour, fat, sugar, leavening agents, egg. liquid, salt, flavors, and spices. Each ingredient has a role to play in the kind of product the baker turns out.

Flour.   The main ingredient in baked goods is flour. Wheat flour is the most common type. However, some recipes call for rye, oats or even corn flour.

Wheat Flour.   Wheat flour contains starch and protein (the part that forms gluten.) Among the varieties available are

Hard-wheat flour.   Hard wheat is "strong" or high in protein.

Soft-wheat flour.   Soft wheat is "weak" or low in protein.

Bread flour.   Bread flour is made from strong wheat that results in high gluten development. It is used for bread and rolls.

Cake flour.   Cake flour is made from a soft, weak wheat used especially for delicate cakes.

Pastry flour.   Pastry flour is a variety that is between cake and bread flour in the amount of gluten it can develop. It is used for cookies, piecrusts, biscuits, and muffins.

All-purpose flour.   All-purpose flour is a combination of 20% cake flour and 80% bread flour. It is the most popular variety for the home consumer. However, professional bakers do not use all-purpose flour. Remember to use the exact specified ingredient.

Rye Flour.   Rye flour comes in light, medium, and dark brown. Because rye flour will not develop gluten by itself, it should be mixed with some wheat flour for bread.

Whole Wheat Flour. Millers grind whole kernels of wheat for this product. The outer bran and germ of each grain are included. Whole wheat flour can develop gluten, but to keep the bread from being too heavy, white flour is sometimes added. Whole wheat flour is higher in fat than white flour and therefore has a shorter storage life than white flour. It needs to be refrigerated.

Fat. Shortening, margarine, oil, lard, and butter are the most common fats. They are used to:

- Add tenderness and richness.
- Improve flavor.
- Help the leavening process.
- Improve keeping qualities.
- Make the grain distinct and the texture tender.
- Make a flaky product (piecrust).
- Add moisture or hold moisture as an emulsifier.

Types of Fats in Baking. There are four types of fats:

Hydrogenated vegetable shortening. This colorless, flavorless shortening has very desirable characteristics for baking. It is plastic, pliable, and holds the shape of the dough. It is used for many purposes. It melts only at high temperatures.

Butter or margarine. Flavor is an advantage that butter and margarine have. They also get soft at room temperature. However, they are not as pliable as shortening and are hard to handle in doughs.

Lard. Lard is fat rendered from animals. It is very plastic and has a distinct flavor. It was a traditional favorite in pie doughs of the past. However, many bakers have turned to hydrogenated vegetable shortenings.

Vegetable oils. Oils are liquid at room temperature and are used mostly in breads and rolls. They are not popular for cake batters because they spread through batter too thoroughly. There are some cake recipes, however, that do call for oil. These are high-liquid, sponge cakes.

Sugars.   In addition to adding sweetness and flavor, sugars have these important characteristics:

- They help yeast to grow.
- They help the creaming and whipping processes.
- They add fineness of texture to baked goods.
- They add tenderness to the grain of baked goods.
- They help hold moisture and prolong freshness.
- They help develop crust color.
- They add energy value or calories.

Types of Sugars.   We usually think of sugar as that white granular stuff, but that is actually just one of many kinds.

Granulated sugar.   The most common type of sugar for baking, granulated sugar is popular for cakes and cookies. It makes a uniform batter and supports high quantities of fat.

Powdered sugar.   Also known as confectioners sugar, it is used mostly in icing and in some cakes. Confectioners sugar comes in many degrees of fineness. The classification 4× is used for dusting and is the most coarse. The finest type, 10×, is used for fine icing. The most common type, 6×, is used for a variety of icings and toppings.

Brown sugar.   Light or dark brown sugar adds a rich color and special flavor to bakery. It also makes products more moist than white sugar.

Molasses.   Molasses is a syrup left in vats after white and brown sugar are refined from cane sugar. Molasses has a rich, heavy flavor. Color varies from light to dark. Molasses adds moisture and helps keep freshness.

Honey.   Honey is a sugar syrup produced by bees from nectar. Honey has a distinct flavor and color. It is expensive and is used for special baked products.

Leavening Agents.   Whether it is baking powder, yeast, or egg foam, the effect of a leavening agent is to mix air into a product. Air cells in baked dough or batter give baked goods their texture and lightness. The goal of the baker is to use just the right amount of leavening. Too little will make a product that is heavy, coarse, and tight. Too much leavening results in a product that is crumbly and open.

Air Leavening.   There are two ways to incorporate air into a batter.

Foaming.   Eggs are whipped or beaten to form a foam. Flour is blended with the foam. Angel food cake is an example in which egg whites form the foam. In a sponge cake, we use whole eggs. In both cases, the leavening agent is air trapped inside the bubbles.

Creaming.   When fat and sugar are whipped together, air is trapped throughout the mixture. This process is called creaming. It is the method used in cake and cookie making.

Steam.   Popovers, cream puffs, piecrust, and puff pastry all use steam as the leavener. Water in the batter or dough turns to steam when the product is heated quickly. The steam expands and pushes out the flour structure. As a result, the product rises. Most baked products do not depend on steam alone for leavening. Cake, for example, rises due to creaming, baking powder, and steam.

Chemical Agents.   A variety of chemicals produce gas to leaven baked products.

Baking soda.   The chemical sodium bicarbonate (baking soda) reacts with acid and liquid to make carbon dioxide gas, which does the leavening. Heat is not necessary to make the reaction happen. However, heat will speed up leavening. Common acid foods that are used in baking soda recipes are buttermilk, vinegar, chocolate, honey, molasses, and fruit. If there is too much soda in the recipe, the extra amount can cause a bitter flavor. Soda starts producing gas as soon as it mixes with acid. Therefore the batter must be baked at once. If not, the gas could all be released before the batter gets to the oven.

Baking powder.   Baking powder is a mixture of chemicals that react with moisture and heat to produce gas. They do not need an acid ingredient. Single-acting baking powder starts to make gas as soon as it is mixed with liquid. It must be used in products that are baked right after mixing. Double-acting powder has two gas-producing chemicals. One begins to make gas when mixed with liquid. The other starts working when the mixture gets hot. Together, the chemicals release gas throughout the baking process. Baking powder is usually the leavener in cakes. It is important to keep baking powder dry when storing.

Baking ammonia. Like baking powder, baking ammonia needs moisture and heat to start producing gas. It does not have the aftertaste of baking soda or powder because all gases are released. It is used for thin products such as cookies.

Yeast. Yeast is a single-cell plant that multiplies quickly when it is mixed with water and a small amount of sugar. When the yeast cells multiply, they ferment and make carbon dioxide gas and alcohol. Alcohol evaporates during baking but the carbon dioxide gas makes the product rise as it is trapped in the gluten network formed by flour. It is important to have the right temperature for yeast to grow. It grows well between 75 and 90°F. At 100°F, the growth of yeast cells slows down. At 140°F, the cells are killed.

The most common reason for failure of a yeast dough product is too much heat. Yeast cells die and do not produce gas to push up the dough. Be sure to let dough rise or proof in a controlled temperature environment.

Yeast comes in two forms, compressed moist or dry. In addition to producing gas, yeast also adds flavor to dough.

Eggs. Many baked products contain eggs. They add to the structure of the product and help produce a smoother batter. They also add flavor and nutritive value.

Be sure to consider eggs when calculating the total volume of liquid in a recipe. Eggs add moisture to the product since they are 70% water. As we said earlier, eggs also produce a foam and incorporate air. In addition the yolks add color and fat.

Liquids. Liquid ingredients have many functions in baked goods. They mix with protein in flour to form gluten. Liquids produce steam, which helps the leavening process. They dissolve and help mix dry ingredients together. They add moisture, flavor, and tenderness. They help browning and slow the staling process. Water and milk are the most common liquids in baking.

Water.   Water is basic in bread baking. For best results, make sure water does not contain a high percentage of minerals (hard water.)

Milk.   Milk adds texture, flavor, nutritive value, color, and keeping qualities. Buttermilk is often used in quickbreads. Some recipes call for dry milk, which is mixed with other dry ingredients. Whole milk contains fat that should be considered as part of the total fat in the recipe.

Salt, Flavorings, and Spices.   These ingredients add to the quality of the finished product.

Salt.   Salt adds its own distinctive flavor. It also brings out the flavor of other ingredients. In addition, salt strengthens gluten formation and controls the rate of yeast action (fermentation.)

Flavors and Spices.   Flavoring ingredients such as vanilla, lemon, or orange add flavor, aroma, and sometimes color. They may be natural or artificial flavors. Spices contribute to the taste and smell of the product. Depending on the baked product, spices used include cinnamon, mace, nutmeg, caraway, anise, allspice, poppyseed, coriander, ginger, cloves, and fennel.

Making Breads

Nothing attracts a customer like the aroma of baking bread. Fresh bread is an important part of our culture. It also has international appeal and is as popular today as ever. Fresh bread is not only an asset to the menu, it is also a marketing feature. Biscuits, muffins, and sweet rolls are much more appealing than plain toast on a breakfast menu. Fresh Italian bread completes any Italian meal better than a slice of sandwich bread. Even a cafeteria meal is more interesting with fresh cornbread or rolls.

Yeast breads and quickbreads are the two major types of bread. Yeast is the leavening agent in yeast breads, and chemical baking agents are used for quickbreads.

Making Yeast Dough. Two kinds of doughs are made with yeast. Rich doughs and lean doughs. Lean dough is another name for basic bread dough. It may contain only yeast, salt, water, and flour. Often, though, there is a small amount of shortening, eggs, and sugar. The liquid may be milk instead of water.

Rich doughs contain more fat, eggs, and sometimes sugar than lean bread doughs. They are used for sweet breakfast rolls and coffee cakes, Danish pastry, and some dinner rolls. Some rich doughs become even richer during the mixing process. The baker rolls in pieces of hard butter or margarine to make a layered, flaky dough. Such a flaky, rich dough is used in French croissants and some rich pastries.

Yeast Dough Mixing Methods. The most important goal in mixing yeast dough is to develop gluten. As we said earlier, the amount of gluten depends on the type of product. It is also important to distribute the yeast throughout the dough and combine all ingredients. The result should be a uniformly smooth dough. Bakers use two mixing methods for yeast doughs.

Straight dough method. All dry and liquid ingredients are mixed together at one time.

Sponge method. First the baker mixes some of the ingredients with yeast. This mixture ferments for a time. Then the fermented, bubbly "sponge" is mixed with the rest of the ingredients. A second fermentation period follows.

Ten Steps for Making Yeast Breads. Follow these important steps to produce fine-quality yeast bread:

1. Weigh all ingredients. You can measure water, milk, or eggs by volume. Just remember the rule "one pint per pound."

2. Mix dough with a dough hook. It is the most important piece of equipment in a yeast dough operation. The goal is to blend ingredients without overmixing or undermixing. It takes experi-

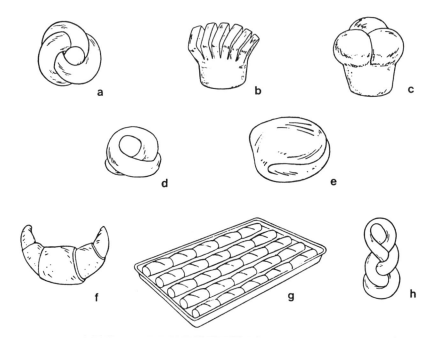

Examples of shapes for dinner rolls: (a) Double knot; (b) butterflake; (c) cloverleaf; (d) single knot; (e) Parker House; (f) crescent; (g) pan; (h) braided.

ence to know when a bread dough has been mixed just long enough. The dough ball will feel smooth and elastic, not sticky or dry.

Note: You may need to add extra flour to prevent sticking.

3. Let the yeast ferment and cause the dough to start rising. Remember that yeast works best between 75 and 80°F. During the fermentation process, the flour protein, gluten, absorbs water and becomes smooth and elastic. The dough should double in volume. It has fermented enough when you can stick a finger in the dough and the dent remains. If the dough does not rise, the yeast has probably been killed by too much heat.

4. Punch dough down by folding in the sides to the center. Then press down the dough mass. Punching down helps release some gas so that the fermentation process does not stop. It also keeps dough temperature even so that trapped pockets of heat do not develop. In addition, the punching process makes gluten strands longer and more elastic.

5. Round the dough by shaping into smooth, round balls. This step helps retain gases and forms a skin that prevents stickiness.

6. Bench the dough or allow it to rest for 8–12 minutes. Fermentation will continue and gluten will relax to make dough easier to handle.

7. Shape dough for baking. Weigh the shaped loaves or rolls to be sure they are the same size.

8. Proof dough in a proof box set at 90–100°F and 80–85% humidity. Dough will increase in volume because the yeast is still fermenting. It is ready for baking when double in size. That should take 15–45 minutes.

9. Bake dough at 375–425°F. The time depends on the size of the loaf or roll, richness of dough, and desired color. Changes that take place in baking include:

- Browning and formation of crust
- Rapid rise of the product (oven spring)
- Death of yeast cells when the temperature reaches 140°F

Table 23.1 lists some common problems in yeast bread baking, and possible causes.

10. Cool and store baked products. To cool, remove from pan and place on cooling racks (loaves) or baking sheets (rolls) Steam and alcohol (a by-product of yeast fermentation) will escape. Keep cooling loaves away from drafts or the crust will crack. For a

Table 23.1: Yeast Bread Problems and Causes

Problem	Possible causes
Poor shape	Improper shaping; too much dough; not enough rising time
Heavy	Not enough fermentation; yeast failure; too much flour
Cracked crust	Dough too stiff
Crumbly crust	Bad fermentation; no salt
Loaf too small	Too much salt; not enough yeast; oven temperature too high
Coarse texture	Yeast failure; fermentation problem
Loaf too large	Not enough salt; too much yeast; rising time too long

Table 23.2: Yeast Products Quality Standards

Texture	Moist, tender, not doughy
Volume	Light in proportion to size
Appearance	Shape right for product, crust evenly brown and free from cracks and bulges
Flavor	Light, ingredients blended, not yeasty

soft crust, brush with butter. Store hard-crust loaves or rolls at room temperature. Do not wrap. Use as soon as possible. Wrap soft-crust loaves or rolls or hold in a covered container until used. If you will not serve within 8 hours, freeze breads and rolls. Table 23.2 lists standards of quality for good yeast breads and rolls.

Quickbreads.   Quickbreads are quick and simple bakery items that require little skill to prepare. They are an important part of the foodservice operation. Some even build the reputation of the restaurant.

The quickbread category includes biscuits, muffins, hot cakes, waffles, popovers, cake doughnuts and fruit breads. They are all made from batters or doughs leavened with something other than yeast. Most quickbreads contain flour, baking powder, salt, sugar, shortening, eggs, and liquid. Different amounts of ingredients and different mixing methods result in many different products. The standard mixing method for many quickbreads is the muffin method.

Muffin Method.   Muffin batters contain a high proportion of flour. There is not much shortening or sugar. To mix, first blend dry ingredients together well. Add liquid and mix just enough to blend ingredients. If the batter is mixed too much, extra gluten will develop. The product will be tough. Other signs of overmixing are tunnels in the product, peaked tops and a smooth crust. Undermixing is nearly as bad as overmixing. The product will be very crumbly and the volume will be poor.

Good-quality muffins have rounded tops, an evenly coarse interior, no tunnels, and a rough surface, like the texture of cauliflower.

Biscuit Method.   It is traditional to make biscuits by cutting solid shortening into a mixture of flour, salt, and baking powder

Table 23.3: Quickbread Product Quality Standards

Shape	Uniform, straight sides, muffins, slightly rounded tops
Size	Uniform, double volume of batter or dough
Color	Even golden brown, free of spots
Crust	Tender, moderately soft, free of excess flour
Flavor	Pleasing, well blended, with no bitterness
Texture	Tender, moist, light

sifted together. The shortening is evenly blended when the mixture looks like pieces of uncooked rice grains. Finally, add liquid all at once and mix the dough until soft and pliable. To develop a flaky texture, knead the dough on a lightly floured board for 30–60 seconds. Knead lightly, with finger tips.

Other products made with the biscuit method are some shortbreads, shortcakes, and scones.

Hotcakes. Hotcakes are made from a thin batter, baked on a griddle. The batter is high in liquid, usually 1 C liquid to 1 C flour. Because of that, gluten does not develop easily. However, in recipes that call for less than 1 C of liquid per cup of flour, overmixing can easily cause toughness. Hotcakes are mixed using the muffin method. Liquid is blended into the sifted dry ingredients.

Quality of Quickbreads. Good muffins, biscuits, and other quickbreads have definite characteristics as shown in Table 23.3.

Biscuits. Good biscuits have even sides and level tops. The color of the tops is golden brown. Biscuits should have a layered texture, flaky and light. The flavor should be slightly sweet, with no bitter taste from too much baking powder.

Muffins. Look for good golden brown color. The tops should be lightly rounded with no peaks. Texture should be smooth and light with no tunnels inside. Flavor should be sweet. Table 23.4 lists common problems with quickbreads.

Merchandising Breads and Bakery

The aroma of fresh baked goods is their best advertisement. Some operations deliberately route the bakery vent over the en-

Table 23.4: Quickbread Problems and Reasons

Problem	Reason
	Biscuits
Tough	Overmixing; not enough fat; too much liquid
Dry	Not enough liquid; overcooking
Crumbly	Too much fat
Hard crust	Overcooking; temperature too high
Uneven color	Incorrect placement in oven; uneven oven heat; biscuits too thin
Irregular shape	Too much liquid; dough not rolled to uniform thickness; improper cutting of dough
Heavy	Too much mixing
	Muffins
Tunnels	Too much mixing
Heavy	Not enough leavening; not enough fat
Tough	Overmixing; not enough fat

trance to the restaurant. Other effective merchandising techniques focus on service.

Serve a small fresh loaf of yeast bread on a cutting board with each dinner. Or have a waiter or waitress circulate with a bread basket of fresh rolls, biscuits, muffins, or fritters. Whatever the specialty, it will be a favorite of guests if the bread is always fresh and top quality.

24
Desserts

For many people, dessert is a natural part of a luncheon or dinner meal. Ending the meal with something sweet is common practice. Dessert is chosen according to the meal it accompanies. It can be as simple as a bowl of pudding or as complicated as a 12-layer torte. We usually choose a light dessert to follow a heavy meal and a heavy dessert to follow a light meal. The cost may be low or extremely high, depending on the ingredients and skill required for preparation.

Four types of desserts dominate dessert menus in this country: cakes, pies, puddings, and specialties. Quality depends on following directions. It is important to use the right equipment and mixing methods.

Objectives and Terms

Objectives. This section should help you:

- Describe two types of cakes.
- List the four steps in cake preparation.
- Describe two cake-mixing methods.
- Describe quality standards for cakes.
- Describe one method of making piecrust.
- List characteristics of quality piecrust.
- List other common types of desserts.

Terms to Know

Butter Cake. Cake that includes fat creamed with sugar. It is leavened with a chemical leavening agent.

Foam Cake. Cakes leavened by beating air into eggs.

Angel Food cake. A foam-type cake that uses beaten egg whites as the leavening agent.

Sponge Cake. A foam type cake that contains beaten whole eggs or yolks as the primary leavening agent.

Batter. Combined ingredients such as flour, eggs, sugar, and liquid, which are spooned or poured into a pan to bake.

Icing (Frosting). A coating or filling for cakes that has sugar as its main ingredient.

Glaze. A thinned icing that is poured or dripped over desserts.

Pastry Crust. A mixture of flour, shortening, and a small amount of water, rolled thin to line a pie pan.

Filling. A flavorful mixture in a piecrust.

Pudding. A dessert made from milk, sugar, thickening agent, and flavorings.

Cakes

Cakes are sweet, baked desserts made predominantly of flour. The goal is to have an attractive product that is even-textured. It should have melt-in-the-mouth tenderness and flavor. The two common types are butter cakes and foam cakes.

Butter Cakes. Butter cakes contain a substantial amount of fat in addition to flour, sugar, eggs and leavening. The proportions of ingredients in a butter cake are very important. The weight of sugar should be greater than the weight of flour. The weight of shortening should not be greater than the weight of the eggs. And the weight of the liquid should be 1½ times the weight of the sugar. That sounds complicated, but most butter cake recipes have those proportions built in. If you find a new recipe and you are not sure it will be a good one, apply the formula given in Table 24.1 before bothering to try the recipe.

Table 24.1: Standard Proportions in Butter Cakes

Ingredient	Proportion
Sugar	Weight more than flour
Fat	Weight less than eggs
Liquid	One and one-half times weight of sugar

In years past, butter was the shortening used in cakes. We still call them butter cakes, even though the shortening may be margarine or hydrogenated vegetable shortening.

Butter cakes should have a golden brown, tender, thin crust. The inside or crumb of the cake should be fine, free of tunnels, and moist. Color will vary depending on the type of cake.

Foam Cakes.   Foam cakes are leavened with air that is trapped in beaten egg bubbles, or foam. Sponge or chiffon cakes contain some shortening. Angel food cake is a foam cake that contains no shortening. All should have an even grain and be moist.

Cake Preparation Methods.   Just as breadmaking has its special, required steps, so does cakemaking. The four basic steps are mixing, panning, baking, and cooling.

Mixing.   Mixing is the most detailed of the four steps. The purpose is to mix ingredients well, form air cells, and develop a good grain. There are four different mixing methods:

Conventional or creaming method.   Use this method for all butter and pound cakes. Cream fat and sugar together first. Whip them until sugar partly dissolves and air is beaten into the mixture. Then beat in eggs. Finally, add dry ingredients and liquids alternately. This helps the batter absorb the liquid. The end result is a thick batter that will not pour. Spoon it into the pan.

Two-stage method.   This method is simpler than creaming. Mix together dry ingredients and shortening. Fat particles will coat flour particles. Add part of the liquid, blend, then add the rest of the liquid. The batter will pour easily. When baked, the result is a moist cake with a tighter, more velvety grain than a creamed cake.

Whipped method. Whipping is the method used for foam cakes. In sponge cakes, whip whole eggs. Then blend in sugar and flour. For greater volume, warm the eggs to about 100°F before whipping. For angel food cake, whip egg whites to soft peaks with part of the sugar. Then add flour mixed with the rest of the sugar. Cakes should be light and spongy.

Package mix or dump method. Packaged cake mixes come ready, needing only water or sometimes water and eggs. Just dump the liquid into the packaged mixture and beat for the correct length of time. Results are consistent with good volume, texture, and tenderness. Flavor is a matter of individual taste.

Panning. Spoon batter into pans and bake as soon as possible. If you hold cake batter for any time, gas from the leavening agent will escape and there will be a loss of volume. The correct panning method depends on the type of cake.

Butter cake. Grease pans for butter cakes. After greasing, dust with flour. Tap excess flour out before adding batter.

Sheet cake. Line sheet cake pans with special greased paper (parchment.)

Angel food cake. Never grease an angel food cake pan. The batter must cling to the clean, dry sides of the pan to rise.

Sponge cake. Grease pans slightly.

For all types of pans, fill one-half to two-thirds full. Overfilling causes cakes to run over the sides of the pan. When this happens, the top will collapse.

Baking. Set oven temperature between 350 and 375°F. For best results, preheat for about 5 minutes. Be sure that shelves are level and keep pans separated in the oven. Air should circulate all around pans. Do not disturb cakes until they have set. They will

Table 24.2: Quality Standards for Cakes

Shape	Symmetrical, all sides same height; butter cake—rounded top, no cracks or peaks, foam cake—level
Surface	Smooth, uniform light brown
Texture	Butter cake—tender, moist, and velvety; foam cake—feathery and spongy
Weight	Butter cake—light for size; foam cake—very light for size
Grain	Fine, free from tunnels
Flavor	Delicate, no bitterness or other off-flavors

fall if shaken while the batter is still liquid or semiliquid. Cake is done when:

- Cake shrinks from the side of the pan.
- Top resists finger pressure (springs back when pressed).
- A toothpick inserted in the center comes out clean.

Cooling. Cool butter cakes on racks for 15 minutes. Then loosen sides and turn cakes over on rack to cool. Cool foam cakes upside down in their baking pans. This will help keep the volume. Table 24.2 lists quality characteristics of cakes and Table 24.3 lists common cake problems and their causes.

Table 24.3: Cake Problems and Causes

Problem	Cause
	Butter cakes
Too dark	Oven too hot; too much sugar
Too light	Oven too cool
Sticky crust	Not enough mixing
Poor volume	Too much liquid; oven too hot
Large holes	Leavening not mixed through
Soggy	Cooled too long in pan
	Foam cakes
Heavy	Eggs beaten incorrectly
Tough crust	Oven too hot; too much sugar
Tough texture	Overmixed
Coarse	Too much leavening

Icings. When the cake has cooled, it may be ready for decorating. Icing is the most common type of cake decoration. It helps improve appearance, flavor, and keeping qualities. There are many varieties of icing. Choose one that is appropriate for the occasion. It should be creamy and pleasing in flavor. The two types of icing are uncooked and cooked.

Uncooked Icing. Uncooked icing is a mixture of sugar and fat. If those two ingredients are simply blended, the texture is like fudge. If they are creamed together, the icing is fluffy and light. Butter cream icing is an example.

Butter cream. To make butter cream icing, blend butter or other fat with fine (10×) confectioner's sugar in a ratio of one part fat to four parts sugar. Add cream to make the icing smoother. Vary the recipe by adding flavor ingredients such as rum, vanilla, almond, peppermint flavors, or fruit juices.

Cooked Icing. Cooked icing may be made with granulated or confectioners sugar. Sugar is cooked with water to make a syrup. The consistency depends on the amount of liquid.

Simple cooked icing. This icing is similar to fondant used in candy filling. It is used on small cakes.

Boiled icing. Boiled icing is like a meringue. It is used to make fancy swirls.

Glaze. Glaze is a flat (not fluffy) icing used for Danish pastry and coffee cakes.

Pies

Pies are popular desserts in many foodservice operations. Whether it is a fruit, cream, chiffon, or ice cream pie, the most important part is the pastry crust. The standard of good pastry is tenderness and flakiness. That sounds easy but it takes a lot of skill and practice. The trick is to combine ingredients in the right way.

Apple pie is a dessert favorite throughout the country.
Courtesy: Kellogg Corp.

Ingredients.   Standard pastry ingredients are flour, shortening, salt, and liquid.

Flour.   Use a flour especially made for pastry. It will develop just enough gluten for structure and flaking. Do not use bread flour. It has too much gluten and will make the pastry tough.

Shortening.   A hydrogenated shortening is very plastic. It should produce the most flakiness and tenderness.

Salt.   Salt adds flavor and helps to firm the dough. Be careful not to use too much salt. It toughens gluten.

Liquid.   Water is the usual liquid. It is necessary to develop a small amount of gluten. Use cold water (about 40°F). Too much water makes pastry tough.

Mixing Pastry.   The key to good pie pastry is mixing the flour and shortening correctly. Tender pastry needs very little gluten development. Coat flour particles with fat to keep gluten to a minimum. Use as little water as possible, but there must be some water in order to make pastry flaky. The solution seems to be to use a minimum of water; and keep it cold. There are two traditional methods for mixing pastry: flaky and mealy.

Table 24.4: Pie Pastry Problems and Causes

Problem	Causes
Shrinkage	Too much water; overworking
Not flaky	Shortening too warm
Soggy	Bottom not baked enough
Tough	Overmixed; too much water; not enough fat

Flaky.   Use this method for top crusts and pie shells. Cut shortening into flour until pieces are the size of peas. This will produce thin layers of fat when rolled.

Mealy.   Blend shortening and flour well, until particles are like small grains. Less gluten will develop and the crust will become less soggy. This is a good crust for cream or custard pies in which filling bakes with the crust.

Table 24.4 lists common pie problems and their causes.

Types of Pies.   Although there are hundreds of pies, there are only a few basic types.

Fruit.   Fruit pies contain fruit, fruit juices, sugar, and usually a thickener. Apples, cherries, blueberries, and peaches are favorite fruits for pies.

Custard.   Custard pies usually contain a single crust and a stirred or baked custard. The custard is often flavored with coconut, bananas, pumpkin, pineapple, lemon or nearly any other fruit.

Chiffon.   Gelatin and whipped egg white are the base for most chiffon pies. The chiffon mixture can be flavored with fruit, spices or liquor. As a result, a wide variety of pies belongs to this single category.

Puddings

Puddings come in many flavors. They may be inexpensive instant puddings or expensive, from-scratch delicacies flavored

Bread pudding is a flavorful mixture of milk, eggs, and bread. This version is topped with peaches and a crumb topping.
Courtesy: Cling Peach Advisory Board.

with brandy or fresh fruit. Most puddings are low cost and easily prepared by employees with average skills. Puddings may contain starch or egg as the thickening agent.

Starch-Thickened Puddings. Cornstarch is the thickener in many cream puddings or *blanc manges*. Such a pudding can also be the base for pies or other desserts.

Egg-Bound Puddings. Heavy steamed plum puddings were popular in earlier times. Bread puddings and custards are other examples of puddings in which egg is the thickening agent.

Cheesecake topped with fruit is a rich, creamy specialty dessert.
Courtesy: Borden Inc.

Gelatin Desserts

Some gelatin desserts are no more than thickened gelatin with fruit. Others include ingredients that completely change their flavor and texture. A Bavarian cream, for example, contains the richness of heavy cream. Stirred egg custard is added to gelatin for a Spanish Creme.

Specialty Desserts

The dessert menu may include many other products. Some restaurants serve plain cheese with fruit, ices, cheesecake, and fried desserts such as crepes, fritters, or regional favorites. Be sure the desserts you offer provide a good return for food and labor costs. An enterprising foodservice operator can improve profits with a variety of desserts. Serve crepes with ice cream or combine fruit and fritters. For even more splash, flame the desserts. Your spectacular flambés will be the talk of the town.

To make desserts pay off in your operation, merchandize them well. Use a display case or dessert cart to showcase your specialties.

Index